# RENGSANGGRI

*Family and Kinship*
*in a Garo Village*

## By Robbins Burling

Philadelphia
University of Pennsylvania Press

7325
Printed in Great Britain by
Fletcher & Son Ltd., Norwich

# Preface

SOME ETHNOGRAPHERS ARE ABLE to return from the field and write a monograph with a single central thesis, perhaps a test of a psychological theory, or a new insight into social structure. Sometimes I envy these people for their single-minded organization and sense of purpose, but I am not one of them. I did go to the field with what I felt was a reasonably coherent plan. I wanted to study the operation of a special form of cross-cousin marriage in a matrilineal society, and I spent a large part of my time working on this very problem. But people never behave in exactly the way ethnographers expect. Some of the hypotheses which I took to the field proved untenable, while many unexpected matters kept obtruding themselves upon my work; so in defiance of neat plans made in advance I ended like most ethnographers in collecting as much information as I could about a wide variety of subjects, and much of this material has found its way into this book. The result is a descriptive study of the Garos, or more precisely, of one Garo village as I saw it between October 1954 and October 1956.

Nevertheless, not even the simplest description is possible in the absence of some over-all organization. One can write a book without a single thesis, but one cannot write without a plan, and my plan has grown out of the interests which first attracted me to the Garos. Having decided to study these people because of their unique combination of kinship traits, particularly their matrilineal descent and their matrilateral cross-cousin marriage, I had committed myself to a society where complexities of kinship were likely to be inescapable. Perhaps someone who was interested in other things would have found less kinship and possibly more religion than I did; but to me kinship and social structure remained the most interesting aspect of their culture. Consequently these subjects form the core of the resulting book. My interests center around the definition of the significant social groups in the society, their composition, their activities, and their inter-relationships. Given such a focus, there are two obvious methods of organization: to begin with the largest group and work down to the smallest, or to begin with the smallest and work up. I have chosen the second alternative, simply because the data seemed to fall into place more readily that way. I have not been entirely systematic; the data of later sections are sometimes anticipated in earlier discussions, and certain fundamental data would fit nowhere except at the beginning— i.e., location, ethnic relationship, a description of the natural and supernatural environments in which the people live, and the manner in which they cope with these environments. Once these are taken care of, I move on to marriage, the family, and the more elaborate kinship groups of the society. I hope this will provide a coherent picture of the Garos and their way of life. I hope in particular that the reader of this book will be able to sense the way in which this culture limits the choices of the individuals who live within it, so that, given his upbringing, and given the behavior of the people around him, a Garo hardly has any choice but to act like a Garo. And I also hope that I have avoided being so scientifically objective as to hide my feelings of affection and admiration for my friends of Rengsanggri.

I have little patience with ethnographic reports which use so many foreign terms that the reader is required to learn a large portion of the language in order to understand what is being said. I have tried to keep the use of Garo terms to a minimum, but in order to preserve the meaning of the Garo I have used English words enclosed in single quotation marks as translation equivalents for Garo words. Thus when I write 'uncle' I do not mean those relatives usually referred to by that word in English, but instead those relatives to which the Garo word *mama* refers. 'Headman' should not carry the connotation of the office of chief or village leader in any other society, but simply be accepted as an equivalent for the Garo word *nokma*.

When Garo terms have been used, I have with a certain reluctance given them in the missionary orthography which has become well accepted, rather than in what I regard as a somewhat more accurate phonemic transcription. In the long run, I believe that this practice will lead to less confusion. I have used local units of weight, measures, and coinage throughout. The Indian rupee was officially valued at approximately $.21, and during the time of my field work it was still divided into sixteen annas. Garos used the standard "seer" of north-eastern India, which is equal to slightly more than two pounds, and the "maund" of forty seers, or about 83 pounds. Certain English measures, notably the yard and mile, were in general use by all Garos.

*     *     *

The number of people upon whose good will and cooperation an anthropologist is dependent defies listing, let alone adequate mention. No one sacrificed so much for the sake of my field work as my wife Sibyl. She spent three months of our two years in India in the hospital and many more months as a convalescent. I hope I realize how fortunate I am that she looks back on our years in India with more pleasure than horror.

My teachers at Harvard guided me toward and through the research which is reported here, and through the dissertation that preceded this book. I must single out in particular Douglas Oliver, who helped to direct my anthropological interests both by pointing out areas of study which I found stimulating and by more formally instructing me in the analysis of society. George Homans, Cora DuBois, John Pelzel, and John Roberts all helped, either by instructing me before I went to the field, or by listening to me talk about the Garos after I returned and by helping me to develop insights into my material. My colleague Ruben Reina read a preliminary draft of the book and gave me innumerable cogent criticisms.

The entire financial support of my field work was derived from a Foreign Areas Training Fellowship of the Ford Foundation. More than most Ford fellows, I had reason to appreciate the Foundation not only for the generosity of its grant, but for the readiness of its staff to help out in the crises, large and small, that can hinder field work. Of the numerous representatives of the Indian and local governments who assisted me, I can mention only Shri S. M. L. Bhatnagar, who was then Deputy Commissioner of the Garo Hills District, and Captain Williamson Sangma, at that time the Chief Executive Member of the Garo Hills District Council. Both these men extended all the cooperation that they could give and helped to make me welcome in the Garo Hills.

To the members of the American Baptist Foreign Mission Society my family owes more than is possible to convey, both for their friendship and for their professional assistance at times of personal emergency. I must mention especially Dr. and Mrs. E. Sheldon Downs and Rev. and Mrs. James M. Wood of Tura, Garo Hills, and Dr. and Mrs. Alvin Mundhenk and Miss Alice M. Townsend of Gauhati, Assam, all of whom helped us in their own ways. Without their tolerant acceptance of myself and my family, life in Assam would have been very much more difficult, if not impossible.

The people to whom I owe most of all, however, must remain anonymous, simply because there are a quarter of a million of them, and even to select out the few hundred who helped me most would take more room than is permissible. The Garos are a friendly and hospitable people. They were patient with my strange ways and stupid blunders. They were as curious about me as I was about them, and were always ready to talk and to spend time answering my prying questions. They made me welcome in their homes by serving me hundreds of cups of tea and glasses of rice beer. There is no way in which I can ever begin to repay them for their help and their friendship.

R.B.

# Contents

# Illustrations

# List of Maps and Diagrams

# RENGSANGGRI

# I

# The Place and
# the People

ASSAM IS THE NORTHEASTERNMOST of the fifteen constituent states of the Republic of India. To-day it is almost severed from the rest of the nation by East Pakistan, which was carved out of what had been British India. This gives the present state an artificial isolation, cut off to the north and east by the massive wall of the Himalayas and the mountains of the Assam-Burma border, and to the south and west by the frequently inhospitable border which divides the present India from Pakistan. Only a narrow strip of territory now connects Assam with the rest of India, but politically it is no less a part of India than its sister states. This has a secure topographical basis in the fact that the lowland of the Brahmaputra Valley, which gives Assam its geographic unity, opens out into Bengal, and from there joins with the great north Indian plain. Thus Assam's present geographic isolation is to a considerable extent a recent and artificial phenomenon. Culturally, too, Assam belongs to India, for the valley has allowed people and their customs to penetrate into Assam from the rest of the country. To-day the valley is occupied by people who—while vigorously maintaining their feeling of distinction from the Bengalis and other Indians to the west—are still, by comparison with the people in the hills around them, very much a part of the general Indian civilization, and who share with other Indians many of their cultural traits. Though the restrictions of caste are said to be milder in Assam than in any other of the Indian states, the Assamese, as the people of the plains are called, are still divided into castes not unlike those in other parts of the country. Except for a few Moslems, most of these plains people are Hindus and follow at least some of the dietary and social prescriptions of that religion. Racially they are not much different from the rest of the north Indian population, and they speak a language which, if not quite mutually intelligible with Bengali and Bihari to the west, is like them and like all the major languages of north India in being derived from Sanskrit.

The great ethnographic diversity of Assam, however, is found in the hilly country that surrounds the valley in all directions except to the west. The people of the hills are divided into geographically separate tribes, speaking dozens of different languages. There seems no reason to doubt that these "hill tribes" represent, in part at least, the remnants of an earlier population and culture, which may even have covered much of the plains region before the immigration of the distinctive Indian civilization now found there. The hill tribes actually form the last western outpost of the type of culture found in much of the mountain area of Southeast Asia. For as long as 2000 years the culture of India and the culture of these tribes have been in contact, sometimes violently and often with considerable exchange of both cultural traits and genes, but by and large the distinction between plains man and hill man in Assam remains.[1] The traits of the hill people that have been taken over by the plains Assamese are mostly of a rather superficial sort, but one can at least speculate that it is partly the influence of casteless peoples such as live in the hills that has prevented the more extreme forms of caste from developing in Assam. Linguists recognize many lexical items and a few grammatical ones in Assamese that seem to be derived from some of the local branches of Tibeto-Burman.[2] Along the upper river, even the plains people occasionally show a trace of mongoloid ancestry.

Still, it is in the hills of the state where the cultural links with southern and Eastern Asia are most marked. All of the hill people are strongly mongoloid. Some show clear evidences of mixture with people like those of the plains, and an occasional individual even looks vaguely negritoid or australoid; but in most, the predominant element is mongoloid. The Khasis to the south of the river speak a Mon-Khmer language, but the other hill languages fall into a number of branches of Tibeto-Burman, and all have their linguistic relatives to the east. All of the hill tribes are agricultural, but most of them rely upon the slash-and-burn technique. Most are dependent primarily upon rice, though many grow a large assortment of other grain and root crops as well. Most of them are characterized by a relatively unstratified social organization, with a notably independent status of the women. They tend to be organized into unilineal descent groups, and for some obscure reason the area shows a remarkable concentration of matrilateral cross-cousin marriage.

The line of hills which lies to the south of the Brahmaputra River is known as the Shillong Plateau. Less impressive in elevation than the mountains north of the river or than those along the Burma border, it stretches for about 150 miles from east to west and for about fifty miles from north to south. The high point of this line of hills is in the center and east, the country of the Khasis, where in places the elevation is more than a mile. This has allowed Shillong, the capital of Assam, to become a popular hill resort which in the past attracted many Europeans to the district. The western end of the Shillong Plateau lies in the bend of the Brahmaputra River where, after flowing almost due west through lower Assam, it turns south to join the Ganges and to empty into the Bay of Bengal. Here are the hills which are occupied by the Garos. The present political district of the Garo Hills corresponds closely with the topography—

AREA SURROUNDING GARO HILLS

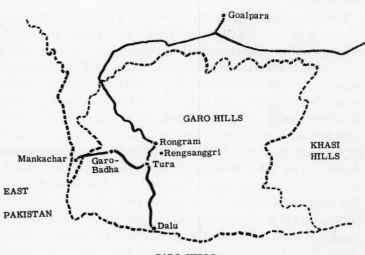

GARO HILLS

that is, the district ends exactly where the hills end. Its boundary also approximates the ethnic boundary between the Garos and other groups. In area the district is about seventy miles long from east to west, and fifty miles from north to south, forming an irregular rectangle.

The first European sources to report in any detail on the Garos date from about 1800.[3] They describe a savage and warlike people addicted to head-hunting, but already having regular market relations with the plains. Even then the Garos exchanged cotton for dried fish and salt; all of these are typical items in the market trade today. These earliest British observers reported the Garos to be honest and independent, and showed sympathy for the difficulties they occasionally encountered in dealing with some of their neighbors in the plains.

As the power of the British government of India increased in Assam, the problem of unadministered hill areas became ever more acute. There were periodic raids from the hills that could not be effectively controlled. For many years administration of the Garo Hills was delayed by the extremely serious malaria which was, and still is, characteristic of the district.[4] Finally, however, in 1867, the district was occupied, permanent headquarters were established at Tura, and peace was rapidly achieved. The American Baptist Missionary Society sent missionaries to the Garo Hills almost immediately after the government was established, and these were followed, in this century, by Catholic missionaries, with the result that today between one-quarter and one-third of the Garos are Christians, the largest number of them Baptist.

The British reserved the use of force to themselves and their officials. They established in Tura the office of Deputy Commissioner, which until the time of Indian independence was filled by a Britisher. Law courts were set up for the peaceful settlement of legal disputes, and though most of these were settled by Garo petty officials coming under the administration of the Deputy Commissioner, he himself sat as judge in the court of appeals. The government also undertook to build and maintain roads, to establish reserved forests, and to control trade and the markets. At first, education was left largely to the missionaries, but gradually the main responsibility for education has also been shifted to the government.

With Indian independence, the old Deputy Commissioner's office was inherited by the successor governments of the State of Assam and the Republic of India, and the office has been maintained, but since independence has been occupied by plains Indians. The constitution of India which was soon adopted provided for a new governmental body, an elective District Council, with powers of taxation and responsibility for many governmental affairs, including, specifically, all matters relating to customary Garo law. In 1956 the new District Council and the old office of the Deputy Commissioner were both functioning governmental departments.

The population of the district according to the 1951 census was 242,075, of which 190,901 gave Garo as their mother tongue.[5] Most of the non-Garo-speaking population of the district is concentrated around the edges, leaving most of the interior almost ethnically pure. In fact, the only people other than Garos who are at all dispersed throughout the district are a few Nepalis living in widely scattered settlements. They are recent immigrants who maintain large herds of cattle and sell milk or manufacture ghee. Another 50,000 Garos were listed by the census in other parts of Assam, mostly in the districts immediately bordering the Garo Hills, and about 40,000 live in the adjacent districts of East Pakistan.[6] Except for a few recent emigrants, then, the Garos form a geographically compact population. If they are distributed through a number of districts, this is largely because the borders of the district do not coincide perfectly with the area occupied by the tribe, though the borders were intended to do this as well as possible. The census reports of the district have shown an increase in every ten-year period since 1901, when the population was returned as only 138,274, just over half that shown by the most recent census. Part of the increase is probably due to immigration from other districts, but most is surely the result of natural expansion which—in spite of an appalling death rate, especially among children—seems to be keeping pace with the rest of India.

Virtually all of these Garos live in small agricultural villages of ten to fifty or sixty houses with a population which is rarely more than about 300. Generally the houses are built close together, while the village land stretches out on all sides, and villages are usually spaced a mile or more apart. Traditionally the Garos have lived by slash-and-burn agriculture, but for the last fifty years or so, an increasing number of small river-bottom areas have been brought under wet rice cultivation. Wet fields are scattered and seldom extensive, but they help to allow a mean population density of 77 per square mile for the whole district. Where low land is used for permanent cultivation, it is used almost exclusively for wet rice, mustard, and jute; but shifting cultivators plant a wide assortment of crops, including rice, millet, maize, many root crops, vegetables, and gourds, as well as the cotton, ginger, and chili peppers which are largely sold for cash.

Physically the villages consist of a number of substantial bamboo family houses, together with associated granaries, wood sheds, and pig sties. The houses are long and narrow, with the front door at one end, and when possible they are oriented in such a way that several of them converge on an open yard which covers the top of a small hill. The backs of the houses radiate out over the descending slopes. A single village may include several such yards, each with its cluster of houses. Chickens and pigs, dogs and cats run freely through the villages in the daytime. Cows are generally tethered and all are shut in at night as protection against wild animals.

Scattered about in non-Christian villages are decaying remains of old sacrificial altars, which must be built new each time a sacrifice is performed. Sacrifices occur on a number of special occasions throughout the year which mark important points in the agricultural cycle, but they are also performed irregularly as the main method of curing disease. Anything from an egg to a cow may be sacrificed according to the symptoms and seriousness of the complaint. Sacrifices provide an opportunity for the cooperation of a number of households, and they usually culminate with a meal at which the sacrificed animal is eaten. Posts erected in memory of the dead stand in front of many of the houses. Bamboo boxes filled with rice and bedecked with pots, baskets, and gourds may occasionally be seen; in these a few of the bones of the dead are kept between the cremation and the post-funeral ceremony.

Every Garo considers himself a member of one of five matrilineal descent groups which, ideally, should be completely exogamous. Two of these groups, however, are so small and so strictly localized as to have no relevance for most purposes, and many Garos have never heard of them. A third, which is called Momin, is somewhat larger but is still confined to a limited portion of the Garo area. Earlier observers who knew about the Momins but had not heard of the smaller groups, sometimes classified the Garos as having a system with three exogamous descent groups. The remaining two groups, Sangma and Marak, are found wherever Garos live, and in more than half of the district they alone exist. In these areas every person belongs to one or the other of these two major exogamous divisions. Since only these two groups were present in the area on which this study is based, I shall refer to them as "moieties" for the rest of this work, though if all the Garos are considered, this term would hardly be appropriate. Membership in the moiety, as in all of the smaller descent groups, is acquired automatically from one's mother.

Each moiety is divided into numerous named divisions which can be called sibs. These name groups frequently include many thousands of people and extend over far too wide an area for all the members to cooperate or even to know of each other's existence. Since the moieties are exogamous, no evident function is left to the sib, though Garos do feel more strongly about a breach of sib exogamy than about the necessity for moiety exogamy. The sib amounts to little more than a name group, but by virtue of the name it is one of the few kin groups with completely unambiguous membership.

Each village is the seat of at least one local lineage of one of the matrilineal sibs. The members of that lineage—all of whom, of course, have the same sib name—are all more or less closely related to each other and all have special rights to live in and use the land of that village. Some villages include just one main lineage together with a few wives and many husbands who have married its members. Other villages, however, have two local lineages, which always represent two different sibs of the opposite moieties. In such cases members of the two local lineages share equally in the right to live and work in the village as well as in the right to bring their spouses to live there.

Though the village is built around a matrilineal descent group, it is not organized exclusively around a group of either co-resident related men or co-resident related women. Most frequently a man lives in the village of his wife, but, as will be explained in detail later, a significant minority of women must live in their husbands' villages.

Within the village some households consider themselves more closely related than others, and members of such households are more likely to give each other assistance than are more distantly related people; but the final kinship unit, the group providing one's most constant associates and companions, is the household. The household is the primary production and consumption unit, and one's daily activities, from work in the fields to eating and sleeping, are most commonly carried on with other members of the same household.

The greatest part of my work with the Garos was carried on in the village of Rengsanggri. This village lies in the valley of a stream called the Rongram, about ten miles to the north of

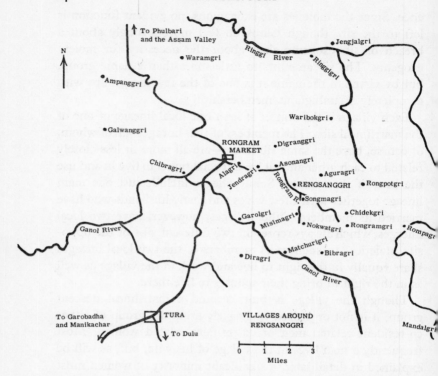

N

↑ To Phulbari
and the Assam Valley

• Waramgri

Ringgi River

• Jengjalgri

Ringgigri

• Ampanggri

• Galwanggri

• Waribokgri

RONGRAM
MARKET

• Digranggri

Chibragri •

Alagri •
Jendragri •

• Asonangri

Rongram R.

• Aguragri

• RENGSANGGRI        • Rongpotgri

• Songmagri

• Garolgri

Misimagri •

• Chidekgri

• Nokwatgri    • Rongramgri        • Rompagri

Ganol River

• Diragri

• Matchurigri

Ganol River

• Bibragri

To Garobadha
and Manikachar

□ TURA

↓ To Dulu

VILLAGES AROUND
RENGSANGGRI

Mandalgri

0      1      2      3
Miles

Tura. It is on the border of a section of the hills which until recently had no schools or missionary activity. Although the people of Rengsanggri have made regular trips to the Tura market for many years, their life seems relatively unaffected by the modern influences of the church, of school, or of new agricultural techniques. The village itself had sixty households and was therefore about as big as a Garo village ever becomes. Its people referred to themselves as "Matabeng", a local subdivision of the Garos which they described as "not quite Matchi" (a group to the east) and "not quite Abeng" (the name of the subgroup covering the western third of the district). In my observation, however, their culture and social organization did not seem to differ to any significant degree from any of the

Abengs, and in only a few ways from that of the groups to the east. Rather than complicate this account by calling these people Matabengs—as they themselves do only on the unusual occasions when they need to distinguish themselves from their neighbors—I shall simply call them Garos. It must not be forgotten, however, that my work refers most specifically to this limited area.

The accompanying maps show the village of Rengsanggri and its neighbors. Map 3 shows most of the villages which are near by or which have important ties with the Rengsanggri people. Map 4 will give an idea of how houses are arranged and oriented in a typical, though comparatively large village. The houses are numbered according to the serial numbers used in the appendices. In all cases the numbers are placed at the front end of the house. Households 21 and 38 each occupied two buildings, the smaller of which are labeled with an "a" on the map. "B" indicates the bachelors' house, and "G" a small guest house.

All of the groups which have been mentioned—village, household, lineage, and the others—will be described more fully in later chapters. First, however, it is necessary to consider in more detail the natural and supernatural environments in which the Garos live and within which their social organization is embedded.

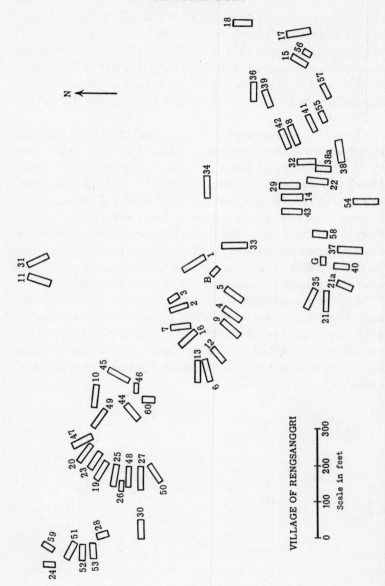

VILLAGE OF RENGSANGGRI

Scale in feet

0    100    200    300

# II

## Nature and the Gods

### THE FIELDS

THE SHILLONG PLATEAU CATCHES the full force of the
summer monsoon as it moves north from the Bay of Bengal, to
spill into the hills. This makes the area just south of Shillong,
including the neighborhood of Cherapunjee, the rainiest known
area in the world. Tura, the district headquarters of the Garo
Hills, is at the western extremity of the Shillong Plateau and
receives only about one-third as much rainfall as Cherapunjee,
but this still amounts to about 140 inches per year, most of
which falls between the beginning of June and October. This
pronounced rainy season imposes its pattern on Garo agriculture, so that most crops must be planted near the beginning
of the rains. In Rengsanggri, land is used for two consecutive
years before being abandoned to jungle for another six or eight.
The first year all the crops are planted together, but during the
second the land is devoted exclusively to rice. Since a new
patch is opened each year, two fields are always simultaneously
under cultivation, one planted to mixed crops, the other to rice
alone, and weather and insects permitting, all crops should be
available for harvest each year.

Well-recognized boundaries separate the land of one village
from that of its neighbors, and within its own boundaries each
village has a reasonably well-defined tradition of land rotation
of its own. In Rengsanggri this was so systematic that by remem-
bering the order in which land had been used in the past, any

villager was able to predict which fields would be used for several years in the future. In general the rotation goes in a counter-clockwise direction around the village. Each plot was named, sometimes for an important event that had occurred there, and so the villagers could easily discuss plans for future cultivation. They also remembered clearly where they had cultivated before, and an event several years earlier could be most easily dated by recalling that it happened while they were cultivating in a particular field. Even longer periods might be remembered in this way, and men who had been married into a village for many years could estimate the time by pointing out that they were now cultivating in one area for the third or fourth time, even though they would never be able to count the exact number of years.

The two-year agricultural cycle begins when the section that has been fallow the longest is apportioned into household plots. Like the choice of the fields as a whole, the apportionment is made largely on the basis of tradition, since most households expect to use again the plot they used the last time around. This does not imply permanent land ownership, since readjustments always have to be made to allow for any increase or decrease in the size of families since the fields were last used. It does a family no good to claim more land than its available labor can cultivate, but families which have increased are always free to take an additional plot out at the edge of the fields, if they cannot take over parts of plots which smaller families no longer need. Occasionally people take more land than they are able to handle adequately, with the result that after a year of cultivation, abandoned patches, scattered here and there in the fields, mark the places where the weeds have gotten out of control. The steady increase in population has meant that land has been left fallow for ever shorter periods, and presumably it is becoming less capable of continued cultivation. This may result in a crisis in the future, but the crisis has not yet come. So far limitation in the available labor has prevented extreme competition for land.

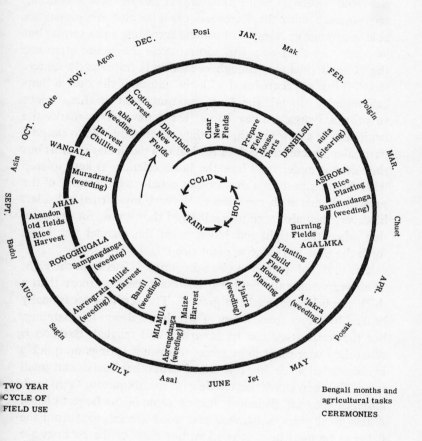

TWO YEAR
CYCLE OF
FIELD USE

Bengali months and
agricultural tasks

CEREMONIES

The agricultural tasks which follow assignment of the plots to households are precisely defined, and are followed with considerable regularity. The Rengsanggri people have a nodding acquaintance with the European calendar and are sometimes able to arrange government business according to its terms; but in describing their own agricultural cycle they more often use the Bengali calendar, though even this is imperfectly understood. They are acquainted with the names of the twelve Bengali months, though the Garo pronunciation of them might surprise a Bengali. They know that a new moon marks the beginning of a new month, and they are usually able to assign a particular agricultural task or festival to a particular month; but they do not understand how the lunar calendar is kept in step with the solar year, and they cannot usually tell the name of the present month with confidence. Beyond any formal calendar, however, they also note natural signs: they know, for instance, that when the bright red blossoms of the mandal tree burst forth the time has come to plant rice.

The first real work is to clear the jungle. Usually in the eight or so years since the field had last been used no more than a thick scrub has covered the ground. The scrub is occasionally broken by larger trees, a few of which are always left standing, but the scrub itself can be luxuriant and tangled. Bamboo is often the major plant to be removed since it springs up quickly in abandoned fields, but it is mixed with other bushes and small trees. The men attack this tangle with the ubiquitous Garo bush knife, or they use their iron axes on some of the largest plants. A few good poles of bamboo and wood are salvaged from the fields to be used in construction, but most of the cuttings are simply scattered about on the ground to dry. The cutting is hard work, and the men must work at it off and on for about a month, through most of January. As in all agricultural tasks, each man concentrates his energies on his own field but may sometimes trade labor with a friend.

Once cut, the fields are left to dry in the gradually warming sun of February and March. Some of the people's time is then occupied in working on the old fields, but nothing can be done in the new ones until they are ready to be burned. Men do make preparations for their new fields, however, by collecting bamboo and prefabricating it into mats and other structural parts, which will be used to construct small field houses after the fields are burned. Though the weather is usually very dry and dusty at this season, rain is not unknown, and if it should rain just before the burning is scheduled, the fire may have to be postponed until the fields have had a chance to dry again. Occasionally the fields get too wet to burn properly, and the crops then suffer seriously. This is less of a danger in the Rengsanggri area than in some other parts of the district where the burning is usually held later. The villages near Rengsanggri generally burn their fields around the latter half of March, and almost every evening at this time of year the sky in one direction or another is aglow, as village after village decides to fire its fields.

Though villagers coordinate many of their agricultural activities, the burning (a'sua: a'a 'ground,' sua 'burn') is the only point that demands coordination for technological reasons. Since all the year's plots are adjacent to one another, it would be impossible to burn one without burning its neighbors as well. Moreover, sparks fly far enough that even the village may be endangered, and precautionary measures must be taken by the village as a whole. On the morning of the fire, one person from each household joins a work party which circles the new field, making a path between the uncut forest and the dried brush, to ensure that the flames do not spread too far—though the danger is not great since even at this dry time of year the forest is wet enough to resist any widespread fire. The threat to the houses in the village, which are built of highly inflammable bamboo and thatch, is much greater.

The fields which the Rengsanggri people cleared in 1956 bordered the village, and the fire was therefore more dangerous than in some years. It was kindled without ceremony at the bottom of the hill on which the plots were located, and then a few men lit bamboo torches and walked along the bottom edge in either direction and then up the two sides, lighting the edge as they went. The fire worked its way inward and upward, and only a few people had to help kindle it. A few others stood about at the bottom of the fields, on the path from which the first lighting was done, but everyone else stayed in the village, protecting the houses from flying sparks, and gazing at the fire from there. At least one person sat on the roof of every house, but several climbed on to the houses nearest the fields, while others climbed on to granaries and even little wood sheds. Each person went equipped with gourds full of water and a broom with which to splash the water on to the roof as a precaution against its catching fire, and of course to douse any sparks that should alight. Most of the people also took their most valued possessions out of their houses and piled them in the open courtyard, and a few whose houses were closest to the fields emptied them completely until the danger had passed.

The villagers watched the fire with interest and excitement. They eagerly noted its progress, exclaiming when it burst out into large flames, and noting especially when the fire reached their own patch; but the excitement was over in two hours, for the fire had reached the top of the fields, and except for a few smouldering logs it had died down elsewhere. Even twenty-four hours later, after the first crops had been planted, some logs continued to smoulder. Tree stumps and the larger branches never did burn up entirely, but the smaller brush and bamboo were quickly consumed, and left the entire field covered and blackened with ash.

The fire is generally held late in the afternoon or evening, when dusk allows stray sparks to be caught more easily; and early the next morning people must rise and prepare for sowing the crops and for the day's ceremonies. Each woman cooks a supply of food in her house, but instead of serving it there she wraps it in banana leaves and carries it to the field. The men's first job is to circle the borders of their individual plots, and in cooperation with their neighbors to define the boundaries. These have, of course, been agreed upon since the plots were first distributed, but burning alters the character of the land and permits a more final demarcation. Wherever possible they place boundaries either along stream beds or along the ridges of small hills; when the division is not marked by some clear natural line, the neighbors lay a series of poles, salvaged from the refuse of the fire, along the boundary that will separate their fields. After this, to move the sticks is said to cause blindness.

Once boundaries are established, each family builds a small altar and honors the god Saljong by sacrificing an egg near the place on their own plot—generally at about the center—where they will build their field house. One man only, the *nokma* or 'headman' who acts as ceremonial leader of the village, sacrifices a chicken. Only when the sacrifice is complete can the sowing begin. All those seeds which can be broadcast are mixed together in the same basket. The major constituent of the mixture is millet (*misi*), but there are also the seeds of chili peppers (*jalik*) and, in smaller quantities, those of melon (*te'e*), eggplant (*baring*), and other vegetables. The men and youths broadcast this mixture over the entire plot. As they sow they let out an occasional lusty whoop, so that from all up and down the still blackened fields shouts are to be heard. Sowing so soon after the fire means that the ashes can blow over the seeds and cover them—which, it is said, makes them grow more successfully. The women in the meantime begin to plant maize (*meraku, mibol, mikop*). Since this involves making a hole with a pointed stick held in one hand and tossing in a few seeds with the other, it cannot be done so quickly as the broadcasting, which may be completed within an hour or two. When the men have finished, the family gather at the place of the sacrifice, where they eat the food which the women have cooked beforehand, and drink the rice beer they have carried to the field for the occasion. A bit of

R—B

rice and curry is placed by the altar, as an offering to Saljong, the god, and then the family "eat with Saljong," squatting in the open near the offering place. People soon begin to circulate about the fields, visiting neighbors and offering drinks of rice beer back and forth. It would be considered rude not to offer a drink to anyone who passes by, and everyone rapidly waxes gay. Shortly before noon, after perhaps five hours in the fields, people make their way back to the village in a thoroughly festive mood. A few must take naps to sleep off the rice beer they have already consumed, but others visit their neighbor's houses informally and continue drinking; the next few days are spent in celebrating the festival of *Agalmaka.*

After the celebration the people return to the fields and to steady labor. For a week or so the men work at building a small hut in the middle of their own plot, using the bamboo poles, matting, and thatch which they have prepared in the preceding months. If there is fear of elephants, they may also build huts in some of the trees that have been left standing. Tree houses, like the houses on the ground, are made of bamboo and thatch, but they are braced across the branching limbs of a tree at a height of as much as fifteen feet above the ground. A bamboo ladder is constructed to give access to these watch towers and places of refuge. Without the danger of elephants probably no one would bother to build tree houses, but once built they are pleasantly cool on hot evenings, and families occasionally cook and sleep in them even if elephants are not an immediate danger. The field houses make it possible for all of the ordinary tasks of the villagers to be carried on in the fields as well as in the village, and if the fields are inconveniently distant from the village, some families live in them for several days at a time.

While the men are building these huts, the women work steadily at planting. They must first finish the planting of maize begun on the morning after the fire. They cover most of the field with maize, so that it grows up interspersed with everything else. Several varieties are known, including a popcorn, and others differ in size, color, and time of ripening. Women must also plant the root crops. These include several varieties of taro (*ta'a*), for which the women must dig holes with a hoe in which the seed taro can be placed. Sweet potatoes (*ta'malang*) are planted similarly, but only in low wet places near a stream. Sweet manioc (*ta'bolchu*) is generally planted only along the boundaries of the fields; it grows into a higher and bushier plant than most other crops. Since people with neighboring fields often plant manioc on either side of their mutual boundary, double hedges of manioc mark many of the borders during part of the growing season. Gourds (*rai, pong*) and some varieties of squash (*te'e*) are planted beside the field house, and are allowed to climb over its walls.

Two cash crops, ginger (*eching*) and cotton (*kil*), are also planted in the new fields. Ginger is planted in the same manner as other roots crops, but cotton must wait until the field houses are built since a man and woman must sow it cooperatively. Alone of the crops which are planted by making a hole with a dibble for the seed, cotton requires two people, one to make the holes and another to follow and put in the seeds—since these, it is said, are so big that it is difficult to get them into the hole if one must be alternately tossing them in with one hand and wielding the dibble with the other. Though other crops replace cotton in some areas, it is the main cash crop for the Rengsanggri people, and they distribute it over the entire area of a new field.

Other crops are planted in smaller amounts. Bananas (*terik*) are set out here and there in the fields. The fruits ripen throughout most of the year, though animals sometimes get them before the people do and they do not form an important part of the diet. Many vegetables are planted: sorrel (*galda*), onions (*rasin*), occasionally tomatoes (*baring belati*, literally 'foreign eggplant'), several varieties of broad pod beans (*genasu*), sugar cane (*grit*), and others. Individually these are not important, but they add variety to the diet as well as confusion to the fields, since they are planted more or less indiscriminately rather than in individual plots.

Several weeks are required to complete the planting, and there follow about two months of the most tedious work before the harvest begins. The rice fields, having been planted first, need the first cultivation, and as soon as this is finished the first weeding in the new fields must begin. This cultivation, called *a'jakra* (*a'a* 'field'; *jakra* 'right hand,' 'first.') may last from May into early June. Removing the weeds from the fields is not only strenuous, but demanding of considerable skill. With so many different kinds of plants mixed together in the fields, one must have a ready knowledge of the characteristics of both crops and weeds at all stages of growth to be able to separate one from the other; but Garos, with a name for every weed as well as for every crop, are trained to this task from childhood. Both men and women share in the weeding. They use a short-handled hoe with a simple iron blade, and as always when working in the fields they start at the bottom and work up the hillside, so that wherever the land is steep, as it almost always is, they can work on a patch that is somewhat above the level of their feet. Weeds grow rapidly, for this is the season when the rains begin. Rain becomes increasingly frequent through May, and in June the monsoon usually becomes firmly established, bringing occasional torrents and a welcome drop of 10 or 20 degrees in the temperature, and settling the dust which plagues the dry season. Cultivation continues even in the rain. In the heaviest showers, people take refuge in their field houses; but they cannot afford to neglect their work for long, since if they fall behind the weeds may get out of control and the fields have to be abandoned.

The first important crop to start ripening is maize; this may happen as early as June, though the main harvest is not until a month or two later. Some maize is eaten at this time of year, and if supplies are low it helps to tide families over until the other grains become ripe. Children especially may be given some corn on the cob for a treat, and everyone enjoys popcorn occasionally. Some maize is also used for brewing beer, though less often than either millet or rice. Most of the crop is sold in the market to Bengalis for 8 to 10 rupees per maund. (One maund = 83 lbs; one rupee = $.21.) Some households get 30 or 40 rupees from their sale of maize, depending upon their harvest and how much they choose to sell. A few ears of the first maize to be harvested are hung up on the outside of the front wall of each house as an offering to the ghosts of dead members of the household. Later, as other crops ripen, the first of each to be picked will similarly be hung on this wall. Aside from funerals, this is the only ritual where the ghosts of the dead figure specifically.

Another cultivation, known as *bamil*, now takes place in the new fields, and by the end of July the millet starts to ripen. Both men and women go to the fields to harvest the millet, which is a far more important crop than maize and may yield as much as 40 maunds. There is little market demand for millet, however, and almost all that is grown is consumed locally. The chaff from the first millet to be winnowed, which is bright yellow, is allowed to fall over a winnowing basket in which all the hoes and sickles used by the household for cultivating are collected, until the chaff nearly covers the tools. This ceremony, called "feeding the tools," is carried out only with millet. The millet is stored in the granary, and is eaten throughout the year. It is often mixed with rice, and the poorer people must use a relatively larger proportion of millet, which though much relied upon is the less desirable of the two grains.

A third cultivation, *sampang danga*, which follows the millet harvest, generally takes place in August. At this time many vegetable crops are taken from the fields more or less continuously, but a good deal of attention must also be paid to the old fields, where the rice is ripening and where it will soon be harvested. In late September or early October, following this cultivation, the new fields are given yet another weeding, *muradrata*, which unlike any of the previous cultivations is done with a sickle. A sickle is quicker and easier to use than a hoe, and hoeing is no longer required since so many of the crops have been taken out of the fields by this time. Moreover, the rains now begin to slacken, and the wild luxuriance of the weeds declines. Manioc ripens but is harvested only as needed since it spoils if not quickly eaten. If not harvested, it remains usable for many months.

The greatest of the annual festivals, *Wangala*, which ushers in the most beautiful time of year, generally occurs in October. The rains peter out, and the weather becomes sparkling and clear. The nights are then crisp and the days delightfully sunny. There is little rain, but it will be two months before the world dries out enough so that dust again becomes a problem. Taro can be harvested at this time. It can be stored in baskets in the house for several months. Gourds are picked and dried in the sun. Women use large bulbous gourds for storing water, and smaller ones with long slender necks are used for dippers to serve rice beer.

Some time after *Wangala* there is still another cultivation of the fields (*abia*). By then, the only important crops left in the fields are chili peppers and cotton. A few chilis may have been picked for immediate use as much as several months before now, but most are left until just before the cotton harvest or are even collected simultaneously with cotton. The harvester may carry a small basket into which he puts the chilis while he puts the cotton into a larger basket. Chilis are dried for two or three weeks, usually on the roof of the field house, and then stored for use in the house or taken to market to be sold. Women gin a portion of their cotton, but only enough to obtain seed for the following year. They use little wooden gins consisting of two rollers geared together and operated by a wooden handle. Strands of cotton are fed into the space between the rollers, like clothes into an old-fashioned wringer. The seeds are too big to fit between the rollers and are squeezed out of the cotton, which passes on through. The ginned cotton is sold, though the price does not exceed that for unginned cotton by enough to make ginning worth while if it were not for the seed. It is tedious, back-breaking labor, one of the few jobs I ever heard a Garo complain about. Every woman must spend several days at this, usually toward the end of January, and at this time the high-pitched wooden squeak of the gins is heard all day throughout the village. The cotton gin is the only practical use of the wheel made in conservative Garo villages today, though children make toy wagons, and trucks visit the markets.

Each year people collect some of the cotton stalks and burn them in order to obtain the ashes, which are apparently rich in soda. The ashes are stored in small conical baskets. Water poured through these drips out from the bottom point of the basket, and the solution with its accumulated soda is used in most Garo cooking. Garos say that it "softens" the food. The cotton harvest completes the use of the fields for the first year except occasionally for some root crops, especially sweet potatoes, which may be taken out still later in small amounts.

In January or February the men clear a new plot of land, but the previous year's fields must also be subjected to a second cleaning, known as *auita*. From now on these fields are called *a'breng* ('second year fields') to distinguish them from the newer *a'dal* (*a'a* 'field'; *gitdal* 'new'). The women scrape together little piles of sticks and brush—any remaining organic matter, of which there is not much, for this is the dry season, when all plants grow slowly and many wither away. The burning of these little piles of collected rubbish adds a note of desolation to the fields, for afterward there is hardly a green thing left, except for the occasional isolated tree that has escaped the clearer's axe. Field houses still stand, and women still dig an occasional tuber, but the general aspect of the fields is one of complete barrenness.

In March the fields are again put to use, this time exclusively for rice (*mi*). Rice is the most important and by far the most

valued crop of the Garos, and more ceremonies and lore are
connected with it than with any other. Garos recognize many
varieties of hill rice. These differ according to their time of
ripening and the size, shape and color of the kernel, and there
are both glutinous and non-glutinous types. Men invariably
referred me to their wives when I inquired about rice varieties,
since women take charge of the selection and preparation of
seed for planting, and each must spend at least a day sorting and
preparing it. They pointed out over a dozen varieties to me,
though each family plants no more than four or five. Everyone
plants a small amount of glutinous rice in a low, relatively wet
part of his fields. Glutinous rice is considered particularly good
for making rice beer, though it is also eaten on a few festive
occasions. The rice should be planted before the new fields are
burned, though not everybody finishes completely by that time.
Rice, like maize, is planted with the aid of a pointed dibble, but
unlike that of maize, the planting is done by both men and
women. The seed is carried in a small basket tied at one side of
the waist. Handfuls are taken from it and a few grains are skillfully tossed into each hole. Another person follows with a hoe,
uprooting any meager growing thing that may have escaped the
previous clearing, but not consistently covering the seeds. This
operation is called *samdimdanga* (*samdim* 'weed'; *danga* 'cultivate'). The rice planting takes a week or ten days, during which
the entire field is covered with seeded holes spaced six inches to
a foot apart, each containing about three to six grains of rice.

As in the first year of cultivation, the fields must be repeatedly
weeded during their second year. The first weeding (*a'jakra*)
takes place toward the end of April or the beginning of May.
In these old fields, as in the new fields, it is done when the crop
is first appearing. The second weeding, (*abrengdanga*, *abreng*
'old fields'; *danga* 'cultivate') is generally done in June, and the
final one (*abrengrata*, *rata* 'cut'), in July or August. As with the
*muradrata* cultivation in the new fields, for *abrengrata* a sickle
is used instead of a hoe. With only a single crop the work of the

old fields has less technological variety than that of the new: one must simply cultivate repeatedly to prevent the weeds from choking the growing rice plants. But several ceremonies are connected specifically with the rice crop, marking stages in its growth, and specifically designed to insure its well-being.

The rice harvest begins in early September. Virtually everybody in the village turns out to the fields at this time and all must work for at least a week before the harvest is finished. The rice is gathered by milking the grain from the plant with the bare hands. The grains of the varieties of rice grown under shifting cultivation are attached so loosely to the plant that they fall easily into the hand. The grain is first placed in small baskets which the harvesters tie to their waists, and which are periodically emptied into larger baskets. When these are full, the stronger young men carry them back to the village and deposit the paddy in the household's granary. It is stored here, to be used as needed throughout the year. Except that cattle may be allowed to graze in these fields, they are then abandoned. Some portions of the field houses, such as bamboo matting or wooden posts, may be salvaged and carried away for use in the new field house which will have to be built in a few months; but older portions are simply left to rot, and by the time the fields are to be cleared again little will be left. Weeds spring up quickly and soon turn the fields into a thicket, useless even as pasture.

Rice is certainly the most important single crop all through the Garo Hills. Some villages and areas within the district produced a slight surplus of rice, but during the years I was there, Rengsanggri had a slight deficit; this was made up by purchases at the market or, more often, from neighboring villages which had a surplus. Garos cannot estimate their rice production with any degree of accuracy. The crop is variable from year to year and also from household to household, depending both on the size of the fields and on the efficiency with which the weeds are kept down. Garos estimate that the yield should be ten or more times the amount of seed used. They themselves never measure the amount of their harvest except by the number of basket loads, and these are of variable size.

When women cook rice, they measure the amount with a bamboo tube or, sometimes, an old cigarette tin, which they know through experience to contain the amount the family needs. They are not able to estimate closely the weight or volume of this rice. I weighed the rice eaten in a day by a family of nine. The family was Jengnon's, which consisted of two adult men, three adult women, and four children who probably averaged less than half an adult portion each. The dry weight of the rice they consumed was about $3\frac{1}{4}$ seers (40 seers equal one maund, and thus one seer is just slightly over two English pounds), which would come to almost $\frac{1}{2}$ seer per day per adult, and probably did reach $\frac{1}{2}$ seer per adult male. Plains people, who are more used to estimating consumption in standard units, frequently give $\frac{1}{2}$ seer as the daily requirement of an adult male. Garos probably like to approximate this standard, but if rice is in short supply they may substitute millet for part of it. A family of this size, which is somewhat larger than average, would require about five or six seers of paddy per day (weight before husking) or perhaps fifty maunds (4000 lbs.) per year.

Garo estimates of what their crop *should* be run as high as 100 maunds or more, though they never weigh it. They habitually say their actual crop is poor, however—it is uncouth to say the harvest was good—and the rather exaggerated estimates of the possibilities help to convince them of the meagerness of even the best years.


FOOD AND DRINK

Though most crops are grown in the fields, a few people keep small gardens near their houses and most men possess a few trees somewhere in or near the village. Village gardens must be carefully fenced against wandering animals and sometimes must even be watered in the dry seasons, so many men prefer not to bother with them. They yield a few vegetables, but never add major quantities of food to the diet.

Fruit trees are more important. In some villages oranges (*kumila, narang*) or areca nuts (*gui*) have become important cash crops, overshadowing even cotton. Oranges have not been grown successfully in Rengsanggri, and areca palms are recently introduced and still scarce, but other fruit is grown for local use in considerable quantity. Whoever plants a tree always has a special claim to its fruit, but no one denies to others the right of picking it for immediate use. Generally when a fruit is in season there is an ample supply for everyone, and since there is little cash market for most kinds, no one is proprietary about the crop. Jackfruit (*tebrong*) is the commonest, and almost every man owns a few jackfruit trees. When the fruits ripen, everyone gorges himself for two or three happy if occasionally dyspeptic weeks. Other fruit trees—among them pomelo (*jambura*), lemon (*temachu*), papaya (*modipol*), guava (*kompiram*) and tamarind (*cheng*)—are found in smaller numbers, and are often eaten mainly by the children.

All Garo families fish occasionally, and gather wild plants from the forest to lend variety to their cuisine; and most of them also keep a few domestic animals. Cattle are the largest of these, though even they are diminutive by American standards, seldom being more than waist-high to their owners. They are never milked, but are kept as sacrificial animals—a purpose for which they are prized above all others—and to supply meat. Garos sometimes raise calves, but they need more cattle for slaughter and sacrifice than they actually raise themselves, and their requirements are met by purchasing cattle in the market from Moslem traders who drive them in from the plains. Cattle are let loose to forage in the old fields after the rice has been cut, but during the growing season, and at night throughout the year, they are kept tethered in a special extension which is built in front of a house to provide a room for them, though it is used for general storage as well. While they are thus tethered the owners must bring them forage; this consists largely of the shoots, sprouts, and leaves of bamboo, which grow wild in profusion. Once each day water must also be brought.

Pigs run freely through the village during the daytime, but are prevented from entering the fields by the fence which surrounds it. At night they are enclosed in special bamboo sheds built for them by their owners. Garos feel that it is impossible to keep pigs in the house as they do cattle because the pigs bring in too many fleas. The chaff from rice and millet is systematically collected and fed to the pigs, and the mash from which rice beer has been poured off is also saved for them. Of course, pigs also scavenge about the village and help clean up the garbage, which is always thrown indiscriminately from the houses. They are occasionally bought or sold, but the villagers raise just about enough pigs for their own use and rarely buy any or sell any in other villages or at the market. Pigs are not ordinarily killed except at sacrifices, but these come so frequently that pork is a fairly regular item of the diet.

Chickens are the commonest of all domestic animals. These colorful birds are similar to the jungle fowl that live wild in the surrounding forests. Garos do not systematically feed chickens but let them scavenge freely. They manage to get a good many of the husks and even the kernels of rice, for when paddy is spread on mats to dry before being pounded and winnowed, chickens are always about. The women constantly chase them away, but never succeed in protecting their grain entirely. Chickens are enclosed in small cages at the front of the house at night, primarily to protect them against marauding animals.

Ducks require more care, and are kept less often than chickens. They must be given cooked rice in both morning and evening if they are to grow fat enough to taste properly. They often get the burned rice from the bottom of the regular cooking pot. The sixty households of Rengsanggri at one time had

67 cattle, 116 pigs of all sizes, about 200 chickens, 48 ducks, and 6 goats.

A few people also keep cats and dogs. Cats are desirable as mousers, and watchdogs are valued, but both are also regarded with a moderate warmth as pets and are usually allowed to sleep inside the house with the family, rather than in the cattle room to the front. Cooked rice must be fed to dogs and cats, and thus they are an expense that many people are unwilling to bear. I was told that dogs are occasionally sacrificed and eaten, but dog sacrifices are certainly much rarer than those of cattle, pigs, or chickens, and I never witnessed one myself.

Most Garos do some fishing in the streams and rivers that cut through their country. The people of Rengsanggri are fortunate in living beside a good-sized brook, so that—particularly during the dry season, when the water is low and fishing easy—fresh fish give variety to their food supply, though they are never plentiful enough to be a real staple. The fish they catch are never more than three or four inches long, and are often smaller. Many fishing techniques are used. Some men have circular nets which they throw while wading in the water. The net sinks toward the bottom, its weighted edges descending most rapidly, and with luck a small fish or two is ensnared as it goes down. Two or three people, either men or women but most often youths, may cooperate in poisoning fish. This is accomplished by blocking off a portion of the stream, diverting the fresh current away from it, and repeatedly pounding, wetting, and repounding a particular kind of bark in order to obtain a foamy extract which stupefies the fish. A few small fish rise to the surface, flopping so sluggishly that they can be quickly seized by hand. When the water is very low, a group of ten or more, again most often young people, may simply move upstream in a body, using scoops more or less randomly, hoping to pull out a fish, and turning rocks over to see what animal life may be available underneath. Individual men set out fish traps which may be left overnight.

A less usual method of fishing requires the cooperation of a large number of people, and even becomes a gay social event for most of the young people of a village. They literally bail out a small pool in a stream, which is dammed off from above to prevent more water from flowing in, and from below to prevent the fish from swimming away. This done, the young people take turns bailing out the water and throwing it downstream. When the water level is sufficiently reduced, everybody plods out into the mud, turning over rocks and digging in the pools of water that remain to extract whatever fish, fry, or tadpoles may have been left helpless by the receding water.

Three men in Rengsanggri owned antiquated guns. They occasionally shot a jungle fowl or, rarely, a larger animal such as a deer, but hunting afforded a barely significant addition to the diet. No other hunting devices were ever used. The forests do provide many wild crops—leaves, herbs, bamboo shoots, etc.—which lend variety to the cooking though they do not add much bulk. Banana leaves from plants that have gone wild in the jungle are collected in large numbers, since Garos use them as plates to hold their food at meals, throwing them away after a single use.

To these foods which Garos raise or gather themselves are added dried fish, salt, and occasionally small amounts of spices, tea, sugar, and candy which are bought at the market. Each meal consists of a boiled grain—rice if possible, but if necessary including a variable proportion of millet—and a side dish of curry. The most common everyday curry is made with a few dried fish, some tubers or other vegetables, and enough chilis to burn even Bengali tongues. For special occasions meat is substituted for the dried fish, but whichever is used, it is always combined with vegetables or fruit of some sort. Beer brewed from rice or millet is consumed on all occasions of importance. Even a casual visitor may be made welcome with a glass of beer if the family has some recently brewed, and for large ceremonies and festivals it is indispensable. Women brew the beer by first cooking the grain and then spreading it out on a mat in the back of the house. Yeast, which is grown by seeding finely ground rice flour with old yeast, is sprinkled over the grain and then thoroughly mixed with it. The mash is then placed in a large earthenware pot, covered with a tightly tied banana leaf, and set to one side in the back of the house to ferment for two to three weeks, or until it becomes fragrant and ready to drink. Then a basketry sleeve is placed vertically in the center of the pot, and water is poured down through the mash so that it filters into the central well, while the sleeve holds back the mash. The beer, which is dipped out of the well with a gourd, may be refiltered through the mash a number of times. Depending upon how much water is used and how fresh the batch is, the brew varies from slightly stronger to considerably weaker than American beer. When sweet it is palatable and refreshing, but it is variable and can sometimes be very sour. The first taste of a new pot of beer is always critically made, and the drinkers solemnly pronounce on its quality. Everyone except the Christians drinks rice beer, and Garos hold their liquor well. The usual reaction is an increase in conviviality, booming good nature, and eventually sleep. Alcohol rarely leads to violence or even to quarreling.

Every Garo smokes. Little Indian cigarettes, *biris*, are purchased in the market, but Garos sometimes grow their own tobacco and roll it in newspaper or in a leaf. Even more frequent is a mixture of molasses with tobacco purchased loose at the market, which is smoked on a water pipe or hooka. Garos buy hookas consisting of a coconut base, which is filled with water, and a turned wooden stem on top of which is placed a pottery pipe bowl. In this bowl the tobacco mixture is placed and covered with glowing coals. The smoke is drawn down the stem, through the water in the coconut, and out through a hole into the mouth. Garos also make themselves similar pipes out of bamboo, and the gurgle of these hookas accompanies all social gatherings. These pipes are invariably passed around among all present, as are cigarettes, for smoking is a social act and it would be unthinkably inconsiderate to smoke in anyone's presence without offering a puff.

## TECHNOLOGY

The most impressive objects manufactured by the Garos are unquestionably their houses. These are really only huge baskets made of bamboo and set on posts. The largest may be 80 feet in length, but they are seldom more than about 15 feet wide exclusive of the width of the great overhanging eaves, and some are no more than 25 feet long by 8 or 10 feet wide. The size of the house is the best single criterion for judging the economic status and the related social position of the family but all houses in the Rengsanggri area, whether large or small, are built in much the same manner and with the same internal arrangement. The front entrance of the house is at one end, close to ground level, while the back end is often high off the ground over the slope of a hill. The main section of the house is framed with bamboo poles, which support a thatched roof and walls and floor of split bamboo matting; and the entire structure sits on top of a jumble of wooden posts. This is the perfect house for this country of earthquakes, for while it may tremble it is much too flexible to break.

At the front many houses have, as has previously been mentioned, a special room for the cattle. This, unlike the rest of the house, has no floor but the cleared, packed-down earth. Before this room, under the overhanging eaves, the women spend many hours pounding and winnowing the family's supply of rice, and it is here that everyone gathers to chat in the mornings and evenings. The main portion of any house but the smallest is divided into two rooms: a larger central section where the family cooks, eats, and visits, and to the rear a smaller, more private section which serves as a sleeping room for the oldest married couple of the household. The main room is dominated by a central fireplace built on a platform of earth and surmounted by a shelf where cooking provisions can be stored. Smoke from the fireplace is allowed to seep out through the thatch and the chinks in the woven bamboo wall. If the air is still, the smoke may not escape rapidly and the house may fill uncomfortably with smoke; but more often the smoke rises rapidly to pass through the ceiling. Since the people sit either on the floor or on low stools, they are usually below the smoke and thus are bothered by it only when they must stand up to move around. An additional fireplace is often placed in one of the front corners of the main room, and sometimes there is a third one in the sleeping room so that it can be kept warm in winter. The walls and ceiling are hung with the family's possessions—baskets, tools, cooking and eating utensils—and two or three bamboo poles suspended from ropes serve as racks to hold the family's spare clothes and blankets when these are not in use. Pots containing threshed rice and other staples line one wall to the front, and pots of brewing rice beer stand at the back. Several low stools may be arranged around the wall, pushed out of the way when not in use. At least one old head-hunting sword is stuck into the back wall of every house, and one or more shields may lean against the wall below the sword. Nobody now living can remember head-hunting but everyone has heard of it, and all take a certain delight in recalling the bravery of their ancestors. The sword and shield are now reduced to little more than symbols of the household, but they stay in what is the most honored spot in the house. At large gatherings men use a sword and shield in solitary dances, and swords are used occasionally in the ritual sacrifice of animals; but otherwise they rest idly in their place on the back wall. On certain occasions the householder places a few piles of rice on the floor in front of them, and pours rice beer over the rice, as an offering to the gods and spirits, before the guests take their share.

The middle room is the public room, but while the much

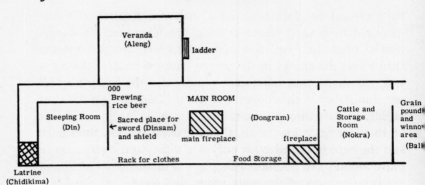

TYPICAL RENGSANGGRI HOUSE

smaller one at the rear is more private, visitors enter it readily if there is some cause to do so. It is used by the oldest couple or by an old widow of the house, while the younger couple and the children sleep in the main room. It serves also as a storage place. Most families have at least one chest, made of wood or cheap metal, which is usually kept padlocked. The family heirlooms—gongs, treasured pieces of ancient cloth, and jewelry—are kept in these and taken out only on special occasions.

Behind the sleeping room, and reached by a narrow passage, is a small latrine constructed simply by leaving an open lattice for a floor. Being at the very rear of the house, it is high up off the ground, and it allows family members, and their guests at large rice-beer drinking parties, to avoid having to forge out into the jungle at night or in the rain. When necessary hot water is poured over and through the lattice to wash away the odor.

Most, but not all, of the houses have a veranda which can be reached from a small door in the side wall or by a ladder reaching up from the ground outside. Here women can do some of their work in the pleasant sunshine of winter. They can sit here to gin their cotton or spread out the mash when they are preparing rice beer. Men use the veranda as a platform for loading cotton into baskets. Beyond any such mundane purpose, however, the porches are also fine on summer evenings when one wants to get away from the cooking fire and to catch as much of the breeze as possible. Here friends and neighbors gather casually for a chat after the day's work, and on gala occasions the veranda can hold the overflow of guests. When tired from dancing, the young people frequently gather on someone's veranda to joke and tease and flirt.

When newly built, the color of the houses is a warm tan. In the hot season the new houses in each village stand out brightly from the rest, but a single monsoon weathers them to the darker gray of the older ones. Anyone may build a house more or less wherever he pleases, though no one would care to build a house too close to another, or in the middle of an established courtyard. There is always room for expansion at the edge of the village if there is danger of crowding in the central part.

The arrangement of the house emphasizes both the unique organization of the family, and its relationship to the rest of the village. On the one hand, the very form of the house sets off the family from everyone else. A house has no windows and its doors are closed at night; and no one, day or night, enters another's house without first calling out to announce his presence. On the other hand, houses are built partly in order to entertain, and it is for this reason as much as any other that rich men must have big houses. The central room is designed to accommodate visitors, and the verandas, though used for many other purposes, are most often built with special thought for guests. Garos visit each other's houses constantly, not only during large festivals, but also on petty errands or simply for casual gossip; but the social boundary between one household and another is never ambiguous, but is as distinct as the physical boundary of the house itself.

Each family also has a few small buildings—granaries, field houses, pig sties, or wood sheds—but none of these approach the elaborateness of the houses. Almost everything else that the Garos manufacture is made from bamboo. As a raw material bamboo is exceedingly versatile, and many of its varied physical properties are put to use. Its hollowness makes it suitable for various types of pipes and containers. By knocking out the nodes of a long piece and fixing one end in a tumbling stream, Garos produce an available supply of running water. Each village has a few such spots where people bathe, wash their cooking pots, and fill their gourds. A useful container is made by cutting a section of bamboo with one node left in the bottom. Garos store many things in such containers and on some festive occasions they also use green bamboo sections to cook in.

Bamboo is extremely tough when whole, and can be used as structural members for all sorts of construction. But it splits easily in a lengthwise direction, and can be shaved down to extremely thin, flexible strips. These are used to join larger pieces; a house is literally tied together with them, and stands without a single piece of metal or even a wooden peg.

Finer and more carefully smoothed strips of bamboo are the basic element in most kinds of Garo basketry. These include delicate baskets for carrying rice, one of which may take an entire day to weave. Rougher baskets may be made more rapidly, and openwork baskets used for carrying cotton are produced so quickly that Garos can afford to give them away with the cotton when it is sold. Other baskets are designed for a multitude of special purposes: small round openwork baskets for carrying chickens; small, closely woven ones for carrying seed while planting, somewhat rougher ones which can be pinched closed for fish; larger ones for chili peppers, and still larger and coarser ones for firewood. All except the smallest of these are designed to be carried from a tump line, and the basic material is always bamboo, though small quantities of cane are used in the finest of them. Winnowing baskets, scoops, mats, and children's toys are all made from bamboo. Great skill is required to make these objects, and it is the only skill which Garos point out as specifically requiring instruction. All men learn to make baskets, but it is recognized that some men attain a greater degree of proficiency than others. For all the skill required, however, little imagination is shown, for Garos invariably follow a fixed and well-known pattern in their bamboo weaving.

Bamboo leaves are sometimes used as thatch, and are given to the cows as fodder. Dried bamboo makes excellent kindling, and a bunch of bamboo can be used as a first-class torch, though wood makes a more even and long lasting cooking fire. Young bamboo shoots provide an excellent addition to the diet. It is no wonder that Garos have a hard time imagining a country without bamboo.

Most Garos are much less proficient at working with wood. Mortars for pounding rice are made from a cross section of a large tree trunk, with a hole carved out of the center. Pestles are wooden poles, the height of a man; to loosen the husks, the women rhythmically pound the paddy contained in the mortar. Drums are made of a hollowed and carefully shaped piece of wood with rawhide stretched over the end. The largest house posts are made from tree trunks, but these are at most roughly finished. Rather than labor over a post, one looks for a tree with a straight section or with a well placed fork and uses it with as little shaping as possible.

Older Rengsanggri people can remember when a few other items of daily use were manufactured. They once used belt looms for weaving, and even spun some of their own cotton. They wove the blue cloth stripes with red and white which was traditional both as skirts for the women and as loin cloths for the men. Spinning seems to have disappeared completely, but in some villages a few women still use belt looms, and more elaborate treadle-operated hand looms have been reintroduced from the plains. Today, however, most Garos depend upon mill cloth. They are particularly fond of a dark blue cotton cloth, from which women make simple wraparound skirts tucked in at the waist and falling below the knees. The same color or another may be used for turbans, which are worn wrapped around the head so as to leave the crown exposed. Men often continue to wear the brief loin cloth, but short pants are becoming increasingly popular. Both men and women often wear knitted cotton T-shirts, which are usually black. Shoes are a sign of real sophistication.

In Rengsanggri bark is used only to make tump lines, though in some areas a very rough bark blanket is made. I was told that many years ago bark cloth was sometimes used for clothing, but it is no longer considered fine enough to wear. Few Garos manufacture pottery today, though in one remote section of the hills women still coil clay into large pots of a sort much prized for brewing rice beer. Other pottery, which is mass-produced on potters' wheels in the plains, is purchased from traders. Older men can also remember when Garos worked their own iron and made their tools, though I never heard of smelting. Today even the working of iron has been abandoned. Cloth, blankets, pottery, metal cooking pots, and tools are all obtained from the market, and without the market Garos today would hardly know how to survive.

### SPIRITS AND GODS

Their technological skills and knowledge enable the Garos to draw sustenance from the natural environment in which they live. They are also surrounded by a spiritual environment, and though the Garos are remarkably uncertain of its nature, they know that they must behave in appropriate ways toward it if disaster is not to overtake them. Other than *me'mang* ('ghost',) the Garos have only one general term, *mite*, for supernatural beings; but this covers both beings whom we would call gods and certain lesser, quite different nuisances, which hardly deserve to be known by any term more dignified than spirit. The latter, distinguished from the gods as "the *mite* that bite," are numerous and ubiquitous, and when they bite they cause disease. Beyond this, little is concretely known about the *mite*, and the usual response to a request to describe them more fully is "We don't know what they look like because we can't see them. What do you think about them?" Garos were puzzled, for instance, by the question of whether the spirits were male or female. Such questions simply do not arise, and in the Garo language it is possible to talk about a spirit without being forced to choose a third person pronoun indicative of gender. There is no question but that they cause disease, however, and just enough is known of their habits, even if not of their appearance, to allow such action to be taken against them that they will be persuaded to stop biting and permit the sick person to recover. The symptoms of the disease indicate which spirit is causing it, thus allowing those concerned to choose the proper kind of sacrifice. Any Garo can name a few *mite*, along with the disease that each produces, the place where it lives—or at any rate the place in which the sacrifice to it should be performed— and the manner of the sacrifice. A few men who are more interested or skilled in these matters can give dozens of names. *Susume mite*, for instance, causes alternate chills and fever, a frequent complaint in this malarial country, and to drive it away an altar of bamboo and leaves must be built in the yard in front of the house. A pig or chicken is sacrificed at this altar, and the animal is eaten. When a spirit known as *but* causes an attack of dysentery, a small boat is built of bamboo, dabbed with the blood of a sacrificial animal, and floated down the river; and the spirit is supposed to follow it. Other *mite* are held responsible for paleness, lassitude, skin diseases, and all the other aches and pains which plague the Garos. Each can be pacified with a special form of sacrifice.

These *mite* live in many places. Some dwell in the village, others in the jungle, near a tree, or by a stream or waterfall. A fork in a road is a favorite place, and powerful *mite* are said to live on mountain tops. All are dealt with in the same general fashion, though the details of the sacrifices differ. Several men usually spend about two hours building an altar. Most altars are built of bamboo and leaves, but the precise form depends upon the particular spirit to whom the sacrifice is to be directed. Once the altar is built, a ritually skilled man must offer an egg, a chicken, a pig, or even a cow, depending upon the seriousness of the disease and the demands of the *mite*. This priest kills the animal in a ritually prescribed manner, and smears the blood on to the altar. He recites a number of chants while standing or squatting before the altar, and usually pours a bit of rice beer on to the ground as an additional offering. At a sacrifice to cure disease, as on other occasions when animals are ceremoniously killed, the priest inspects their viscera for omens. If the proper portion of a chicken's intestines prove to be filled, for instance, the prognosis is good; otherwise it is bad. While the priest is performing the ritual, the men who have helped build the altar sit around, chatting and joking, with no outward signs of respect or attention. There is no ecstasy and no sleight of hand, and the sick person is not even necessarily present. When the formalities are completed, the helpers prepare the animal and cook it into a curry. Rice is boiled, and all of the helpers share in the ensuing meal. Typically, the entire sacrifice, from the time the participants first assemble to the time they finish the feast, takes three or four hours. Afterward the participants go to their own houses. They are not supposed to go to their fields for the whole day, though they may do chores about the house. Sacrifices of this sort are the commonest kind of ceremony performed by the people of Rengsanggri. They involve only a half dozen or so neighbors and relatives, and they are held whenever the need arises. Occasionally two or three may even be held on the same day if several people in the village are sick. Altogether several hundred sacrifices are likely to be performed in the village of Rengsanggri in a single year.

Sacrifices are usually quite effective, for within a few days people usually feel much better and are able to go back to work. Some spirits are more stubborn, however, and may demand a larger animal, or sometimes developing symptoms may show that a mistake had been made about the identity of the biter, and so another sacrifice must be performed to a different spirit. If the village should have an unusual number of sick people, more dramatic procedures may be tried. The men of the village may all cooperate by going to the jungle and attempting to catch a monkey. They are not experts at this and the monkeys are elusive, but by surrounding the animals, using sticks, stones, and sometimes even a gun, they may be able to get one or more. These, if not killed in capture, are soon dispatched, for they bite too much to be carried back alive. While the women closet themselves at home behind closed doors, the men drag the monkey systematically around the village, pausing before each house, and then suspend it from a pole near a river, in the hope that the spirits will leave them alone for a while. Of course, in spite of all efforts some people die. Some spirits are simply too strong, and kill their victims no matter what efforts are made to drive them away. Garos realize that even the best of their sacrifices cannot dissuade them.

However vague the Garos may be on the characteristics of the spirits, they have no doubt of their existence. The fact that other people do not perform sacrifices, or sacrifice in a different manner, has no effect upon the value placed by the Garos on their own procedures. I once heard a Nepali negotiating to buy an animal to be used in a ritual. A Garo asked him curiously whether the ritual was to be directed toward a Garo spirit or a Nepali spirit, and the answer, that it would of course be a Nepali spirit, seemed entirely reasonable to everyone. It is even doubtful how much effect Christianity has on the belief in spirits. Certainly the belief does not suddenly cease, even if sacrifices do.

Christians, and other Garos who live in close contact with the plains people, use jungle medicines and even modern western medicines more often than the people of Rengsanggri. Even in Songmagri, one mile away, medicines are said to be more popular than in Rengsanggri. A few jungle medicines are known in Rengsanggri, and the people occasionally make use of western drugs when they are available, but overwhelmingly the most frequent method of dealing with disease is sacrifice.

Not all supernatural beings are so uniformly malign as the biting *mite*. Most of the others, the "creating" *mite* as they are occasionally called, are more or less neutral if not positively friendly. They are a bit more remote from daily life, but harmony between men and these gods, as they can be appropriately called, must be maintained by several annual sacrifices. There is confusion among the Garos as to how many of these gods exist and how many names each one has, and it is quite impossible to decide whether two names stand for two different gods or for two aspects of the same god, since Garos describe them now in one way and now in the other. Rabuga, Ranaga, Tatara or Dakgipa, are used as names for a god who is believed to have made the world and man. Dakgipa, in fact, means quite literally "the one who makes." These names are called out in the course of sacrifices to ward off disease, but the sacrifices are directed primarily toward the lesser biting spirits, and not toward Rabuga. Saljong is a name referring to a god who presides over crops. Some identify Saljong with Rabuga, but others are inclined to regard him as distinct. At any rate, it is specifically to Saljong that most of the annual sacrifices are dedicated, particularly those that are held in the fields. Saljong controls the water and the rain, and the growing of all things. When the dried fields are burned at the beginning of planting, Saljong sees the smoke of the fire and comes to join the people as they worship him in their fields. He supervises them as they fix the boundaries, and he blinds the people if they later move the markers—the only example of supernatural punishent for immoral behavior that I ever heard of. Saljong is not an ordinary biting spirit, and the blindness which he causes is incurable, but he is more intimately concerned with the daily affairs of the Garos than the somewhat more remote, if abstractly speaking no less powerful Rabuga.

There are other gods, though none quite so important as these. Susume and Salgera are said to be brothers. Susume is associated with the moon, and may blind people or lame them, but the diseases caused by this god can be cured by sacrifice. Susume in fact holds an intermediate position between the ordinary biting *mite* and the creating *mite*. Salgera (*sal* 'sun') is associated with the sun and is less troublesome than his brother, and so he receives no sacrifices. A goddess with the names Nuring, Noting, Miring, and Mikal is sometimes considered to be the wife of Rabuga, but she is not an important figure. Minima, literally 'mother of rice,' is a guardian of that important crop. The gods who bear these and other names are sometimes described as though tied to each other by kinship bonds, but at other times they seem to be simply different names of the same god. The Garos are vague about any more definite characteristics. They tell a few stories about the gods, some of which have a bearing upon the origin of the people themselves, but different men tell varying or even conflicting stories. Many people simply admit their ignorance of the details of the pantheon. As with the kinship ties of their more remote ancestors, people believe that there must somewhere be a truth among the suppositions concerning gods and the origin of men, and that one should be able to find an expert who could be asked if one really needed to know what the truth was. But remote origins have no great importance today, and in daily life it is enough to know that Saljong should be worshiped several times each year by calling his name and by pouring rice beer on the ground before an altar built in his honor.

Garos also display uncertainty as to the fate of the soul after death. It does seem that the mode of death affects the destiny of the soul, for those who die unnaturally in an accident or from an unusual disease, or who are killed by a wild animal, have difficulty in reaching the country of the dead; thus they may stay to haunt the place where they die, apparently holding something of a grudge against those who are still living. Ghosts are expected in strange places, especially at night, and while these are not related to specific persons, Garos suggest that ghosts are responsible for the spooky sensations one has at night. Even those who die naturally must undergo a perilous journey to get to the land of the dead. An ogre called Nawang waits at one road junction on the way, and he will allow the dead person to pass only if he is propitiated with earrings, and for this reason most tradition-minded Garos are careful to wear earrings at all times so as to be equipped if they should need them. There is reputed to be a lake along the road where the dead people all bathe. The lake is black with ashes, since so many recently cremated people bathe there. Eventually, however, the soul finds its way to the land of the dead. Perhaps the soul enters the belly of a woman there and is born. As far as anyone knows, it lives in much the same fashion as it lived in this world, for that world probably has houses, and fields and cotton, and eventually the people who live there, die too. The country seems to have an unusual number of boulders lying about, but babies cry, pigs squeal, and firewood is cut. Some Garos claim to have heard these things, but anyone who actually sees them would surely die. This after-world is described as the "country" of the dead people, not as a really different world. In describing it people point vaguely up, but more toward the top of a mountain than to the sky. Some Garos avoid one of their mountains because it is believed to contain this abode of the dead. However, a Garo hardly speaks of these things without doubting and hesitating and admitting that he doesn't really know because he hasn't seen the things himself.

Side by side with this concept of an after-world is the belief that the soul can somehow be born again into this world, and even into the same family. Occasionally people recognize a sign, such as a birthmark, which shows them that a baby has been reborn from an earlier existence, since someone else may have had similar marks. A soul occasionally deserts a man's body and enters a woman's womb to be reborn, without the first man's actually dying. Naturally the man grows thin and weak, and if nothing is done, he will die when the baby is born; and if the baby does live to be born it is likely to cry a great deal. However, the ailing man will probably recognize his difficulty, and preventive action can be taken. A string must be suspended from the back to the front of the sick person's house, with another string dangling from it toward a pile of rice on the floor. Altars must be built and sacrifices made. If at some point the string should dip slightly, this is a sign that the soul has returned along the string, and the string must be quickly cut so as to prevent the soul from escaping down it again. The baby will of course die before it is born, but the people doing the ceremony to retrieve the soul need not know where this is happening. Garos are puzzled as to why souls should act in such a peculiar way.

The belief in the transference of the soul from one person to another also figures in the custom, when a man or woman dies, of presenting a gift to the house where he or she was raised. The gift is explicitly destined as a sign for the soul, to allow it to find its way back to the house where it had been born once before. When challenged to reconcile a belief in an after-world with that of rebirth in this world, Garos may suggest that after living out its life in the after-world, the soul's turn may then come to be born again here; but mostly they find it unnecessary to try to reconcile the two beliefs.

No suggestion is made that a man's behavior in this world affects his later destiny. Spirits and gods are amoral, and punishment for wrong behavior comes in this world or not at all. One treats the spirits and gods with respect and circumspection because they can cause sickness and crop failure, but they do not send these as punishment for immoral behavior. Morality has a more pragmatic basis. Nothing is wrong unless it hurts someone else, and one may expect that the other person and his family will take action against the wrongdoer. One need not wait for punishment from the gods.

Garos had difficulty in understanding the suggestion that evil men might manipulate supernatural forces to bring harm to other men. A few said that they had heard of such things among their neighbors, but no Garo gives a moment's thought to being himself endangered by witchcraft. Spirits need no encouragement to bite. Garos even take a rather casual attitude toward tiger men. Everyone knows that some people who live normal lives in the day change into tigers at night and in their roaming may be a menace to others; but I have been cautioned against saying anything to a woman suspected of changing to a tiger at night, not because I would be endangered but because it would be impolite of me to call attention to the woman's unfortunate condition.

There are other ways in which a Garo maintains his peaceful relationship with the supernatural beings which surround him. Some crops must not be eaten before a certain ceremony. One doesn't beat drums while the rice is ripening, for to do so might offend the spirits or gods and bring suffering to the transgressor. But the Garos are hardly oppressed by fears of the supernatural, and the usages they follow are so taken for granted that they cause little feeling of deprivation. Moreover, one man's transgressions harm only himself, so no one need keep a watchful eye on other people lest they bring down the fury of the gods on the whole community. This salutary attitude allows each man to conduct his behavior with little fear of moral disapproval from others, and helps to keep the Garos from getting too worried about the horrible effects of some offence to the gods. Most ceremonial behavior is concerned with repairing things that have gone wrong, not with prevention.

The annual festivals, however, do have ceremonies which are designed to preserve harmony with the supernatural, though the festivals include far more than rituals. They coordinate the agricultural activities of the people, marking out significant stages in the annual cycle, and they provide occasions for the most joyous celebrations of the year. Solemnity has no part in

Garo religion. Even sacrifices are carried out in a matter-of-fact, almost secular manner; while at the annual ceremonies rice beer flows more copiously than at any other time, and with feasting and dancing everyone enjoys himself to the fullest.

For most of the Garos, including those of Rengsanggri, the greatest festival of all is *Wangala*. This usually comes in October, but since each village sets its own time, there are two or three weeks during which *Wangala* is being performed in one or another near-by village. The celebration even of a single village lasts many days. *Wangala* comes after most of the harvest is well finished, but it is less closely tied to the agricultural cycle than any other festival. It comes, however, at the end of the rains, and the beginning of the cold season, when work in the fields slackens, though a few chilis and some cotton remain to be picked. The festival comes in the same season as the *Pujas*, which are celebrated by the neighboring Bengali and Assamese Hindus. Garos are aware of the parallel and sometimes even refer to their own celebrations as the "Garo *Puja*" but this does not imply that the Garos are worshiping the same gods, or that their ceremony closely parallels that of the Hindus.

Preparations for *Wangala* begin well before the celebrations are due. Cows must be purchased from the market to provide meat for the feast. Many people now buy new clothes in order to be elegant for the celebration, and men usually repair their houses; in particular they are likely to build or repair their verandas to make room for their visitors during the festival. On the day preceding the first ceremony, the village is busy with the slaughter of cows. Several households usually cooperate in buying and killing a cow, and divide the meat which is obtained. Slaughter is a messy business, but it is done in the midst of the village, and the butchers display about as much squeamishness as they do in paring their fingernails.

In the evening the first entertainment takes place at the bachelors' house, where the young men act as hosts to all the other villagers. As many men as can fit crowd into the bachelors'

house, and the youths serve them beer, rice, and curry
prepared from a cow that they have bought and butchered
themselves. The women and large numbers of children crowd
around outside, and they too share in the feast and drink. The
first few dances of the festival follow the feast, but they are only
a preview of what is to come.

The next day is called *churugala*, for the first real ceremony
when rice beer (*chu*) is poured (*rua*) as an offering to Saljong.
The *nokma* ('headman') performs this ceremony in his own
house. Banana leaves are spread out in a square around the
central fireplace; upon them a white squash, a ginger root, an
onion, and a taro tuber, each cut in half, are spread, along with
cracked rice, and thus "shown to Saljong." None of these vegetables are to be eaten before this ceremony. Rice beer is offered
to the gods at the back of the house. Everyone drinks and beats
the gongs and drums. This is not the main ceremony, however,
and not all the men of the village attend. Some are always too
busy with other preparations.

After this ceremony the *nokma*'s house is decorated. The
women of each house prepare fine rice flour and mix it with
water to form a paste. In the *nokma*'s house the posts and beams
are first marked with finger dots of rice paste. If the men can
reach the ridgepole, they decorate it with rice-flour prints of the
whole palm. Afterwards the bachelors go about the village helping the men of each house to decorate it in the same way. When
new, the flour looks bright and white, but as the months go by
it yellows and blends with the yellow of the bamboo, though it
never disappears completely, and after several years one may
see several layers of this *Wangala* decoration. Only a new house
built within the current year is entirely without it.

The main ceremony comes the next day, and is called
*satsatsoa*, literally the burning (*soa*) of the *satsat*, a bark which
gives a strong odor of incense when it is kindled. *Satsatsoa* is
also performed by the *nokma* in his house, and a larger crowd of
villagers assembles than for the earlier *churugala*. As always on

**1** Few parts of the Garo Hills District lie at an altitude of more than two or three thousand feet, but the ground is seldom level. In most of the district the jungle has been periodically cut so that patches of cultivated land are interspersed with patches of jungle of varying ages.

ch village consists of clusters of houses which are usually arranged und one or more open courtyards.

**3** Although the front ends of the houses are built close to ground level, the backs frequently radiate out over the descending slope of a hill, and must be supported by a jumble of posts.

**4**
Tree houses are built
the fields to serve
lookout towers a
places of refuge agair
marauding wild el
phants, but they a
pleasant and cool on
hot summer evenin
and are sometimes ev
used for cooking, ea
ing, and sleeping.

**5** Each village where the traditional religion is still practiced has at least
one bachelors' house. They differ from the ordinary houses in having
their front built high from the ground and in being open on one end.

**6** One of the main jobs that must be done at any kind of construction is the shaping of pieces of bamboo to be used in the building. Many older men sit to one side for most of the day and do nothing but shave off the thin, flexible strips that are used to tie the larger pieces of the house together.

**7** Younger men frame the building and then weave the bamboo matting to make the walls. That old posts have been reused in this building can be seen from the spots of rice-flour paste which decorate them and which are left over from previous *Wangala* celebrations.

**8**

The back wall of each house is adorned with a head-hunting sword held in a bamboo cup. The doorway in which Ringin sits leads to the back room, which is used for storage and sleeping.

**9**

The main room is dominated by its central fireplace, which is built on an earth platform and surmounted by a shelf on which cooking materials are kept.

**10**

The ceilings are used to hang many of the people's possessions. This keeps them out of the way when not needed, and in the case of the baskets places them where they get a maximum of smoke from the fire, which helps to preserve them.

**11** On the morning after the fields are burned each family starts planting and each performs a sacrifice and eats in its fields. Rice beer is served liberally to anyone who passes by.

**12**

ors are sometimes fed rice and
by hand. This is a gesture of
tality, but it also provides much
ement.

**13**
Much of the daily work is assigned to women. One of their regular jobs is pounding rice, which they must do throughout the year whenever the family supply of husked rice runs low. The pounding dislodges the husk from the grain, which is then winnowed in baskets such as those lying on the ground beside the mortars.

**14**
Women also collect wood for the cooking and heating fires. There is no shortage of wood in the jungle, but it must be chopped and carried.

**15**
Fields must be con tinually cultivated t prevent the weeds from overwhelming the crop and women share thi job with the men.

16

All baskets are made by men. This man is making the large rough type used for carrying cotton. He is squatting on the part that will become the base, and will soon be ready to draw the ends parallel to each other to form the sides of the basket.

**17** Men sometimes fish with round nets, which they throw into the water in the hope of entangling small fish. The stream is the Rongram River near Rengsanggri as it appears during the dry season, when the level is low and the fishing is best.

men know how to butcher. Several families generally share the
at of a single animal and weigh out their portions on a balance like
s one.

**19** At a few festivals men prepare the food. They usually cook outdoors
in big metal pots. Daily cooking is done indoors in smaller pots by the
women.

**20** The high point of many festivals is the dancing. Dancers (especially the girls) dress with great elegance in their best clothes and jewelry, and tie sprays of feathers into the backs of their turbans.

**21**
Each festival requires an altar which the men build for the sacrifice. This is one of the largest altars ever built, and is to be used for the den'-bilsia ceremony.

**2** The Rongram market place is permanently occupied by only a few families of Nepalis who operate tea stalls, but on Friday mornings throngs of people converge upon it to buy and sell their crops and manufactured goods.

Garos sell their bulk crops, such as cotton and ginger, to traders, but occasionally they offer smaller amounts of vegetables, for example the eggplant which these people have put on display, to other Garos.

**24** The old and the young are well cared for. Children are usually held in the arms or tied on with a cloth but when they are left alone for a few minutes they sit still and almost never try to crawl away.

**25** It is more practical to put shi small children than pants bu body worries about modesty o about the cold weather and r effort is made to keep cloth children until they are six or years old when they can be into covering themselves.

**26**
Nangmi, one of oldest women in Re: sanggri had such p eyesight that she co do little work exc tend her grandchild and do familiar hou hold chores.

**27**
Miman was a man of about seventy, who had never been wealthy but who had a certain reputation for his skill in performing sacrifices.

**28** Mingcheng (left) and Gagan had let their hair grow, wore earrings and turbans, and slept in the bachelors' house, all signs of the increasing independence of youths of their age.

**29**

Naban was the oldest man in Rengsanggri. At one time he claimed to be 100 years old, but a year later the claim had gone up to 110. Unfortunately he was quite deaf and his mind was failing so he could supply little information; but his body, though wispy and weatherbeaten seemed indestructable.

**30**

Aling was one of the more successful of the Rengsanggri men. He had many children and his household was the largest in the village.

**31**
Gan'mi, the wife of Jengnon, the second *nokma* of Rengsanggri, stands with her son beside their field house.

**32**
Wilwil had divorced her first husband many years before, and had raised an adopted daughter who had become the co-wife of her second husband. The two women lived in such harmony that they were cited with approval by the Rengsanggri people.

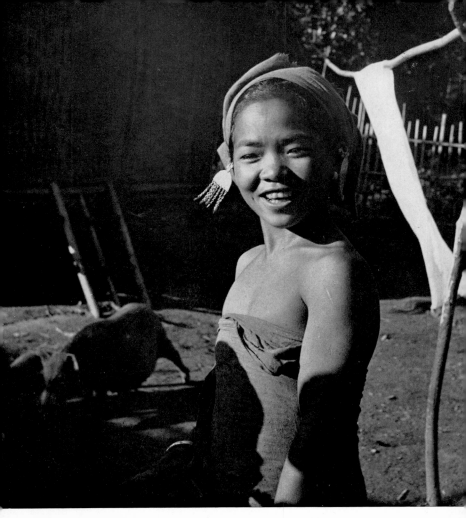

**33** Songdi was about twenty years old and had already had three children all of whom had died.

such occasions, the men sit at the back of the house and the women collect in the front. Curry and rice mixed together, and rice beer, are served in liberal quantities. The rice and curry are served by hand. The server carries a tray with the mixture and places a palmful directly in the mouth of the guest. This can be the cause of much merriment if the guest protests that he is not hungry, since he may be virtually forced to open his mouth in order to prevent his face from being smeared with rice as the full hand inexorably approaches. After this first small feast, the men beat the drums and gongs, and the young boys and girls crowd into the front of the house carrying their drums and beating them in a steady throbbing rhythm. The *nokma* carries in some powdered *satsat* and burning twigs and lights the bark, which fills the house with its fragrance. Suddenly a man fires a gun outside the house, the *nokma* extinguishes the flame, the drummers reduce the intensity of their rhythm and file back to dance in a circle at the back of the house, while the girls form a crowded circle in their midst. The burning of the *satsat* is destined to attract the notice of the god Saljong, who, it is hoped, then ensures that the harvests of the following year will be good.

This is the climax of the biggest festival of the year. After Saljong has been honored at the two ceremonies, all that remains is to spend three or four days in feasting on the slaughtered cows, drinking rice beer, and dancing. Before the festival is finished every household in the village twice acts as host to any villager who wishes to come. Most of the older people circulate during the day, when they are served beer, rice, and curry, while the younger people do their visiting at night, when they not only eat and drink but spend much of their energy in dancing. The houses are visited in a fixed sequence. The villagers always begin at the house of the *nokma* and proceed systematically from house to house until the entire village is covered. No centralized planning is needed, even though the feasting lasts for several days, since each household can predict

R—C

from the course of events the time when they are to expect the crowd, and prepares accordingly.

*Wangala* is one of the three festivals at which group dancing takes place. This occurs in the courtyards in front of the houses, where people like to keep a sizable cleared space for this very purpose. Both married and unmarried people take part, though dancing is generally felt to be most appropriate for the young, especially those who are unmarried. Group dancing is almost exclusively a night pastime, and may continue intermittently until dawn.

The dance figures are stylized pantomimes of everyday activities. In one, the girls pretend to cut off their heads, letting them flop to one side in imitation of cutting down a tree. In another, a girl dances with one boy and then moves to a second in a way suggesting that she has been stolen away by a new lover; and in fact, such boy-and-girl teasing is an element expressed in many of the dances. Groups of girls always dance more or less opposed to groups of boys, though they pair off now and then temporarily; and there need not even be equal numbers of the two sexes dancing. Each boy carries a drum suspended from a cord around his neck, and maintains a steady and sometimes intricate rhythm while everyone executes the various steps and patterns. Though the boys and girls approach one another re peatedly, they never quite come into physical c ontact, apparently teasing each other by coming as close as p ossible without touching. Some people are recognized as being more skilled than others at dancing, and not all are equally enthusiastic. People drop out when tired and rejoin when they wish to, for no specific number is ever required. Rice beer drunk in copious quantities frees the dancers of some of their shyness, and allows them to continue their strenuous sport for many hours. The boys and girls associate far more freely than on ordinary working days, and the closest public intimacies ever indulged in come during the breaks between dances when they sit together and pass around rice beer, betel nuts, and tobacco.

They talk, joke, engage in a mild sort of horseplay, and have a certain superficial physical contact with members of the opposite sex which would be out of the question at other times.

Older people dance less often, but they visit the houses of the village in the daytime and feast with food and drink. These drinking parties at *Wangala* are times for good-natured relaxation, talk, and merriment. Men gather at the back of the house and rice beer is passed around to them. The guests sit with their backs to the wall, rarely standing up except to go and come, and talk animatedly with their neighbors, growing more and more friendly as they drink more beer. As the rice beer is served, more and more water is poured through the mash and strained out to drink. The beer grows weaker as water is added, but this makes progressively less difference to the drinkers. At intervals the assembled drinkers take up gongs, which the host provides from his own stock if he is rich enough or borrows if he is not, and beat out various rhythms. Besides the gongs, there are usually a small bamboo flute, a trumpet made from a buffalo horn tied to a long bamboo tube, and the *nokma*'s small sacred drum, which is carried from house to house and beaten. Festivals such as *Wangala* are also occasions for the telling of stories, especially the mildly competitive stories in which two people alternately chant, each trying to outdo the other in the cleverness and obscurity of his phraseology, to the amusement of all bystanders.

When all the rice beer in the village is gone, the celebration ends. By that time most people are ready to go back to the work of tending the fields that have been neglected for a week. A few enthusiasts may troop off to another village to get in a few more days of dancing and drinking, but most of the people return to their daily activities until the next festival comes around.

None of the other ceremonies are as elaborate or protracted as *Wangala*, but they include many of the same elements. Most of them are held during the hot or rainy seasons, rather than during the cold season, in part no doubt because most ceremonies have something to do with the agricultural cycle, and because plants do not grow in the cold season—though one man suggested to me that there were fewer spirits around in the winter. The annual ceremonies which are performed in Rengsanggri, in addition to *Wangala*, are as follows:

*De'nbilsia*, (*de'n* 'cut'; *bilsi* 'year'). This marks the completion of the clearing of the new fields, is held in January or early February, and lasts for only one day. It is held at the house of the *nokma*, where in the morning many of the village men gather to build an elaborate altar, and where at about midday the *nokma* sacrifices a goat. Following the sacrifice there is a feast which features not only the meat of the goat, but also beef curry.

In the afternoon most of the villagers join in this feast, and the men then beat gongs and one by one some of them dance with a headhunting sword inside the *nokma*'s house.

*Asiroka*. This inaugurates the planting of rice in the old fields. The ceremony begins with the slaughter and distribution of a cow which has been purchased cooperatively out of contributions by all the villagers, and a small sacrifice by the *nokma* in the village. Following this is a day of rest, during which no person should go to the fields; and this is followed in turn by the day of the main ceremony, when each man sacrifices an egg in his own fields, calling upon Saljong to witness him, and several of the richer men of the village sacrifice something larger, usually either a chicken or a small pig. Less wealthy villagers attend one of these sacrifices and share in the ensuing dinner. The sacrifice is followed by another day of rest, and after that all the people plant rice in their fields.

*Agalmaka*. This ceremony is performed just after the burning of the fields, and is second only to *Wangala* in importance. On the morning after the fire, each family sacrifices an egg for the sake of the growing plants in its own field, and the *nokma* sacrifices a chicken. Then, after the first broadcast planting has been completed, everyone returns to the village. That afternoon all drink and feast in the house of the *nokma*, and then as at *Wangala* the older people circulate from house to house during the day, the younger people visit the same houses at night, and everyone eats, drinks, and dances for several days. Fish is considered the proper food for *Agalmaka*.

*Miamua*, (*mi* 'rice'; *amua* 'sacrifice'). This ceremony lasts only one day, and is usually held at the end of June or early in July, after the rice has grown tall but has not yet started to ripen. The *nokma* sacrifices a large pig in his field, and the villagers gather there to help with the preparations and to share in the feast. In the afternoon they return to the *nokma*'s house in the village and make music with gongs, flutes, and buffalo horns; but they do not dance.

*Rongchugala*, (*rongchu* 'a preparation of rice cooked until dry and crisp'; *gala* 'to throw'). This is the first of the three ceremonies which mark the latter part of the growing season. It is generally held in August, and follows the final cultivation of the rice in the old fields and the harvest of millet in the new fields. The *nokma* offers *rongchu* in his house by spreading it on banana leaves. This sacrifice is followed by eating, drinking, and the playing of gongs at each house, but not by dancing. Rice and dried fish are proper foods for this festival. Sugar cane and limes are displayed as an offering, and these are not supposed to be eaten before this ceremony.

*Ahaia*. The second of the three autumn ceremonies is held in September, after the rice harvest has been completed. Each household sacrifices a fish in its own field and then once again the rounds of the village are made with eating, drinking, and music at each house. This time, however, the young people dance, and the whole festival may take several days. They cannot dance at the earlier festivals because it is improper to beat the drums while the rice is growing, and without drums dancing is impossible. Besides, it is likely to be uncomfortably hot and too rainy for dancing much earlier. Red glutinous rice must not be eaten before *Ahaia*. *Wangala* follows about a month later.

Garos thoroughly enjoy these festivals. They look forward to them eagerly and remember them with pleasure. But life does not consist of one long binge, and most days are spent less boisterously, working in the field, building houses, and going to market.

# III

## First Marriage

GAROS MUST DEAL NOT only with the natural and super-natural worlds but with the world of other men, and the rest of this book will be concerned with the way in which they carry out this latter task. Like all men Garos organize themselves into groups of various sorts. In a society such as theirs, where specialized political or economic institutions are rudimentary, kinship groups take over many of the functions of control, production, and exchange which may elsewhere be the prerogative of more specialized organizations. It is for this reason that kinship bulks so large in the life of the Garos, and thus most of the remaining chapters are to deal with various kinship groups. The smallest kinship group is the nuclear family, and the family is initiated with marriage. This makes marriage a convenient starting-place for the description of Garo social organization.

### COURTING

When Garo boys reach the age when they start to do some work, or as they express it, "when they get old enough to want to wear a turban," they are expected to become a bit unruly. These youths, it is said, "cannot sit still," and are always thinking about girls. Girls are seldom quite so irrepressible as boys, but they too grow a little wild at the same age. Everybody expects this to lead to occasional problems, and no one is greatly surprised when a girl becomes pregnant, though neither does anyone really approve. Adults told me that they thought it would be better if young people would stay quiet and behave themselves properly, but, they said, "After all they are young, so what can you do?" While recognizing that premarital sexual relations can lead to personal difficulties, and even to legal disputes and monetary fines, Garos are tolerant of human weaknesses.

The activities of the young people are seldom severely restricted. Any girl has many opportunities of escaping the supervision of her parents if she really wants to. Boys sleep in a separate bachelors' house from the time they are about twelve or fourteen and are hardly supervised at all. Though unmarried boys and girls do not associate as freely as adults, they have ample chance to see each other and even to speak briefly together in their own village, or on occasional trips to neighboring villages. Moreover, the weekly market attracts people from all the surrounding area, and this is the best possible place to look over members of the opposite sex. Many a flirtation starts with a trip to market, and this is one of the many reasons why Garos so regularly make the trip.

A boy who is interested in more than a shy look and a giggle needs to take the initiative in approaching a girl. Boys are first attracted by a girl's appearance, and they like shiny straight hair and dark eyes. They say that the light eyes of the Europeans look like those of a goat, but they admire a light skin. The face should be round without prominent cheekbones, and the nose should not be squeezed too flat against the face. The waist should be comfortably smaller than either the bust or the hips, and the muscles of the calf should taper down the leg, and not be all caught up in a bunch at the top. All boys can admire a girl's looks, but the next steps are not clearly marked. Only at the dancing which accompanies village ceremonies do boys and girls have the chance to become familiar with each other without direct sexual involvement, and this is one reason why dancing, like going to market, is so popular.

In talking with a girl, particularly at dances but also on ordinary days, when duties require or allow a conversation, a boy can make some judgment of whether a girl is attracted to him by the way she replies. They say that if she replies "sweetly," he may feel that she is pleased with him. Boys always come to village dances equipped with the leaves, nut, and lime out of which the betel mixture commonly chewed by Garos is prepared, as well as with *biris*, little commercial Indian cigarettes. They offer these to the girls to "soften them up." If the girl accepts and acts in a friendly way, it may give the boy courage to go on to suggest sexual relations. A boy seldom initiates negotiations toward marriage, since even if he wants to the culture does not provide him with accepted channels, but he does have recognised ways of suggesting sexual relations. A boy may touch the girl rapidly and briefly on the leg or arm or, less ambiguously, on the breast. This last is risky since if the girl is really offended by the suggestion, she may go to her father or village authorities, and she has the right to demand and receive a compensation from the boy of about five rupees. This happens rarely, probably only when a boy is grossly forward with a girl who has given him no sign of friendliness at all, but the possibility does add excitement to a flirtation. Even a girl who is favorably disposed, or at least not irritated, is likely to feign displeasure at first and to say "*Hut!*" to the boy—a term used, among other things, to chase dogs away—but if she is really favorably inclined, they may eventually agree to meet later, or the boy may simply go off and afterward the girl will follow him to a private spot. Sexual relations may occur at any time of the day or night and at any place, in the village, fields, or jungle, where privacy is possible.

Boys, and men too, frequently make some gift, often a few rupees in cash, to their lovers. They hardly think of this as a real payment, but rather as a gift showing gratitude for her favors. If the affair lasts over a long period the number and value of such gifts should be correspondingly increased. Girls, and even married women, have enough control over money to make such gifts worth their while. A married woman can manage to buy things, perhaps saying that she earned the money by selling something—rice beer, for instance—or else juggling the prices of things she buys, saying that they cost less than they really did, if the question of money should ever come up.

I cannot make any reliable estimate of the frequency of either premarital intercourse or adultery. Neither is fully condoned. The societal ideal of desirable behavior is certainly to confine sexual relations within the limits of marriage, and a girl who has been pregnant is markedly less desirable as a wife than one who has not. Virginity itself, however, is not prized, and most people have had some sexual experience before marriage.

A premarital affair occasionally serves as a prelude to marriage, though since marriage is first proposed by the girl, or by her family, rather than by the boy, it is not considered the proper or desirable way. The girl may suggest whom she wants as a husband, and her family will try to obtain him. Undoubtedly some girls, being satisfied with a lover, simply suggest to their fathers that so-and-so would be a fine boy to obtain as a son-in-law, and the fact of an earlier sexual relationship might never become known. Even after a girl becomes pregnant it is often possible to arrange a formal marriage, and this is a satisfactory arrangement involving little disgrace. Occasionally a boy and girl who engage in frequent sexual relations start living together publicly without any ceremony, and are henceforth considered husband and wife; however, the people of Rengsanggri, who are conservative in these matters, frown upon such a "stolen" marriage. When I first went to Rengsanggri, every couple in the village had undergone the traditional ceremony, though there were couples living in near-by villages who had never had a formal wedding. However, most marriages both in Rengsanggri and in the neighboring villages still begin with arrangements and negotiations by the families, and a ceremony which formalizes the union.

A young boy or girl approaching marriageable age faces pressures both for and against marriage. On the one hand, boys in particular prize the freedom of bachelorhood, which as will be shown in the next chapter, is exceedingly great, and both boys and girls are often reluctant to assume the very real responsibilities that go with marriage. There is a Garo proverb: *Mana nona ok; jikna dena kok* (literally, 'mother and sister the stomach; wife and child the basket') implying that some relatives worry about what a man has in his stomach, others about what he brings home in his basket. On the other hand, no boy, and certainly no girl, has any desire to remain single throughout life. Most widowed people are anxious to remarry, without any of the reluctance which young people show. The only people to remain permanently unmarried among the Garos are the mentally or physically disabled. The entire pattern of labor makes men and women deeply dependent upon each other. The older a bachelor becomes the more he is aware of such things, and the less importance he attaches to the freedom he has been enjoying.

Parents are also sometimes reluctant to see their children, particularly their sons, get married. A son leaves the parental household at marriage, and his mother and father may feel the break more deeply than the son. One man gave me a rather stylized account of the advice that parents may give to their young sons: "You are not an expert in cultivation. You will not be able to build your own house. You will not be able to care for your wife. You will not know how to give proper respect to your wife's 'brothers.' You will not be able to cooperate with the husbands of your wife's sisters." One of the very few times I ever saw an adult Garo cry was when a woman first heard that her son had been married. This was not an institutionalized or formal wail, and I was told that mothers frequently do cry a bit when they learn of their son's marriages. They even feel that there is a degree of injustice in the custom that requires them to bring up a son, feed him and clothe him, and teach him to work, but which then takes him away from them to live with and support another family. On the other hand some adults, though perhaps not the parents as much as others, also feel that it is desirable to get people married and settled down and so prevent them from getting into mischief. There is every reason to expect that even a girl who remains unmarried will eventually manage to become pregnant, so it is well to get her established before it is too late. These considerations mean that the boys and their families are usually less eager for marriage than the girls, and appropriately it is the girls or the girls' families who propose the marriages. Boys seem most often to be married in their middle twenties, though Garos are so vague about their ages that this can only be an estimate. Girls are often several years younger than their husbands, marrying in their early twenties or late teens, though rarely the wife may be older than her husband.

## SELECTION OF SPOUSES

Marriage leads to one or another of two contrasting economic and family arrangements, and much that is distinctive about Garo social and kinship organization stems from the differences between them. The contrast is based upon the desire of all middle-aged Garos to arrange their families so that one young couple will live with them in their old age—a couple who will support them and who will eventually inherit their property and assume much of their social position. To achieve this result each Garo couple chooses just one of their daughters to be their 'heiress' (nokna), and she alone of the children will stay in the parental home with her husband and their children. All boys and all other daughters move away at marriage or shortly thereafter, often to a different village. The family members always have a firm understanding before a marriage as to whether or not the couple will act as heirs to the girl's parents and whether or not they will support the parents in their old age. Only rarely are such understandings revised after marriage. The implications of the distinction between these two marriage arrangements will pervade the description of Garo social organization. The differences start from the very beginning of negotiations for a marriage.

Just as there are conflicting pressures for and against being married at all, advantages and disadvantages are likewise seen in regard to becoming an heir. Most young men say that they do not want to become heirs, for the responsibility of caring for one's parents-in-law in their later years, and of maintaining an old, and perhaps respected household may be an awesome prospect. Furthermore, it is recognized that there are personal complications to be faced in living with one's parents-in-law. Since the father-in-law is normally a member of the same matrilineal lineage as his heir, he has a general authority over the younger man. This puts the heir in a sometimes uncomfortable position which boys hesitate to enter, in spite of the economic compensations and the approbation of one's kinsmen which are gained thereby. A boy who agrees to become an heir explains his action by saying that he feels a sense of duty and believes he should help his father-in-law. Older men who have been heirs for many years, however, say that they could not imagine having done differently, and that the advantages of being able to move into an established household and of eventually inheriting all the assets of the household outweigh the responsibilities involved. In fact it would seem that the advantages and disadvantages just about balance each other, so that boys neither compete to become the heir of a rich man nor shrink from the task to the extent that it becomes difficult to find enough boys to assume the responsibility. In practice the system works with remarkable smoothness. Enough boys and girls are found to fulfill the requirements of heirship, while the others do not feel handicapped by their omission.

The first step in arranging a marriage of heirs is the choice by the parents of one of their daughters as heiress. Because they need a girl to perform these duties, Garo parents welcome a daughter more than a son, though if they have many children, they say that they like best to have some of each. However, even if a couple should have no daughters, they can adopt a close relative who will come into their home and assume the duties of an actual daughter.

If a woman passes the child-bearing age without having borne a daughter, or if all her daughters have died, she will search among her close matrilineal relatives for a suitable girl to adopt. Ideally and most frequently the choice falls on the daughter of an actual sister, though the daughter of a classificatory sister, or any other female relative of the appropriate age, whether or not of the formally proper generation, can also be called upon. There is no precisely defined group within which she must obtain a girl, but the more closely related, the more suitable the girl. An adoption is frequently arranged when the girl is as young as ten or twelve, and at a time when the girl can hardly have much choice in the matter. She may immediately move in with the adopting family and be supported by them until grown and ready to marry. This is likely to involve only a move to a neighboring house in the village, one with which the girl has been familiar since early childhood. Occasionally it requires a move to a greater distance, sometimes even to another village, and it may be arranged for the girl to stay with her own mother for a while, perhaps even until marriage, at which time she then finally moves to her adoptive mother's house. The relative wealth of the two families may help decide, for if the adopting family is well off, while the girl's own parents are poor and have many children, they may be glad to have one less mouth to feed.

The formal negotiations for arranging such an adoption require the cooperation of the men of the woman's lineage. Men are supposed to look after their sisters in formal kinship matters, and part of their duty is to make sure that they are properly taken care of in their old age. It is to the general advantage of the lineage to shift daughters about when necessary to make sure that each woman has one girl who will look after her. The whole weight of opinion within the lineage will favor making suitable adoptions. Since the same group of men have authority over and responsibility for both the actual mother and the potential adoptive mother, they will support any necessary adoptions. When the girl actually shifts residence, a number of lineage people, including the adopting mother, go to the girl's house, taking curry, rice, and rice beer, and formally "lead" the girl back to her new house; but the crucial arrangements are made earlier in a less ritualized atmosphere.

Only two of the women in Rengsanggri had been adopted in precisely this way. Rami was taken into the house of her adoptive parents as a girl. She was not consulted about the move but she lived there a number of years before being married, and even helped care for her adopted mother's youngest sons. On the other hand Manmi, who was raised in a different village, continued to live with her real mother until just before she was married, though her eventual adoption had been agreed to many years earlier. Once she was willing to come to Rengsanggri, it was quickly possible to arrange her marriage. Chongrin had already been considered for her husband, and they were married soon after Manmi came to the village.

Most women have at least one daughter of their own so they do not have to adopt another. A single daughter automatically becomes the heiress, but if a woman has more than one, a choice must be made. Garos simply say that they choose whichever girl loves her mother the most, or whichever is the hardest worker; but age also has a bearing upon the decision. The oldest of several girls is rarely chosen since she is likely to be too near the age of her mother, who will have no need of support until she is older. Most people prefer to wait until they draw near the age when they grow feeble before filling the house with a son-in-law and grandchildren. But if the parents so desire, even the oldest daughter may become heiress. Aling had a slightly withered leg, which made it difficult for him to do the heaviest labor. He and his wife, therefore, chose the oldest of their several daughters as heiress so that their household would acquire another adult man as soon as possible. Under more normal circumstances the youngest daughter is a more likely choice than the oldest, but there is no fixed rule either way. Rather, it is a matter for the personal decision of the family members. Since the choice is often made while the girls are still small, they have less to say about it than their parents, though their desires are taken into account if they are old enough. The decision is largely the parents', and especially the mother's.

The alternatives that face a girl are not unlike those facing a boy, except that personal sentiments are apt to be much more important to her. She will either stay in her home and care for her own parents or move out and set up a new household. Only rarely is there any real problem in persuading a girl to accept either responsibility, but the choice must be made one way or another before she can be married, and it is usually made many years beforehand.

Once the heiress is chosen, and once she has grown old enough to marry, the family can start to look for a husband. The initiative in obtaining the heiress's husband rests most directly with the girl's father. The Garos express the situation by saying that "a man always wants to get his own 'nephew' (i.e., *gritang* 'classificatory sister's son') to come in to be his heir, the husband of his heiress daughter." A man searches among the younger men of his own lineage and chooses one whom he would like to bring into his home. His search, then, is like that of a woman with no daughters who must find a girl of her own lineage to adopt. He too must look for a person of his own sex a generation younger and in the same matrilineal lineage as himself. However, since most women have daughters of their own, they do not usually have to look so far. This has been particularly true in the last generation or two, during which the population has been rapidly expanding, and families are some-what larger than would be expected in a static population. Every man, on the other hand, once he reaches the age when he must worry about his future support, must look about among the members of his own lineage for a son-in-law, heir, and replacement. An ideal choice is an actual sister's son, but many men have no sister, or if they have a sister she may have no sons, and even if there are sons of the right age, the preferences and happiness of the daughter, the nephew, and the nephew's parents must all be taken into account. No marriage can be arranged simply because the partners are in the correct genealogical relationship to each other. All concerned must be at least reasonably happy with the choice. This makes it necessary to accept a somewhat elastic definition of 'nephew' (*gritang*) and to look among wider and wider circles of lineage kin until a 'nephew' is found whom both father and daughter like, and whose parents can be persuaded to agree to the match. In actual practice almost all men are able to find fairly close relatives, and so long as arrangements are made and worked out satisfactorily, it does not really matter much whether the 'nephew' is his own sister's son, or a somewhat more remote kinsman.

If a man is acquainted with his own sister's son and likes him, he and the boy's parents may be able to settle the matter with little reference to other members of the lineage, but if he has no suitable near 'nephew', he will investigate ever more distant collateral lines. For this he may require the cooperation of other men of his lineage.

As in the case of a woman looking for an adoptive daughter, a man who searches for a 'nephew' to bring to his home has the advantage of lineage authority on his side. All the members of a lineage cooperate in taking care of each other and being sure that each man is provided with an heir. Though not an obligatory duty, it is at least a proper and worthy act to oblige a 'brother' by giving him one's son, and to oblige an 'uncle' by becoming his son-in-law. The 'uncle's' authority over his younger lineage mates, both his 'sister' (the mother of his prospective 'heir') and the 'nephew' himself, makes it somewhat difficult to give him an outright refusal. His 'sister' may discourage him if she is opposed to the marriage, and in the final analysis he can never force a marriage against the will of the others. One man told me that one of his 'uncles' had tried to get either himself or his brother to come to be his heir. The 'sister' the mother of my informant, seemed to go along with him, never refusing outright, but she also quietly advised her sons to avoid the match since she did not like the girls. In this way she prevented the marriage from taking place. Nevertheless, all members of the lineage recognize that each man must find a younger lineage relative to be his heir, and the weight of opinion will aid a man who wants a 'nephew'. Everyone encourages the 'nephew' to undertake the duty and tries to overcome his doubts.

The actual arrangements most directly concern the girl's father and the boy's mother, who should be at least classificatory 'brother' and 'sister', though the boy's father and girl's mother are also consulted. If there are two or three suitable nephews, the girl is likely to be asked which one she prefers and is able to veto anybody whom she strongly dislikes, although the lineage members can be quite persuasive in urging a girl to agree. It is difficult for young people to decline the arrangements made by their families unless they can offer sound reasons.

Girls other than those destined to become heiresses cannot rely on their fathers to choose a husband for them, but must make their own selection. The initiative should properly come from the girl herself, and her only formal restriction is that she must not ignore moiety exogamy. Unlike her sister who is chosen as heiress, she need not marry into her father's lineage, though this is not forbidden. It is simply a matter of indifference. As a girl moves about her own village, and makes trips to neighboring villages and to market, she sees and hears about eligible bachelors. She goes to dances, not only in her own village but in neighboring ones as well, and has some chance to meet and flirt with boys. Eventually, she should suggest to her father and 'brothers' that she fancies a certain boy, but neither the boy nor the boy's parents need be consulted.

Once a boy is decided upon, the method of bringing him to the girl, and the marriage ceremony itself, are both the same for 'heirs' and 'non-heirs', though no one ever forgets which type of marriage is being undertaken.

### THE WEDDING

I was sitting in Rengsanggri one afternoon when three shy-looking youths from another village wandered in and inquired where they might find Unon. Everybody chuckled, and some-body replied that he might be out in the fields, and suggested that the boys go out there to look for him. The boys walked out in the direction of the fields, until they came over the crest of a hill from which Unon could be seen cultivating in the company of half a dozen other people. Here the boys split up, so as to close in on him from all sides. Unon did not realize his peril until one boy was almost next to him. He started to flee but was caught, and after a brief struggle he recognized the uneven odds, surrendered, and let himself be led calmly to Waramgri, where a girl was waiting, hoping to become his bride. During Unon's brief battle, his fellow villagers ostentatiously continued their cultivating and ignored Unon's plight. Only when the struggle was nearly over did a few of them look up, but even then no one interfered, and as the captors led Unon away they continued their work. This was by no means a lack of interest, but only a studied noninterference; for when I returned to the village after watching from a hearby hilltop, everybody eagerly asked me what had happened—"Did they catch him? Did they take him away?"—with no effort to hide their intense interest and even glee.

I had just witnessed one of the most exciting events in the life of every Garo man, the bridegroom capture, which is considered the only decent way to invite a man to become a husband. The boy should know nothing about it beforehand, though his family must be consulted if he is being asked to marry an heiress.

To begin a bridegroom capture, the father of the girl tells some of the youths of the village that he wants to get a certain boy as his son-in-law. Boys never seem to tire of chasing through the jungle in pursuit of a bridegroom, and will always cooperate by attempting to capture him for the girl. These boys are sometimes loosely referred to as the 'brothers' of the bride, and it is suitable for them to belong to her moiety and thus to the opposite one from that of the bridegroom, though this rule is occasionally broken. Married men occasionally take part, but more often they leave the chase to their unmarried and more adventurous juniors.

A single foray need not lead to a marriage, however, for nobody can be confident of having acquired a husband just because a boy is captured. In fact, most boys put up an elaborate display of reluctance to have anything to do with the proposed marriage. They may be accosted at almost any place— along the road, in the market, or in their own village—but they generally struggle to get away, and once captured use every stratagem to escape. This can lead to chases through the jungle, and to considerable excitement, which is thoroughly enjoyed by everyone except, perhaps, the bridegroom. A boy must usually be seized two, three, or even more times before he is finally willing to admit capture and to settle down as a husband. As much as several years occasionally pass, during which an heir is periodically brought to the girl only to escape again, though a non-heir seldom takes so long. This gives the boy time to consider his prospects, and nobody can be sure of a permanent marriage until he finally surrenders and stays with the girl. Simply running away is clearly no indication that the boy is really turning the marriage down, and in fact, neither the boy nor the girl is free to contract another marriage until he has stated his disinclination in other ways. If a boy is genuinely opposed to the marriage, he will go along quietly, while earnestly explaining to his captors that he is unwilling to undertake the match. In the case of a prospective heir, particularly, considerable family pressure may be brought to bear to persuade him to accept. His duty to his 'uncle' will be pointed out, and the propriety of the match explained. But he, like the girl, does have veto power, and if he insists that he does not want the marriage, the girl's family must eventually accept his refusal and look for someone else. The Garos are convinced that it is nonsense to force unwilling people into a marriage, as this can only be a prelude to future trouble and family quarrels.

Boys will do almost anything to appear reluctant to marry an heiress and thus become the son-in-law of their maternal 'uncle.' Boys shy away from romantic involvement with a daughter of their 'uncle' because of fear of the 'uncle's' authority and of the ridicule which they will receive about this relationship. Those taken as non-heirs are less likely to put on such an extreme show of displeasure. If they wish to be married they run away less often before settling down, and if they are genuinely against the marriage, they can make this clear from the beginning and end the matter promptly. Far too many boys run away and decline a marriage, to allow the conclusion that even non-heir marriages are always or generally preceded by private understandings between the boy and girl. Many men maintain that they had no idea they were about to be captured until their captors actually set upon them, though certainly the news must leak to some men beforehand. In principle neither the parents of a prospective non-heir nor the boy himself need be informed of the coming bridegroom capture, though every boy of the proper age is of course well aware of his eligibility.

Whenever a boy is successfully captured and brought to the house of a girl, the marriage ceremony is performed, though even this does not ensure a real marriage. A boy may frequently run away, sometimes temporarily, but sometimes permanently, even after the ceremony; in fact, he is likely to be guarded much too closely to escape any earlier. As a result some people go through several ceremonies before they finally marry permanently. Panjak had seven boys captured for her before the eighth one, Tanggeng, agreed to become her husband, and some boys are similarly taken to several girls before settling down. Seven refusals is certainly extreme, but no refusal can be considered a divorce simply because the marriage ceremony has been performed. Only after the boy has expressed his willingness to stay and become a husband can it be considered a breach of marriage to leave, but if the boy runs away and is captured again for the same girl, there is no need to repeat the ceremony.

When a boy is brought to a girl's village, his captors lead him into the house of the bride. This most often takes place in the late afternoon, but if the party arrive earlier they spend their time drinking rice beer until early evening, which is the only proper time for the ceremony. A number of people gather at the girl's house. The young men who have captured the boy stay with him continuously, guarding him so that he cannot escape. The girl herself and her family, together with any interested friends, neighbors, and other relatives, all collect. While the precise attendance is not formalized, the parents of the boy never participate, and are usually miles away in their own village. Someone must be present who can act as a priest. He may be a relative, though he need not be, and the girl's father would never perform the ceremony even if he knew the ritual. The girl's father and the priest sit on one side of the central fireplace, the priest behind the father, and the groom sits opposite the fireplace, against the other wall, with his captors guarding him on either side. Other visiting men assemble in their place at the rear of the house and the women gather in the front, where they can help with the cooking if there is much to be done. The bride must stay in the front of the house and cook both rice and curry, so that she can give her prospective husband his first meal. If possible the girl's family should provide a pig, though they cautiously refrain from slaughtering it until they know that the bridegroom has really been captured. The bachelors may suggest that the girl bring rice beer to the groom—to whom they now refer as the 'new man'—and the girl's father eventually suggests that the ceremonial chickens be slaughtered. A helpful neighbor brings in three fowls, one of which must be a hen and one a cock. These are put into a basket and carried in to the priest, who strikes the boy on the back with the cock while reciting a short incantation, and then repeats the action by striking the back of the girl with the hen. All during this time the girl is at the front of the house, working around the fireplace while the boy remains in his place at the side. The priest then cuts the necks of the two chickens, and calls out the names of the boy and girl. He removes the chickens' intestines, and reads them for an omen to determine what prospect of success the marriage has. If the two sections of the intestine hang together, this is an indication that the couple will also remain together; if they are separated, then the couple may also separate; and if the two chickens give different signs, the future remains obscure. The result of reading the omen does not alter the course of the ceremony. A man once suggested to me that boys are more likely to run away permanently if the omen is bad, but this is not inevitable, and if omens influence the proceedings at all, it is to reenforce or allay the doubts of individuals rather than to alter the formal course of events. The girl must then cook the third fowl, the one not used in the ceremony, and must serve this and the rice she has prepared to the 'new man' and to the boys who have captured him. Not all captured boys accept the food that is offered, since acceptance is at least some indication of intention to stay as a husband. Other guests eat the two fowls used in the ceremony, and also any other animals that the family provides. The captors are said to "lead the 'new man' in eating," as they will later lead him in the other activities of the village.

By the time the meal is finished it is generally late in the evening, but the captors then like to lead the boy out of the house and start to show him around the village. They must keep a close watch on him all the time to make sure that he does not escape. They may visit the bachelors' house, where they will briefly beat the drums, and they may go into two or three other houses, but in any event the visits are quite informal. Soon the captors lead the boy back to the girl's house, or sometimes the girl even comes out and suggests that it is late and time to go to sleep, and that he should come back to her house.

So the 'new man' and his guardians all return. The girl lies next to the wall at the rear of the main room, and the boys require the bridegroom to lie down beside her and share her blankets. The others array themselves all around the couple in such a way as to make it as difficult as possible for the boy to escape. The public nature of this wedding night makes sexual relations out of the question even if the boy has decided to stay, while if he is intent on running away he would refrain in any case. Apparently it is impossible for the captors to stay awake and keep guard, and the boy sometimes manages to sneak out of the house after everybody is asleep; but if he wakes the girl as he gets up, she should call to the boys to bring him back, and this can lead to a merry nocturnal chase, in the course of which the groom sometimes escapes entirely.

If the night passes without the 'new man's' escaping, the bachelors again spend much of the next day showing him around the village, and "showing him how to work." On the second day after the ceremony they lead him to his new wife's fields and "show him how to cultivate." The leading of the 'new man' about the village, and "showing him how" to do things, may go on for as long as three or four days. If the boy is determined to flee, he will sooner or later find the chance. If he wants to run away but hopes eventually to be caught again, then he will have to elude his captors by pure stealth. But if he really knows that he wants to have no more to do with the affair, he will make no effort to leave stealthily but will say openly that he wants nothing to do with it. If he can persuade his captors that this is the way he really feels, he will be allowed to go, and the affair will be at an end. Occasionally boys do stay the first time they are captured, but when the bachelors first set out to get the boy, nobody can be certain that they will catch him; and even if they do they cannot know whether the capture will result in a permanent marriage.

If the boy gradually indicates his willingness to settle down and "act like a husband," then after a few days the bachelors start to lower their guard over him, and people begin to refer to the new couple as husband and wife. Only when the bachelors have really ended their supervision can the marriage be consummated, and only then does it become a permanent marriage which cannot be dissolved without subsequent legal action.

After a few days of marriage the couple generally goes together to visit the husband's parents in his village. Occasionally a bachelor still accompanies them to guard the new husband, but often the two of them go alone, a real sign that they are "acting like husband and wife." They eat and drink, and spend a night or two in the boy's village. Then the couple returns to the girl's village, the girl carrying whatever personal possessions the boy may have—clothing and possibly a few tools—which she takes to her house, where the boy will henceforth live. Some Garos, possibly carried away by the logic of their matrilineal system, state that when a boy marries he can take no personal property with him at all. But young men in the neighborhood of Rengsanggri sometimes accumulate many baskets of grain and even a cow or two before marriage, and they are allowed to take these with them to their new family. Other men have little more than their own clothes and tools.

If the boy is taken as an heir, he will move into the household of his wife's parents. He will be expected to make free use of all the possessions of the family, to participate in the work in the family's fields, and to share in the responsibility and in the rewards of the family labor.

A non-heir couple may live with the girl's family for a few months, but during the first year they are married they are assigned a separate plot of land, and they always work this, and make use of the crop obtained from it, independently of the girl's parents. Within the first year they usually build themselves a separate house. If the parental home is crowded with other people they are expected to move out just as soon as they possibly can. If the household is small, they may stay without undue complications for some months or even a year, but the temporary residence of non-heirs with the girl's parents is never more than a makeshift arrangement which lasts only until the young couple is able to build a separate house. Occasionally the problem of crowding can be solved temporarily if the young couple moves into the family's field house, where they live separately until they can build their own house. The girl's parents and other relatives contribute some labor toward building the new house, but usually the economic resources of a young couple are so limited that their first house must be a very modest one. Only after several years of industrious work can they hope to accumulate enough to allow them to erect a more substantial building. Garos point out that a young couple must work very hard when they are first married and especially before they have children to encumber them, or else they will never be able to accumulate any appreciable wealth. From the time the first house is built, a couple is economically independent of the parental home.

As has been pointed out, readjustments in the choice of heir and heiress are only rarely made after marriage. Of the many marriages in Rengsanggri I discovered only two cases in which some readjustment was made or suggested in the responsibilities of heirship. Nemnem and her husband were originally designated as heirs to her parents, Nomi and Rontok. Nemnem and her husband did not fulfill their obligations adequately, however, and when I was there, Nomi, by then a very old lady and a widow, was living in the household of another daughter,

Kandok. To all appearances Kandok was acting as Nomi's heiress. They lived in the same house, and Kandok will surely retain whatever possessions adhere to the house when Nomi dies. But Nemnem is still spoken of as the proper heiress, and her failure to fulfill her duties has left bad feelings which remain today.

Wilson had been recently married as an heir. When I left the district it was said that he and his young wife wanted to set up a separate household and relinquish the duties and privileges of heirship. This case was complicated by the death just before their marriage, of Wilson's wife's father and they had not yet decided whether they would have to remain as heirs as had originally been planned. In all other cases in the village, so far as I could determine, the people originally designated as heirs remained so, while everyone else set up permanently independent households.

Garos say that a marriage is not made by a single ceremony, but that it takes a long time for a boy and girl really to settle down and behave towards each other as husband and wife. They expect that for the first few weeks a boy and girl will be shy of each other, especially in public, but they know that this shyness will grow less as they become accustomed to one another. Marriage almost always uproots a boy much more than it does a girl. In many cases he shifts villages, often a move of several miles, while a girl continues, for a few months at least, to live in her own house. On the other hand, a boy has the freedom to get out of his wife's house, to visit people whom he may know in her village, and to take frequent trips to his own home. Most new husbands manage to find many excuses to visit their parents' village, either in the course of a trip to market, or so as to take part in a village festival or to see a sick relative, or they may go frankly for a visit without any excuse at all. The freedom of men to plan and carry on their work, to go to market almost every week, and especially to visit their parents from time to time, mitigates the sharpness of the break at marriage, but the longer a man lives with his wife and in his wife's village, the more intimately he becomes associated with the life there and the less he identifies himself with the village of his birth. Middle-aged men visit their native village less frequently, and usually for a definite reason, such as sickness or some other family matter necessitating their counsel.

From the time he marries, a man's routine work is entirely centered around the home he shares with his wife. All his money and resources are shared with her, and he will rarely or never work with or for his parents again. A man and his wife make almost all of their meals from food that is cooked in common, and they frequently eat together. They go to the fields together, and spend many hours working side by side. Gradually their emotions conform to these daily affairs, and by the time they have been married for a few years a man and wife have each become the most important person in the other's life.

If husband and wife meant nothing else to each other, their economic interdependence would keep many of them together. If the work of a household is to be kept up, there must be at least one man and one woman to share it, since many tasks are the exclusive province of one or the other of the sexes. Because their work is complementary, both men and women regard it as catastrophic to be for long without a partner. I never heard a Garo man who had passed the period of youthful frivolity pretend that he still longed for the carefree life he had when he was single. When large crowds gather, the men usually sit apart from the women, and so husband and wife are separated; but when they are alone in the house, or when one or two neighbors drop in for a visit, they sit in the same circle, and share in the conversation and laughter. Garos never display affection in public but spouses do display friendship and mutual confidence, responsibility, and understanding. Garo husbands and wives appear to need each other, and to realize how great this need is.

The marriages which have been discussed in this section are first marriages between young people. There are other marriages also, those in which a widow or widower remarries, or in which a second wife is given to a man. The arrangements for these marriages are somewhat different and depend on a number of special circumstances. These marriages will be discussed in Chapter VI, which deals with the arrangements following a death.

### CROSS-COUSIN MARRIAGE AND RESIDENCE

The marriages of heirs are examples of classificatory matrilateral cross-cousin marriage, since a man marries the daughter of his classificatory mother's brother. Because of the importance of cross-cousin marriage in various current anthropological theories as well as in the society of the Garos themselves, it seems necessary to digress long enough to give a statistical summary based on a sampling of actual Garo marriages. As soon as this is attempted it becomes clear that the situation is far too complex to be indicated by anything like simple percentages of various types of marriages. The only meaningful way to define 'cross-cousin' is to accept the Garo definition and regard as 'cross-cousins' not only the actual daughters of a mother's brothers and a father's sisters, but also various distant classificatory relatives. This means that, for instance, two people may be simultaneously "close matrilateral cross-cousins" and "distant patrilateral cross-cousins." Clearly, it becomes essential to define various degrees of the cross-cousin relationship.

The relationship between matrilateral cross-cousins (a man and the daughter of his mother's 'brother') is easily regarded as a function (in the mathematical sense) of the relationship of the boy to the girl's father. If these two are actual mother's brother and sister's son, then the boy and girl are first cross-cousins. If first cross-cousins are considered as type (1), it is possible when considering Garo society to define five other increasingly distant degrees of the classificatory 'cross-cousin' relationship; (2) the boy and girl's father are closely related members of the same

minimal lineage (see Chapter VII) though not direct uncle and
nephew; (3) the boy and girl's father come from the same village
lineage but are not particularly closely related to each other
within it; (4) they come from closely allied lineages of different
villages; (5) they are members of the same named sib though
they do not belong to closely related lineages within that sib;
(6) they belong to entirely different sibs. If moiety exogamy is
consistently practiced, the girl's father and the prospective husband must always belong to the same moiety, and so in the most
extended sense the spouses are still 'cross-cousins.' That is, the
spouses are members of the opposite moiety, and so marriage
between them is not forbidden.

Similarly, six classes can be defined to describe the relationship of the spouses as patrilateral cross-cousins. For this it is
necessary to consider the relationship between the girl and the
boy's father. In this way the degree of closeness as both patrilateral and matrilateral cross-cousins of any married couple can
be explicitly defined, though the actual determination of the
degree of relationship in particular cases may be difficult. The
data on the cross-cousin relationship of the spouses of Rengsanggri is presented in Appendix B. The totals are summarized
here.

In Rengsanggri there were 70 married men with 78 wives,
eight men having two wives. (This does not include widowed
mothers-in-law whom the Garos call 'wives' but with whom
sexual relations are not maintained.) The marriages of these
people included 52 "new marriages." Most of these "new
marriages" were first marriages in which neither spouse had
been married previously. However, a divorced man, unlike a
divorced woman or at least a woman who has borne a child, can
enter into a new marriage without any change in the rules, so
the two cases of remarried divorced men are included as "new
marriages." of these 52, 28 of the couples were married as heirs
and the other 24 as non-heirs.

Considering first the 28 heir marriages, only three were

between first matrilateral cross-cousins but another fifteen were closely related. In another six cases the boy and his wife's father came from the same village, and in one they were at least from closely related villages. In three cases they were from un-related villages, but still of the same sib. All 28 of the heir marriages were then between a girl and a man who was at least a member of the same sib as her father, and in most cases the girl's father and her husband were fairly close relatives.

The picture for non-heirs is very different. None of the 24 non-heir marriages were between close matrilateral cross-cousins. Four were marriages in which the boy came from the same village as the girl's father. In two other marriages the boy was from a village closely related to that of the girl's father, and in seven more they were of the same named sib, though of en-tirely different villages. In the largest number of cases, eleven, the boy's mother and the girl's father were from entirely different sibs. These figures can be summarized in the following table.

### Summary of Matrilateral Cross-Cousin Relationship of Rengsanggri Married Couples

| Degree of relationship of the husband to wife's father | 1 | 2 | 3 | 4 | 5 | 6 | Total |
|---|---|---|---|---|---|---|---|
| Number of Marriages — Heir | 3 | 15 | 6 | 1 | 3 | – | 28 |
| Number of Marriages — Non-Heir | – | – | 4 | 2 | 7 | 11 | 24 |

This is not a large sample, but no elaborate statistical devices are needed to demonstrate the differing constitution of the two types of marriage alliance It is, in fact, exactly what the formal rules of marriage lead one to expect.

The relationship between the wife and the husband's father

is a measure of the closeness of the spouses as patrilateral cross-cousins. When the same 52 marriages are tabulated for the patrilateral relationship, much less difference between the two types of marriages shows up. In neither case does a man have much tendency to marry a close lineage relative of his father, though marriage to a father's sister's daughter, either actual or classificatory, is not forbidden by the formal rules of the society. Classificatory patrilateral cross-cousin marriage does occur, but no pressure encourages that type of marriage in a way comparable to that in which matrilateral cross-cousin marriage is encouraged by the practice of heirship.

Summary of Patrilateral Cross-Cousin Relationship
of Rengsanggri Married Couples

| Degree of relationship of the wife to husband's father | | 1 | 2 | 3 | 4 | 5 | 6 | Total |
|---|---|---|---|---|---|---|---|---|
| Number of Marriages | Heir | – | 1 | 3 | 4 | 5 | 15 | 28 |
| | Non-Heir | – | – | 4 | 6 | 5 | 9 | 24 |

Since the two distinct types of marriages result in different residential arrangements, it is not possible to summarize in one neat word the preferred residence pattern of the Garos. Those who marry as heirs are uxorilocal in that the man moves into his wife's household. In most cases this is the home of the wife's parents, though occasionally it is with her adopted parents instead. These marriages are simultaneously avunculocal, since the boy also lives with one of his classificatory maternal 'uncles.' Since the residence pattern does not result in the systematic localization of all matrilineally related men, as would be the case if avunculocal marriage were carried out consistently, the society can hardly be characterized simply as avunculocal. Furthermore, almost half of the new marriages in Rengsanggri were "neolocal" in that the new couple, not being heirs, set up a new and economically independent household. From the standpoint of the individual household, then, residence may be either uxori-avunculocal or else neolocal, and neither can be considered as "preferred," if "preferred" means anything more than a statistical majority. Different residential arrangements are preferred for different marriages, and both types are essential to Garo social organization. (The residence pattern appears quite different if locality with respect to the whole village, rather than with respect to the household alone, is considered. This aspect will be discussed in Chapter IX.)

R—D

# ⁂IV⁂

## *Becoming a Garo*

WITHIN A YEAR OR so after marriage most women become pregnant, but the Garos recognize some necessary preliminaries: "As a tree must bloom before it bears its fruit, so a woman must have her menses before she can bear her child." Women sometimes have pain and discomfort at this time. An unmarried girl is expected to get over this by herself, and even her first menses are not ceremonially marked, but an attentive husband may perform a small sacrifice to appease the spirits who plague his wife if she is in pain or if the period lasts too long. A menstruating woman is under no formal restrictions, but sexual relations are avoided, and she often wears dark clothes and is likely to spend at least one or two days fairly close to the house so as not to be embarrassed before her neighbors. She has to wash extra clothes, and when these hang out to dry, the women of the village take notice and know that she is not yet pregnant. I was told that the men are seldom so observant.

Garos say that sexual intercourse, not just once but several times, is necessary before a woman can conceive. When an unmarried girl becomes pregnant it is always assumed, probably correctly in most cases, that the girl has had a more or less prolonged affair. Moreover, intercourse need not cease as soon as pregnancy is discovered, but rather it helps to hasten the time of delivery. Garos use the same word for both semen and seed, and describe the woman as being like the earth which nourishes the seed. In spite of this explicit biological knowledge, the biological role of the father is ignored socially, for the Garos say that the affiliation to social groups follows the mother's milk. No particular aspect of a person's body, soul, or social affiliation is believed to come from the father.

A woman recognizes her own pregnancy by the cessation of menstruation. Others say they notice that her breasts swell and that her nipples become darker, though a man hardly mentions such observations except perhaps to his own wife. Especially dark nipples foretell a girl, lighter ones a boy. Young girls sometimes feel sick during the first part of their pregnancy, and they rest about the house; but later they feel well enough to get up and work, and older women who have had many children are no longer bothered even in the early months. A woman usually continues to work while pregnant—"who else would do the work?"—but a really sick woman is given consideration, and like any other sick person she can rest quietly in the house and rely upon others to care for her.

When the pregnancy becomes obvious by the enlargement of the abdomen or when the movement of the baby is first felt, several sacrifices are performed at intervals of a few days or a week. These insure the health of both the fetus and the mother. The woman's husband most often performs the sacrifices himself, but he may call in another man if he prefers. Young husbands particularly feel some shyness in offering sacrifices, and any other person, even the girl's father, can do them for him. It is expected that the father will perform the sacrifices for an unmarried daughter who becomes pregnant, but if a husband does not at least make certain that somebody attends to them, the relatives would surely blame him for any complications that should arise. Four sacrifices are usual at this time, though a sickly woman will warrant more. Each sacrifice is designed to appease a different spirit and as in sacrifices performed to cure disease, an animal must be killed at each, and its blood smeared on a specially built altar. Ideally a goat should be sacrificed at one of these and a baby pig at another, but poverty may force the substitution of a fowl. If the sacrifices are all properly performed the woman should be healthy and have no difficulty with giving birth, but otherwise the baby or even the mother may die.

Predictions of the date of birth are often wide of the mark, but as nearly as possible to the time the parents should brew rice beer, pound rice, and obtain chickens and a pig to be used for the occasion. When a woman notices signs of imminent delivery, such as pain or rupture of the fetal membrane, she returns immediately to her house. If other villagers hear of her labor, they also come back to the village from their fields, and they are expected to be particularly careful to refrain from cutting banana leaves or bamboo leaves from their fields until she has given birth. The woman retires to the back room of the house for the delivery. In most villages a few women are recognized as skillful at midwifery, and one of these generally comes to assist at a birth. A second and unskilled woman, often a sister or some other female relative, assists the midwife. Other relatives gather in the main room of the house, some of the men help with the sacrifice, and the women help with the cooking. If the labor is protracted, chickens, a pig, or sometimes, if the family is wealthy enough, even a cow, may be sacrificed to assure the woman's health. If labor goes so rapidly that there is no time for a sacrifice, then both the opportunity and the necessity for assuring ease to the mother are past, and the sacrifice can be safely omitted. Rapid delivery is considered to be easier for the mother. It allows her to get back to work promptly. The baby, on the other hand, is less likely to be healthy if the delivery goes quickly. For this purpose the husband, or another man, cuts two bamboo knives from a large rafter of the house. Bamboo knives are not otherwise used today, but Garos feel that iron tools are used in too many other ways to be appropriate for cutting the umbilical cord. New bamboo would be less sharp, and the rafters, which are made from the most suitable type of bamboo, provide an accessible source. One of these knives is used to cut the cord, and the other is later taken to the jungle with the afterbirth and left there for the spirits.

In the delivery room of the house a stout piece of bark rope is suspended from wall to wall. The woman may rest lying or sitting down until labor becomes strong, but then she stands hanging on to the rope, while the less skilled of her two assistants sits behind her on a low stool, and helps to support her with her arms. The midwife sits in front and receives the baby, making sure that it does not fall and get hurt, and it is she who cuts the umbilical cord with the bamboo knife. She places the infant on a banana leaf which she has spread out on the floor for the purpose, and washes it with warm water. Finally she catches the afterbirth in a special little bamboo basket which the men have made, and ties it up.

During the delivery the other visitors remain in the main room of the house, and only the two women stay in the back room with the mother. If the labor is prolonged, the husband may come to visit his wife, but at the birth he stays outside along with everyone else, waiting for the news. As soon as the baby is born, the midwife calls out whether it is a boy or a girl. She immediately bestows a name, though this is little used during the first few months of the baby's life.

After the birth, the men build an altar outside the front wall of the house, on the right if the child is a boy and on the left if it is a girl. An egg is sacrificed here with the intention of erasing the filth and pollution to which the midwife has been exposed at the birth. She carries the basket containing the afterbirth into the jungle, where she places it in the fork of a tree, along with the leaves on which the baby first lay and the second of the bamboo knives. She should return by way of a stream where she can wash off any dirt and blood that she has accumulated during the delivery. When she returns to the house the man who has sacrificed shouts for the pollution to leave, and the midwife calls back that it has left. The next day the altar is thrown into the jungle along with the afterbirth. The mother in the meanwhile rests in the back room. Some of the other women present heat water and bring it to her so that she can wash in the unaccustomed luxury of hot water, cleaning the blood and dirt from her legs and body.

Another sacrifice is intended specifically to ensure the closure of the fontanel. An altar is built in the cattle room of the house, and the midwife carries the new baby to it. Here the father or another man sacrifices a large rooster, and the baby is then carried back to the mother. The rooster is butchered and cooked, and the curry, a leaf filled with rice and a gourd of rice beer are taken by a relative or friend to the home of the midwife as a small payment for her services. If a cow has been killed for the mother before the birth, one of the legs is given to the midwife as well, and if a special man is asked to perform the sacrifices, he also receives a leg; but since a cow is not always sacrificed, payment for his assistance is often omitted. Other visitors are fed and given rice beer. Before the birth the mother should not eat, but after delivery she may if she likes, though new mothers are not always hungry.

The mother generally rests quietly for a few days, lying down as much as she likes, and doing little work. The husband must stay near home, and if there are no older daughters to help, he may even do the cooking and care for his wife and other children. Some women recover quickly and are able to go back to work in a day or two, but they are the exception.

About a month after birth, another sacrifice is held and the baby's hair is then cut off. If the parents can afford it, a few relatives come to assist and they kill and eat a pig; but the essential animal of the sacrifice is a chicken, whose blood is smeared over an altar built at the rear of the main room of the house. If the parents cannot afford a pig, they may attend to this sacrifice alone. The father or a friend, using cheap scissors purchased in the market, cuts the baby's hair short all over. When the food has been prepared, portions of the cooked chicken curry, with some boiled rice and rice beer, are taken to the midwife who helped with the birth and to the man who sacrificed at that time, though neither need be present at the hair-cutting ceremony. This is the last formal rite of passage until the marriage ceremony many years later. Both boys and girls have their ears pierced a few years after birth, but Garos ignore the opportunity of making a ceremony of this event. By the time the baby is a few weeks old, the parents forget the exact date of its birth, and in a few years they forget even the year unless they are able to remember which patch of land they were cultivating at the time.

Garo children spend most of their first year in direct physical contact with an older relative. They sleep with their mother, or sometimes when a little older with their father, and during most of the day, when they are not actually being fed or cleaned, someone carries them. From the time the umbilical cord falls off a few days after birth, the mother, father, or an older sibling ties the baby to his or her back, or more rarely on the hip or in front, by means of a long cloth especially made for the purpose. Even small babies not strong enough to hold up their heads are carried this way; but parents never worry about the awful angle at which their heads sometimes droop, and the children survive. If the baby has an older brother or sister of an age between seven and ten or twelve, he or she is often given responsibility for the child during much of the day. In the absence of a suitable older sibling, a cousin or even a more distant relative, either a boy or girl, may be called into service. If so, the older child must be fed by the baby's parents as if he were their own child, though he may continue to sleep in his own parents' house. Often, however, the mother must carry the baby herself, since even if a cousin is available the parents are sometimes unwilling to stand the expense of feeding him. A mother may work in the fields with the baby constantly tied to her. The baby can doze peacefully, or look placidly about if awake, but he rarely leaves his guardian's back.

Some babies learn to nurse more easily than others. Garos do not expect them to suckle much for the first day or two even if the nipple is put into their mouths; but, they say, since there is no milk this early, they could get nothing anyway. Some babies start trying to suckle from the time the midwife brings them back to the mother after the first sacrifice. In a day or so all of them want to suckle and all are able to. It is a rare Garo woman who has difficulty nursing her child. Occasionally the child of a sick mother is given some sugar water or tea, or even cow's milk if it can be obtained from Nepalis, but ordinarily insufficient mother's milk can lead only to the baby's death. I never heard of an attempt to give a baby to another woman to nurse. Infants are nursed whenever they cry or show signs of hunger, throughout the day and night. Parents do not enjoy the night feeding that babies usually demand, but it is unthinkable that a baby should be denied the breast if he cries. At night women sometimes nurse lying down but otherwise they sit comfortably on the floor or ground with their legs either stretched out straight in front or doubled back to one side. A small baby is held cradled against the front of the mother's body, but an older one may sit sidewise in his mother's lap. Nursing appears to be a placid and relaxed experience for both mother and child.

If children get enough milk, their parents expect that they will sleep and not cry, but nursing is said to make mothers grow thin. They also note that while nursing the menstrual cycle is likely to be disrupted, and as long as this lasts they say that another pregnancy is unlikely. By the time the baby is sitting up, however, his mother is likely to become pregnant again even if she continues to nurse, while if the first baby dies most women are said to become pregnant more rapidly. Some women, however, conceive easily and promptly after delivery, and Garos think this is unfortunate both for the health of the woman and for the family because her other work is interfered with. Garos do not desire a surfeit of children, but they also say that a woman who never has any children ages rapidly and cannot be healthy. Every woman should have at least one or two, and as many as five or six children is considered a reasonable number.

When a woman becomes pregnant for a second time her milk may disappear, but sometimes women go on nursing a previous baby right up to the delivery of the next; and occasionally they try to nurse two children at once. They know that the milk is inadequate, and not infrequently one of the children dies; but if this must happen they feel it is better for the younger one to die since it is still only small. A woman who is determined to stop nursing simply refuses to give the baby the breast. The child may cry a great deal for a day or two, but after that it is expected to become reconciled. Mothers seldom force weaning until the baby is almost two years old. This is apparently a dangerous period for the children's health, since they are so dependent upon milk and so unused to other foods that they have a difficult time adjusting to the transition.

The baby may be offered water at an early age, but other food is seldom given until the baby can at least sit up by itself, and generally not until the age of nine months or a year. The mother premasticates the first solid food for the child. Favorite early foods are boiled taro and manioc, and after these come rice, bananas, and maize. The mother generally holds her child on her lap while sitting on the floor, with a banana leaf beside her containing food which she chews, mouthful by mouthful, before spitting it into her hand and placing it in the baby's mouth. Gradually she tries feeding the baby meat, dried fish, and all the other Garo foods. Mothers even feel that they must soon start to give the babies a taste of chili peppers, or else they will never be able to eat them properly.

Rice beer should not be given to babies until they are able to sit up, since younger ones get sick if they drink it, but slightly older ones are not restricted, and it is said that the children like the beer and that it makes the body healthy. Six-year-olds may get decidedly tipsy, but "a child who drinks no rice beer will not have blood." Home-rolled cigarettes are given to children as soon as they are able to puff on them. A thoughtful child nurse will hand his glass of beer or his cigarette to the baby on his back so that it too can have a sip or a puff. Sophisticated Garos who have observed the strange habits of the West see in our refusal to give small children cigarettes an indication that we do not show our love for our children so easily or openly as they. If a child wants to smoke, they think, no adult can be so cruel as to deny him.

Everyone delights in a small baby and will do anything to soothe one that is fussy. The mother, father, or older sibling who carries a baby on his or her back starts to bounce and jiggle it at the slightest peep, urging it to be quiet and to sleep. As a result babies have numerous short naps interrupted by short waking periods—a pattern which extends into the night, when the babies wake frequently for a brief nursing. Perhaps it even extends into adulthood, since Garos have no qualms about lying down in the middle of the day for a cat nap if immediate work is not pressing, and on the other hand nobody ever hesitates to wake another, or tries to be quiet in order to let someone sleep. If husband and wife walk together to the market or to work in the fields, the woman usually carries the baby unless it has been assigned to a child nurse. Fathers help out, most often in the morning and evening, when they also tie a baby to their backs, and they appear to take a decided satisfaction in their duty. Both men and women will bounce a baby and try to make it smile. They seldom roughhouse with their children, but play with them quietly, intimately, and fondly.

In the absence of reliable memory of the day or year of their birth, it is difficult to estimate the age at which stages of growth are complete; but the Garos themselves are convinced that their children develop more slowly than other people's. The Garos look forward to several stages of maturation. Smiling, sitting, and walking are most clearly recognized; but they also speak of the "filling out" which comes in the first few weeks, and of turning over and crawling. They notice when the teeth start to appear and later when they are replaced, and say that teething is apt to be accompanied by diarrhea. They take an unabashed delight in welcoming the first smiles.

At the age when American children crawl, Garo children are much less active, rarely creeping more than a few feet and never with any serious intent to go somewhere. Children are not encouraged to crawl, and before they travel far someone always picks them up and holds them. I never saw a Garo child struggle to get loose so that he could go off and crawl by himself. Even when slightly older children are left to sit on the ground, they usually stay placidly in one place. I had an informant who once brought his three small children with him when he worked for me. His wife was going to the fields, and he knew his work would be quiet so that he could keep an eye on them. They ranged in age from about two to seven but they sat so quietly that I was hardly aware of them. Occasionally the youngest whimpered a bit, and his father would tie him to his back and bounce him to sleep, while he continued talking to me. This and an occasional soothing word were sufficient to keep them content. The striking placidity of children may be partly attributable to the way they are cared for, but it may also be due to malnutrition or disease. Children at this age are subject to various intestinal diseases, hookworm, and most serious of all, malaria. Disease wins out in many cases; but even those children who survive must fight their way through to partial immunity from malaria, and may be debilitated in spite of showing no acute malarial symptoms. In the town of Tura, where Garos get better medical care and possibly a better diet, the children are more active; and even in the villages children above the age of five or so shout and run about in a far more lively fashion than their younger siblings.

Children rarely walk until well into their second year, but adults and older children encourage them to do so as they never encourage crawling. They may let the child practice walking while they hold on with one hand, or after he is a little more steady on his feet, they may squat a little distance away and hold out their arms to encourage him to come. The first early steps of a child are thoroughly enjoyed and applauded, and its falls are laughed at indulgently, but the baby is also comforted afterward. A baby continues to be carried much of the time until he is able to walk proficiently—usually until he is about two years old. Little fixed routine surrounds child care. Not only feeding, but sleeping as well, is a matter of demand. A small baby is encouraged to sleep whenever it wants to, and later when it is old enough to roam freely, a child lies down and takes naps at will, rather than at the suggestion of a parent; and a child may stay up at night as late as he cares to.

The carriers of children are frequently wetted or dirtied. They calmly wipe off the urine and shake out their clothes, but if they can catch the baby in time, they hold him away from their own bodies until he is finished. Stools are more distressing, and they try to hold the baby away when they feel his muscles tighten. If they do get dirty, they wash themselves, and clean the child with a stick or small piece of bamboo. If the stools fall in an awkward place, they clean them away with a stick, and in the house they wash the spot with water. They do not enjoy this but they never express much annoyance with a child who has dirtied or wet, for they recognize that children cannot control themselves.

No systematic effort is made to toilet-train the children, and when I inquired about the matter, people were surprised at my questions, since they regarded such training as both futile and unnecessary. Babies are expected to urinate and defecate promiscuously until they are about two, when they learn to control themselves without any teaching. However, though the adults do not realize it, they do teach the child what is expected of him by turning him quickly away when he begins to urinate or defecate. He also has ample opportunity to watch and imitate older children.

Parents put few clothes on their children and sometimes cannot prevent the child from shedding those they do provide. Some wear shirts, but they almost never try to cover the lower part of the baby's body, since the clothes would promptly be soiled anyway. Occasionally parents buy a small loin cloth for boy or a short skirt for a girl—miniatures of the traditional adult garments—but they do not really expect that the children will wear them. Instead they just drag them about and play with them. They like to buy them, because, I was told, if they do not other people will say, "why don't you get your child a loin cloth," or a little later the child himself may say, "Why don't you get me one like he has." When a child is five or six, adults and older children start to tease him about running around naked. They point to him, laugh, and say "Very ugly"; thus he learns to keep his genitals covered. Adults never expose their genitals even to members of their own sex.

At about two years of age, the unstinting indulgence given a small child begins to change in various ways. For one thing, adults start to play upon the fears of children. There are objective dangers, such as snakes and larger animals, which they must be kept away from. Frightening is an effective means to this end, and Garos speak of frightening their children into obedience. It is always assumed that children will be afraid of strangers and of the dark, and they are told about ghosts and spirits and taught to be afraid of them as well. Garos who have experienced modern medicine threaten their children with an injection, and warn them that the doctor will come if they do not behave. Ghosts or injections may be mentioned in teasing, but this is not really malicious. It is amusing to see a child frightened, and people laugh when they see a face starting to pucker up with tears; but comfort is never denied to the child. In this way the adult becomes a protector who guards the child against the dangers of the world. Repeatedly, when I arrived at a new village, or sat down at a house where I was not known, children would begin to size me up quizzically. A mother would look at her child, look at me, and remark to everybody around, "I wonder if the baby will be frightened." The child would hear the suggestion of fear. He would look at me, look at the mother, and obligingly start to cry. At this point the mother would gather up the child, hold him in her arms, and provide the reassurance that a mother's arms afford. The mothers never made any effort to help the child overcome his fear, never suggested that I was harmless and that it was silly to cry. They did not consciously want to frighten the child, but they were so confident that he would be afraid that they managed to instill the fear they expected. By putting themselves in the position of protector instead of frightener, both the parent and child become convinced that everything possible was being done to protect him. This would seem to increase the child's dependence upon its close relatives, who alone can give him comfort in an occasionally terrifying world.

The age of two, when nursing is likely to stop, when children are carried about less, and when fears can be exploited, is also the age when a younger sibling is likely to arrive. This would seem a situation likely to produce extreme sibling jealousy. The Garos recognize a degree of rivalry among their children, but the signs of intense jealousy are not often obvious. The attitude toward it is likely to be one of amusement, and certainly no effort is made to give the older child compensatory affection. At this age, on the contrary, for the first time, temper tantrums (unlike evidences of fear) are ignored or laughed at, and a child may be spoken to sharply if he does something of which the parent does not approve. A parent may even tease an older child about the younger sibling and encourage, it would seem, his feelings of jealousy. But jealousy is a futile emotion, and children apparently retire into a quiet dependence upon their parents and close relatives, sitting near them, playing quietly, but rarely showing overt signs of revolt or rivalry. Conceivably they are so effectively disturbed by less tangible threats, such as ghosts, the dark, or strangers, that some of the blame is shifted away from younger siblings, or their parents. When the younger brothers or sisters are old enough to be teased, older siblings share in the teasing with impunity, for Garo parents largely ignore it. Indeed every older sibling has explicit authority over the younger ones, and is expected to punish and discipline them when necessary. This may help to ease his feelings of jealousy, since however much an older sibling may resent the presence of a younger one, he knows from very early that he has the authority to discipline the younger one. Very young boys are allowed to rebuke or even slap their younger brothers, and far from being considered bullies, these older brothers are looked upon as wielding the authority proper to older lineage mates.

When an older child carries a younger sibling, he generally shows almost as much unrestrained affection for it as his parents do; however, this is rarely the first child to follow his own birth. Older siblings, especially older brothers, are seldom intimate with each other. They meet for formal matters concerning their sisters or younger lineage mates, but reserve their intimacy for others. Conceivably this is an expression of early family rivalry. Economic arrangements allow brothers and sisters to be independent of each other from early in their lives, so one potential source of rivalry is avoided.

From about the age of five, children exhibit much more freedom, and they run about the village or the fields with only cursory adult supervision. Boys form little groups of three or four close friends who may live in neighboring houses, though real brothers are not usually included in the same group. Small groups of girls may run about the village at the same age, though they are never quite so unfettered as the boys. Children make little carts of bamboo with rough wooden wheels, some-sometimes with the aid of a cooperative father, on which they pull each other screaming around the village. Small animals, dead or alive, are suitable playthings. A child may drag a dead chick about on the end of a string. I once saw a man catch a

lizard and give it to his child of about five who proceeded to
tear off its lower jaw and impale the upper one with a safety
pin. He tied a string to its tail and then prodded it with a stick
to make the barely living lizard walk in this encumbered
fashion. The only emotion displayed by adults who were watching was amusement. A child is occasionally given a cheap
plastic toy from the market, and adults make little bamboo
whirligigs for their children, but none of these things survive
for long and children must more often be content with sticks
and stones or discarded objects which they find about the village. Much of their play is an imitation of adult behavior. They
pretend to cook rice, to go to the fields and work, or to go to
market and bring back salt and dried fish like their parents.
Sometimes they pretend to blow horns and beat drums, and
four or five children may cooperate to imitate a ceremony, or
the way their older brothers would capture a new husband for
one of the village girls. They enjoy making little slingshots and
stalking through the village in search of birds, but I never saw
children play any competitive games. For a number of years the
children have few responsibilities and considerable freedom.
They come home to eat and to sleep, and they spend as much of
their time as they wish with their families in the fields, but they
are under little pressure to learn anything or to help with the
work.

Parents criticize their children when they are at this age, and
can be distressed by them if they are naughty. The limit of
punishment is usually a few shouted words, or a single quick
blow on the head or body with the fist or a stick. This may do
little more than send the child skipping away laughing, but that
at least removes the child and that seems to be enough. They are
quickly friends again, and neither seems to remember the blow
after a few minutes. Later, in formal legal cases, adolescents and
even adults are punished in a more deliberate way, a way reminiscent of the "for your own good" attitude of some discipline in
America. This punishment is administered by male lineage

mates, never by the mother or father, and I cannot imagine a Garo parent taking the same attitude towards his child. A parent's punishment, when it occurs at all, is quickly administered, accompanied by a certain amount of anger and noise, but then quickly forgotten.

Children rarely come to blows with one another, but parents separate them when they quarrel, restrict them if tempted to get into mischief, and keep them away from danger. Life is simple enough, and possessions are so meager that discipline presents a less formidable problem than for people who own many breakable objects, or adhere to rigid routines. Furthermore, while little is expected of children, what is expected is well defined. Any adult may scold any child, so the parents share the burden of discipline with others. As a last resort, even small children may be threatened with the mother's 'brother' or other older lineage mate. Though an 'uncle' may never actually be requested to discipline his 'niece' or 'nephew', a child is taught from an early age to expect punishment from these older lineage mates and to be correspondingly cautious in dealing with them. The older a child becomes and the more serious is his misbehavior, the more likely it is for his lineage mates to take a hand in his punishment.

Girls apparently need discipline, at least formal discipline, less often than boys, and the shift to the jurisdiction of the 'uncles' seems to be less complete for them than for boys. The heiress remains in her father's house and partially under his formal control until he dies. Correspondingly, lineage mates less frequently have to exert their authority. However, if a girl or woman really misbehaves—if, for instance, she commits adultery, which seems to be the main infraction of women—it is her lineage mates, 'uncles' and 'brothers,' and never her father, who berate and punish her.

Both the father and maternal uncle are disciplinarians, then, or conversely a man has responsibilities for both his children and his younger lineage mates. This need not lead to conflict, since the types of authority exercised, and the areas of responsibility, are different. A man must keep his own small children from being naughty, but need act only as a potential threat for his 'sister's' small children. Later his own children will escape from his jurisdiction entirely, but serious infractions by younger lineage mates are his permanent responsibility. Certainly by the time a boy is ready to be married jural authority rests in the status of the 'mother's brother' rather than in that of the father. The 'mother's brother' has the legitimate, constituted authority.

As a child grows older, his emancipation from his parents' home becomes more complete. At the age of five or six he starts to sleep apart from his parents, with a separate mat and blankets. He ranges more widely about the village, and clings less to his parents' protection. A few years later comes the first real responsibility of most children—both boys and girls—that of taking charge of a younger brother or sister. One child generally takes consistent care of the same small baby. So many children die between the ages of being carried and of carrying that those who do survive may carry two or three younger siblings in succession before finally outgrowing this work. A close bond develops between the two children, and adults remember happily the brothers or sisters that they took care of. Occasionally the bond is symbolized much later in life, when a man or woman kills a cow in honor of the person who carried him, though not everyone does this. The two spend many hours together each day. The older one may devise games for the baby, dandle him and jounce him, and try to make him happy. He runs quickly to his mother, sometimes with a certain amount of alarm if the baby starts to cry, so that she can nurse it. Carrying may last for as much as three or four years if the babies keep arriving, and only a few children never carry at all. Their job does not restrict them greatly, since they are free to run about the village and play with their friends, some of whom also have charges; but they must not go out of reach of their mother.

A major step in a boy's freedom comes when he starts to sleep

in the bachelors' house. This is a building constructed primarily by the unmarried youths themselves according to a distinctive plan. The bachelors' house is shorter than most houses, and
is completely open at one end. Each village has one of these,
often located near the 'headman's' house, and it serves as a
center for the activities of the unmarried youths. The drums
hang in the bachelors' house when not in use, conveniently
ready if a group of bachelors feel like an impromptu concert.
It is here that boys learn the arts of drumming, of playing the
flute and jews' harp, and of blowing the horn. The boys may
start to sleep in the bachelors' house even before they stop
having the daytime responsibility of caring for a child; otherwise, they start soon after. This is one step in removing a boy
from the jurisdiction of his parents. Two brothers may both
sleep in the bachelors' house, but they try not to sleep too close
together, for, it is said, the younger one is always conscious of
the authority of the elder, and afraid he may be beaten.

After this, boys spend even more time with age mates. They
relax in the bachelors' house or race each other about the
village. Day-to-day standards now are more often set by the
group of bachelors, and if formal discipline is needed older
lineage mates will enforce it. At about the same age boys let
their hair grow long, start to wear a turban, and are assigned a
special plot in the fields for their own use. These steps occur in
early puberty, but no ceremony marks the transition. In fact
boys take the initiative themselves and decide when they want
to start working more consistently and to act less like a child.
They may even want to do these things before their parents are
willing, while a parent may not, for instance, allow a child to let
his hair grow until he is old enough to keep it clean and free of
lice. But if a child delays too long, everyone will tease him about
being lazy and not beginning to work in the fields as he should.
Though largely free of parental discipline, other pressures
encourage a bachelor to learn the skills of his society. He knows
that eventually he will be married, though he may resist and

postpone this event for some years. Everyone impresses him with the necessity of learning to do all the adult work, and he knows that no one will provide him with food or other basic necessities if he is unable to produce them himself. A bachelor should try to save for his marriage. If his parents are poor, he feels that he must help by contributing some or even all of his income to the family budget. So most bachelors, however much they carouse, also spend an increasing portion of their time in serious and sometimes hard work.

Only after he is about twelve years old does anything like formal teaching take place. The most difficult skill to learn or to teach is basket-making, which the father or some other man must impart to a boy. The instruction consists mostly of telling a child to make a particular basket as he has watched others do and then reprimanding him if he does it wrong. Occasionally a man will demonstrate, but I never saw anyone who was able to analyze and point out the mistakes another was making. If a person makes a mistake in a complex basket, for instance, his instructor will take the basket away, redo it himself, and then tell him to do it that way henceforth. No effort is made to break the complex weaving process down into steps so as to make it easy to understand and learn systematically, although it is recognized that certain baskets are easier to weave than others. Fathers tell their sons to make the easier types first, and then gradually lead them to the more difficult ones. Fathers make little rice-pounders so that their small daughters can practice with equipment suitable to their size, and they may encourage their sons to build miniature houses just for practice.

The other skills of the society are less exacting than basket-weaving, and even less formal instruction is required. A father often teaches his son and a mother her daughter, though a job like cultivating, which is done by both sexes, may be taught by either parent, and nothing prevents other relatives or neighbors or older friends from giving instruction too. The general attitude toward technical education is that it is a process for which the child must take the main responsibility. A parent can tell the child what to do, provide him with a sample or a demonstration, and punish him if he is really lax, but mostly the child must learn these things for himself. A child learns by watching.

Adolescence is also a time when a boy must learn the etiquette of entertaining, how to behave with relatives, and how to participate in village ceremonies. Much of this knowledge is acquired by joining other unmarried youths in activities in which the bachelors have a special role, such as the bachelors' feast which comes at the beginning of the *Wangala* festival, or their decoration of village houses with rice-flour paste.

The most exciting duty of the bachelors is to bring new husbands to the village girls. Several times in the course of a year, but most often during the winter months, bachelors must take time off from other duties to capture a boy and then "lead him in eating" and "lead him in cultivating" in his new village.

In each activity the older bachelors take most of the responsibility and the younger ones follow along, doing as much as they feel able to. Older boys virtually never give outright directions to younger ones, but the younger ones observe the behavior and actions of the older, and as they feel ready, start to do the same jobs. When a new bachelors' house was built, for instance, there was a steady progression from younger to older in the seriousness of their labor and in the amount of it assumed. When posts had to be carried, each boy chose one according to his own size and strength. The biggest post was carried by the oldest, but even the little boys trotted along carrying small sticks. No one assigned these jobs. The boys simply did what they could.

Boys learn to serve food to others and to pass out rice beer, beginning with the most senior person present, according to the social proprieties. Even though they don't always act as a group, each bachelor also helps entertain visitors in his own father's house or in the houses of neighbors and relatives. Bachelorhood is an exciting period in a boy's life. Men look back on their bachelor days with a certain amount of nostalgia and shake their heads a bit at their wildness. When they hear bachelors whooping through the village, the older men grin and say "the bachelors are out of their heads again."

Girls are kept more closely under the eyes of the parents than their brothers in the period between puberty and marriage. They work with their mothers and sisters, learning to cook, to pound rice, to make rice beer, and to exercise all the feminine skills of the society, but they do not have the opportunity to spend as great an amount of time with other girls or in the houses of other people. This does not mean that girls are in any way secluded. They dance in the village ceremonies, they go to market, where they can look the boys over and be looked over in turn, and with a fair frequency they get pregnant before they are formally married.

Most unmarried girls are shyer than boys. They tend to cling more to the protection of their homes and are encouraged to do so. Most young married women are considerably less shy than their slightly younger unmarried sisters. They talk freely to others and are freer both to go about the village by themselves and to go visiting with friends. Marriage for girls comes as a liberating event, while for boys it is a restricting one. One expression of this fact is the custom by which the woman or her family take the initiative in finding a husband while boys traditionally try to avoid matrimony.

Besides technical skills, maturing Garos also acquire considerable intellectual knowledge, though it is not consciously taught. No formal instruction in arithmetic, for instance, is ever given, but Garo men can add, subtract, and do a certain amount of multiplication and division in their heads. They may not be able to read a single figure, but they must know something about calculation in order to buy and sell in the market. All Garos habitually divide the day into its twenty-four hours, but few in Rengsanggri could read a clock, or knew how many minutes an hour contained. A few people in the village could laboriously write their own names and recognize a few letters, but most could not.

Everybody in Rengsanggri had been to Tura and quite a number had been as far as Mankachar, a town about 30 miles west of Tura; but only a few had been further. The most widely traveled Rengsanggri people were three men who had joined the Garo labor battalion in the Second World War, and who had gone all the way to the Assam-Burma Border. Only they had traveled extensively outside of the Garo Hills. Knowledge of geography beyond the district was extremel ylimited. Towns however distant, were always located by pointing, and I was often asked to point out the direction in which America lay, and also to say whether it was really true that it was night in America when it was day in the Garo country. This seemed unlikely, and no reason given for it was very convincing, but there had been rumors.

Garo children also absorb their elders' conception of the proper behavior toward relatives and other people, and of their relation to the supernatural. They observe death with an intimacy denied to Western children, and learn to accept it calmly. Children die so regularly that one cannot afford to let a single death plunge one into lasting depression. Garos casually discuss the likelihood of death in the presence of a sick man. Children, also learn, of course, that sacrifices may ward off death and cure disease, and so should be tried, but they must always be prepared for failure. Man's resources against adversity are always limited.

Much of a man's training teaches him to be independent and self-reliant. Since early childhood he has had responsibility for many of his own actions: the times and amounts of eating and sleeping, the age at which to start sleeping in the bachelors' house, how much to dance and flirt, the amount of work to do in the fields. He knows that after marriage he will not be able to depend upon others for support but will have the entire burden of caring for his family. Every man is expected to bear these responsibilities, and poverty is a natural result of failure to do so. On the other hand, a child also learns that men have responsibilities to others beyond their immediate family: the duty to help others in house-building or sacrificing or in legal disputes. He learns that within broad limits his behavior is his own responsibility, but that if he steps so far out of line as to infringe upon the rights of others that he can expect organized punishment. And so a balance is struck between independent responsibility and duty to help one's neighbors and relatives.

By the time a Garo has reached a marriageable age, he has acquired the technical skills, the social graces, and the intellectual knowledge that will allow him to carry on as a responsible adult. Of course, not all men learn these things equally well. The Garos clearly recognize individual differences in intelligence and they know that some men are simply not capable of well-organized labor. Others they know are lazy, if not stupid. They have no doubt that these personal differences determine to a considerable extent a man's success in life. An incapable man is not likely to become wealthy, and poverty is sometimes explained by saying that the people simply do not have the ability to do better. Personal ability is certainly a prerequisite to success, since all men have the opportunity to learn the Garo skills and knowledge; but even personal ability is not enough, for beyond all human endeavor is a luck or fate that can prevent even the hardest-working man from becoming successful.

# V

## The Household

MARRIAGE ESTABLISHES, OF COURSE, many relationships beyond those within the nuclear family. Since a man generally moves to his wife's house or at least to her village at the time of marriage, the bonds between a man and his wife's relatives are usually more important than those between a woman and her husband's relatives. An heir becomes part of his father-in-law's household and works intimately with his parents-in-law and with other members of the family. The father-in-law is generally a classificatory maternal 'uncle' of the heir. Before the marriage this 'uncle' is likely to have been only one of a number of men occupying this kinship position, a man of the heir's own lineage but approximately a generation older. Marriage brings these two men close to each other, and identifies them firmly with one another. Any son-in-law, but particularly an heir, should do as his father-in-law suggests. No father-in-law can bring himself to be really authoritarian even toward his heir, and no heir would stand for too restricting a rule, but since the heir is a younger but reasonably close matrilineal kinsman of the father-in-law, a built-in authority that would otherwise be absent characterizes their relationship. It would seem to be this that underlies the Garo insistence that a 'nephew' is the desirable, indeed almost the essential, heir. Apparently, the authority inherent between lineage mates forms the only source of authority that can serve as a basis for the relation between father-in-law and heir. Other sons-in-law who are not heirs and are not members of the same lineage live and work separately from their fathers-in-law and do not come under even the mild authority that the heir must accept.

Though they must work together and cooperate in many things, father-in-law and son-in-law are restrained towards each other. A son-in-law never mentions the name of the older man if he can possibly avoid it, even if, as one man explained to me, the son-in-law is the richer and more successful of the two. Avoidance of the father-in-law's name is a sign of formal respect. The father-in-law, on the other hand, does not hesitate to use his son-in-law's name. Unless the younger man's wife or other people are present, the heir and his father-in-law even prefer not to work too closely together in the fields, though this is not prohibited. Frequently they have separate plots of land, and each generally concentrates on his own, though they usually trade a certain amount of labor back and forth. The two men usually avoid sitting next to one another in the house, just as brothers try not to sleep next to each other in the bachelors' house. This mild circumspection apparently helps to forestall friction in a relationship that the Garos feel to be a potentially difficult one. They know that a man and his heir occasionally do quarrel, though such behavior is certainly unseemly. A non-heir son-in-law, being less closely associated with his father-in-law, is less likely to be put into situations of conflict with him, and it is easier to maintain the restraint with which these men should treat each other, but the same sort of relationship holds for them as for an heir and his father-in-law.

The circumspection with which a man treats his mother-in-law is even greater than that with which he treats his father-in-law, at least so long as the father-in-law is alive. A mother-in-law and her son-in-law assiduously avoid going anywhere alone together. Properly they should be accompanied by either the mother-in-law's husband or her daughter. It is not forbidden, at least for brief periods, for a mother-in-law and her son-in-law to be in their house alone together, but they usually try to avoid staying there very long unless somebody else is present as well. Since they are likely to live in the same house, they may occasionally find themselves unavoidably alone. If everyone else is away, a son-in-law may even take a meal with his mother-in-law, but he is likely to eat as expeditiously as possible and then find some excuse to leave. He would never spend a night in the house unless somebody else were present, which of course is usually the case. The two may sit in the same group, but so long as the mother-in-law is present, her son-in-law is usually somewhat restrained. They say that a son-in-law feels very "shy" of his mother-in-law and wishes to avoid any suggestion of improper behavior toward the older woman. Mothers-in-law seem slightly less concerned about these rules, and with the security of their greater age worry less at the thought of a breach in etiquette. A woman might even gently tease her son-in-law occasionally, but she is in no danger of being teased back.

Garos sometimes say that this shyness comes from fear of the father-in-law's jealousy, but that one must also avoid anything that might make the jokes of which he will be the object have any basis of truth. Everyone gets teased about his mother-in-law. So long as one knows that he has been perfectly well-behaved it is possible to laugh these things off, but one always tries to avoid giving grounds for teasing. The Garo theory that the heir becomes the 'husband' of his mother-in-law when his father-in-law dies—even though this relationship includes only the economic aspects of the husband-and-wife relationship and not the sexual—is never far from the consciousness of the parties involved. It makes the son-in-law particularly anxious to demonstrate that even if he may in the future be considered the old lady's husband, at least that time has not yet come.

A non-heir son-in-law has much less necessity for contact with his mother-in-law. For the most part it is easy to avoid her without awkwardness, and at the same time there is less need to go to extremes to demonstrate the avoidance.

Non-heirs, like heirs, never mention the name of either parent-in-law. Failure to avoid these people sufficiently entails no formal sanction. One may encounter irritation on the part of the father-in-law, but far more important is the fear of ridicule on the part of all the members of the community, added to one's own nagging sense of uneasiness.

During the early years of a man's marriage younger siblings of his wife often continue to live in the household. Garos are not so particular as to insist that children marry in strict order of age, so a man's older brothers-in-law and even sisters-in-law may live with him for a year or more. The relations of a man with his wife's siblings are not complicated by the rather strong avoidance practiced with the parents-in-law. One may sit, talk freely, and even joke with the unmarried sister of one's wife, and a wife should not take offense at such behavior. After the wife's sister is married one may have slightly less freedom, because of the feeling that her husband might object if one talked or joked too broadly, but the relationship is still reasonably unrestrained. Similarly the wife's brothers of approximately one's own age can be treated fairly freely. It is considered appropriate to be good friends with these men, though it is difficult to be really intimate with any relative as close as this, and the warmest friendships are more often between men with whom there are no complicating questions of kinship at all.

If the siblings-in-law are separated by great age differences, the relationship assumes the character of that between parents and children. Siblings of the wife who are much younger than she is are like children to her husband, particularly if he is the heir and living in the same household with them. An heir, after all, probably comes from the same lineage as the father of his wife, and he will inherit the father-in-law's property and social status when he dies, so that the wife's younger siblings regard him as a sort of younger version of their father and accept any appropriate discipline from him. After the death of the father, all the heiress's siblings refer to her husband by the term that they otherwise use for a younger brother of their father, and this neatly sums up their relationship with him. He is much like the father, but younger.

A peculiar relationship exists between a man and his wife's brother's wife. The people of Rengsanggri, unlike the Garos of some other parts of the district, consider these two people to be fair game for constant broad joking. A man may be asked with mock casualness how his wife's brother's wife has been lately, or whether he enjoyed his visit with her. To ward off the teasing these two will assiduously avoid each other's company in an effort not to deserve the teasings that will nevertheless come their way.

Because of the residence pattern, a woman is less likely than a man to be closely associated with her parents-in-law. Conflict is here less likely to develop, and careful avoidance is less likely to be necessary; but when a woman does meet her parents-in-law, the relationship is similar to that of a man with his parents-in-law. A woman is circumspect in her behavior toward her husband's parents, particularly her father-in-law, and does not joke with them. She may sit in the same house with her father-in-law, but she should keep a respectful distance from him, just as her husband keeps his distance from her mother.

After a young couple have children, a new set of relationships is also established between the grandparents and the grandchildren, and once again the residence pattern makes the mother's parents more important to the children. The children of heirs live in the same household with their grandparents, while their cousins, the children of other daughters, are likely to live nearby and to regard their grandparents' home as one in which they are freely welcome, where they can be almost as much at home as in their parents' own house. So long as the grandparents are able to do their work in the fields, the parents have the responsibility of caring for the children. Except for a very aged person who is able to do little else, systematic care of the children by the grandparents is not usual. One woman in

Rengsanggri, who was almost totally blind, took regular care of her daughter's baby, while the daughter did her work unencumbered, and a few other feeble elderly people helped out a great deal in keeping the children out of mischief. Other grandparents dandled their grandchildren, and took pleasure in the little babies as all Garo adults do, but they seemed glad to leave the responsibility to their children.

Behavior toward the grandparents is complicated by another of the relationships which is regarded with amusement and which draws considerable teasing by the Garos—that of a boy to his mother's mother. Even small boys are frequently teased about their intimate contact with their mother's mother. People, for instance, call him by his grandfather's name, thereby pl cing him into an improper relation with the grandmother, a..d the thought of this is hilarious to everybody but the boy himself. From the time the boy begins to understand what this teasing is all about, he becomes shy of his grandmother, and tries to keep away from her and avoid as much teasing as possible. He has no shyness with his mother's father, but regards him as something of a disciplinarian. Girls and boys must obey their grandparents or expect punishment. There is no amusement found in teasing a girl about her relationship with any of her grandparents, or in teasing a boy about his relationship with his father's mother, and certainly not with either grandfather. If the father's parents live close enough to be visited regularly, the children can associate with them freely, though this relationship is not emphasized as being a particularly close one. The grandparent-grandchild relationship, then, while it involves strain only in the case of mother's mother and daughter's son, is not the relationship of pronounced freedom and intimacy that it is in so many societies.

One other relative or set of relatives in the grandparent's generation may be significant. This is the mother's mother's brother, and the other men of one's own lineage in that generation. A special kin term designates such people: *mamaachu*, compounded from the terms for mother's brother (*mama*), and grandfather (*achu*). Like the 'grandfathers' they are old, but like the 'uncles' they have the authority of the lineage, and in fact as the oldest male members of the lineage they have particularly great authority, though it does not differ in kind from that of the 'uncles'.

## HOUSEHOLD COMPOSITION

The Garo household may include, at most, a married couple and their unmarried children, together with one married daughter (sometimes adopted), her husband, and their small children. In principle, a married granddaughter and her children might also be included, but the grandparents seldom survive long enough to see their grandchildren married. Rarely, and then for short periods only, more distant relatives or even non-related people are included for various reasons, but most households have only the members shown in the following diagram.

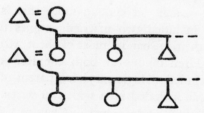

Of course, few households include all the possible relatives, but most are readily understandable as fragments of such a family, i.e., either the residue of living members who have survived from a more complete household, or a young family on the way to becoming a full household. Data on household composition in Rengsanggri are given in full in Appendix A and will only be summarized here.

Of the 60 households in Rengsanggri, seven consisted of

married couples without children. Of these seven couples, five were recently married, and either had had no children as yet, or had none who had thus far survived. One was a middle-aged couple who had never had any children, and one a couple so poor that their two unmarried sons were being fed in other houses and therefore counted as members of those households. Twenty households consisted of a married couple with their unmarried children, making a total of 27, or not quite half, which were simple nuclear families. Nineteen of these 27 nuclear families had been set up as new households of non-heirs, while eight were remnants of once larger households which were still maintained by heirs. Two of the heir families were living as nuclear families because the older couples had moved away (both to the neighboring hamlet of Asonanggri, where they seemed to be moving toward conversion to Christianity, though it was still possible that they would later return and live with their heirs), and in a third case a surviving widow had moved away and remarried elsewhere. In the other five cases of heirs now living alone, the wife's parents had both died. Of the 33 households which did contain more than simple nuclear families, nine included two married couples (a mother and daughter and their husbands) most of them with a number of unmarried children of one or both couples. Another eleven households included a single surviving parent of the wife, and eight households included men with two wives. (These polygynous families will be described in Chapter VI).

Some of these households as well as all the others were, for one reason or another, more complex in their composition. Two households included a recently married non-heir daughter and her husband who had not yet established their own house but were expecting to do so in the near future. One other household included the wife's maternal aunt and her husband, who had recently moved to the village. This was a most unusual arrangement and was strictly temporary. It would last only until the second couple could get a house built for themselves.

Three households included no married couples, but only a widow and some children. Two households included youths whose proper parents were too poor to care for them. Three households included divorced sons. Most of these divorcés were young and had every expectation of remarriage. Finally, two households included miscellaneous survivors of three generations of marriages.

When listed in this manner households appear to have great variety, but actually almost all of them can be quite properly considered simply as variations and slight alterations of the single type of household that the Garos regard as normal. Only seven of the households included people who did not explicitly belong to the ideal family type. Two of these were unusual only in having a recently married or recently arrived couple who expected to build their own separate house within a few months, after which even these households would revert to the standard type. In no case in Rengsanggri, or to my knowledge in any neighboring village, did a man live in his parents' house with his wife, and in no case did two married sisters expect to live for any length of time in the same household.

## ACTIVITIES OF THE HOUSEHOLD

The households are important by virtue of the jobs which they fulfill for their members and for the society. They are residential, they are the primary organization for production and consumption, and they are, of course, the organization within which the greatest part of socialization occurs. Furthermore, they are explicitly recognized by the members of the society to be the building blocks out of which larger residential organizations—most particularly the villages—are formed.

The most tangible evidence of a household is the house which its members share. In all but three cases in Rengsanggri, each household occupied a single house. One ancient widowed man slept apart from his married daughter, with whom he took his meals, in a small shack which he apparently considered preferable to sleeping in the same house with his daughter. Two other households included so many members that one building was not large enough, and had expanded into a second building. In both of these two cases the younger couple slept in a relatively small house built beside the larger one where the older couple slept. Both houses were counted as belonging to the same household, though in walking through the village it would not be possible, without being told, to know which of the houses were annexes to the main dwelling of a large family. The house is the physical seat of the family and is closely identified with it. In fact, in the Garo language, the word *nok* refers both to the physical building and to the organization of people—the family —who live inside it.

The fields are the other important family asset, though these are not permanent possessions since fields are used for only two years at a time. Moreover, a family cannot be limited economically by a shortage of fields, since any family is free to open up as much land as it can use. Nevertheless, during the years any fields are in use, they are unambiguously assigned to a particular household, and in spite of the considerable amount of labor exchanged in agricultural work (see Chapter VIII) each household retains primary responsibility for its own plots. It must do all of the planning and organizing for its own fields, and most of the actual work as well. The members of the family have exclusive rights to the products of their own plots. This fact strengthens the ties within the household and de-emphasizes more extended kinship relations. Everybody has a strong obligation to work for and to support the members of his own household, but owes little of an economic or material nature (as opposed to legal responsibility) to more distant kinsmen.

The independence of the household in subsistence activities accentuates its importance to the individuals within it. Since both men and women have their own tasks, it is difficult to maintain a family without able-bodied members of both sexes.

Husband and wife form the closest of teams. All of the work that either does is for the good of both. A man's obligation to support his wife is a strong one, and one that youths recognize as a serious drawback to marriage. Women too must work for the benefit of their husbands. Husband and wife are the only relatives who never cultivate separate plots.

Garos say that in principle the woman of the family should be the one to hold any money that the family possesses. However, they are inclined to over-systematize their own matrilineality, and maintain on the other hand that everything is owned by the woman, and that the husband can only use his wife's possessions, never really own them. The statement that the family valuables, including money, are held by the woman is one aspect of this over-systematization. Most people readily admit that control of these things depends greatly on the particular family situation; and their modifying statement, that actually whichever spouse is the "smarter" keeps the money, seems closer to the truth. Certainly in many families the man has more responsibility than the woman for whatever cash transactions have to be made, but no man is in a position to be high-handed with the family budget. Rather, he and his wife must agree on the general use of the money as on the general allocation of all the family's resources.

Material goods owned by a couple are essentially family property, though some of them are of course used more by the husband and some more by the wife. Only their separate clothing is really personal property. Since widowed people generally remain in the family of the heir after the spouse's death, such demise does not lead to division of the goods. The question of division of the goods arises only in the case of divorce, and even then the husband usually simply departs with a few items of personal clothing, while everything else is left to the wife. Ordinarily a husband and wife expect to stay married, and their property and resources are completely merged.

Children, when young, are of course dependent upon their

parents. Though the time is not precisely marked, from puberty
onward they begin to have an increasing economic independence from their parents. First, the parents assign a small patch
of land to the child, dividing it off from their own portion. This
plot is planted and taken care of largely by the child, and he will
be considered the owner of the crops grown there. Boys of
fourteen carry their own baskets of cotton to market for sale and
for the most part are able to use the money as they please. Each
year a larger plot is assigned to the child until the household may
even take an extra portion for clearing so the boy or girl will
have enough. By the age of eighteen both boys and girls may
grow substantial amounts of their own crops. I knew of boys
who made more money from cotton than their own fathers. The
separate plots which young people cultivate contribute materially to their freedom. Nobody, certainly not the parents, need
direct the work a boy does in his fields. That work is his own
responsibility and the crops are his reward. So a father has little
authority over his children, particularly over his sons, even in
daily labor. However, since an unmarried person can never be
a complete economic unit, having no partner of the opposite
sex, unmarried sons and daughters receive some assistance from
other members of the family. Mothers help with the woman's
work of their sons' plots and fathers do the same for their
daughters'; or sometimes a brother and sister may help each
other. Children also do some work on the plots of their parents,
and there is never any accounting kept of the amount of work
exchanged back and forth. The parents' plot and the plot of the
children are all considered in a broader sense to belong to the
same household. When, for instance, the sacrifice is carried out
in the fields before planting, each household sacrifices in just
one spot and there is no need to duplicate the sacrifice in each
of the separate plots belonging to the family. But boys and girls
have particular responsibility toward their own plots, and they
take pride in producing a good crop and selling a good supply of
cotton. Until they are married they continue to be fed from the

family kitchen, and many of them contribute from their harvest to the family supply. This is viewed as a contribution and not as a family prerogative in the way that a husband and wife automatically use the food produced by their common efforts. Usually a boy uses at least some of the output for his own use for the luxuries that young people enjoy—fancy clothing, betel nut, cheap cigarettes, and jewelry, and sometimes for favors to lovers or even as a saving toward marriage. By eighteen, boys in particular have a securely independent supply of cash, and they gradually attain economic independence and responsibility even before marriage.

The economies of a middle-aged couple are not uniformly merged with those of their heiress and her husband. It is the rather imperfectly maintained ideal of the society that these economies should be as completely merged as those of husband and wife, but personal difficulties in such a family frequently tend to divide the older and younger couple from each other. The possibility of separating their economies is a means of reducing conflict, if this occurs in spite of the ideal. Those families that do work most closely together speak with a certain satisfaction at being able to get along so well, but many other households separate some of their activities and lose no particular status in the community for doing so. Three different phases of economic activity may be maintained separately or together: cultivation, sale and storage, and consumption. Of these, cultivation is the most likely to be kept separate, and indeed in the great majority of cases where two couples live in one household, they organize their efforts so that each couple has major responsibility toward its own separate plot. This arrangement may be convenient if the older couple had cultivated their plot many years earlier when the same section was previously cleared. They may more or less automatically take it up once again, but with a new son-in-law this is likely to be inadequate in size, so the son-in-law and his wife open a new plot, often at a considerable distance from the old one. No particular difficulty is seen in this, and for the most part the two couples work on their own separate plots; however, like the plot of an unmarried son or daughter, these two are considered general family property in a larger sense, and one sacrifice is regarded as enough for both when the fields are planted. The separation minimizes the sense of uneasiness that sons-in-law sometimes feel when they have to work too intimately with their parents-in-law. Such couples generally work back and forth rather freely on each other's plots and never count closely the amount of work exchanged in order to make certain that they are repaid, as they do when they work with other relatives or neighbors. Rarely, two or more plots are considered general household property and are never allocated to the individual couples.

More households sell their products together and store their non-money crops together than actually grow them in common. Many pairs of couples mix the crops after the harvest and from then on count the entire supply as general household property, but some of them find less conflict in selling their cash crops separately and building separate granaries for the rest. These families maintain separate budgets, keep their money completely separate, buy their clothes separately, and even buy household necessities, such as dried fish, separately. Even these families may cook and eat together, however, each couple contributing supplies to the common mess.

Still other families, not always those that keep separate in all other activities, prefer to cook separately. Even though they store their grain together, some take out their food and prepare it individually and others eat from their own separate supplies. Cooking arrangements need not even correspond to the division of the household into two buildings. Wila and her heiress, Nokan, had separate houses and they cooked individually, though they did go back and forth freely and used each other's belongings constantly. Aling's wife and his heiress daughter, however, continued to eat together even after the daughter and her family moved to a separate house. Finally, Miman's wife and his heiress (who was the daughter of an earlier marriage and actually older than his present wife) cooked separately even though they lived in the same house. All sorts of degrees and combinations of cooperation take place. All the types of cooperation that neighbors sometime engage in are particularly likely to take place between the couples of a single household. These arrangements depend entirely upon their own preferences, though there is some suspicion that if the members of a single household keep separate in most of their economic activities that they may not be getting on as smoothly as the ideal household should. It is nobody else's concern to interfere, however, and one can never really be sure of a lack of harmony without more obvious signs. Furthermore, the arrangements may even vary from year to year, depending upon the fields that are available, the number of children, and so forth.

However much economic separation there may be, the household is still recognized as an important unit. As the older couple grows feeble, the economies merge more completely until there is no distinction between them. Particularly when one of the older people dies and the widow has no partner of the opposite sex to do his share of the work, the older person joins with the younger couple in all subsistence activities. An elderly widow lives in the same house with her daughter and heir, and participates completely in their agricultural work. Although single elderly men are not so common, widowers too are dependent upon their daughters and sons-in-law in all economic matters. This is in fact the primary reason for the system of heirship. It would be considered a profound tragedy for an old person to be left alone.

One other explicit duty of household members toward one another, not unlike the care of the aged, is care of the sick. A frequent reason given for desiring marriage is to ensure care during times of illness. Husband and wife are expected to look after each other, and husbands even cook for their sick wives.

If illness becomes serious, then neighbors and more distant relatives are called in to help with the necessary sacrifices, and relatives other than immediate members of the household occasionally help with the ordinary nursing, though it is more often the household members who fulfill these duties.

The individuality and importance of the household is formally recognized by the government in its collection of a "house tax." For many years the most important tax levied upon the Garos has been a fixed assessment on the house, or more properly household, since those in which the older and younger couple live in separate buildings, whatever the degree of their economic separation, never pay a separate house tax. On the other hand, when a non-heir couple sets up a new household after moving out of the girl's house, one of the signs by which Garos now recognize and also explain their separation is that they must pay a separate house tax. The special position of the household will appear more fully in Chapter VIII, in which various types of exchange which tie the individual households of a village together will be described.

Garos spend the greatest portion of their time working or relaxing in the company of other members of their own household. On an ordinary day people start to stir about their houses as soon as the sky begins to grow light. The first task of the wife's day is to cook the morning meal of rice—or sometimes millet—and a curry, and she may even finish cooking before the sun rises. The family members usually eat in front of the central fireplace. They each have a banana leaf of rice, and another of curry. If they happen to be ready and hungry at the same time, husband and wife and their children eat together, but often family members eat one by one as they find time. One of the women or girls of the house must visit a near-by stream, where she scours her metal cooking pots with sand in the cold water. She also fills a number of gourds with water and carries them back to the house for the day's supply. People often relax inside or in front of their houses for a while in the morning, stretching from sleepiness, smoking, and chatting with the members of their families or close neighbors. It is the time of day when people are most certain to be at home.

Each person must decide to what work he will devote his day. Small jobs, such as minor house repairs by the man, or gathering firewood by the woman, may be done at odd moments before and after the field work, but most of the day is usually spent on a single major task. If the couple go to the fields the entire day is spent there; if a woman pounds rice, she spends all day at it; if a sacrifice must be performed, those who help do no other major work on that day. The choice of work for any one day comes as a resolution to the requirements of numerous conflicting duties. On a January day, a man may have clearing to do in the new fields; his wife may want to rake up the brush in the old fields, but she may also need to pound and winnow rice if the family's supply is getting low. If it is a bright, sunny day, she may feel that she should take advantage of the weather for pounding rice and leave the fields for another day, though weather is less of a problem in January than in the rainy months. If a relative or friend is building a house, the man may feel that it is more urgent that he help him than go to the field; or someone may get sick, and require his help in making a sacrifice. If it is market day, everything else may be dropped for a trip to market, though people with pressing work may even skip the market. Often husband and wife go together to their fields, and sometimes other members of the family join them; but at other times various responsibilities separate them. Somehow enough days must be found to finish all of the varied work necessary to keep a household going.

By an hour or two after sunrise people have finished their breakfast, have smoked a relaxed pipe at home, and are ready for work. In some months, a large proportion of the villagers go to the fields. They drift off singly or in small groups, making their way to their own fields or to the field of the people with whom they are cooperating that day. Field workers take some rice and curry left over from the morning's cooking, and at about midday they sit in their field houses and eat a cold lunch. Sometimes they also boil up a pot of manioc or sweet potatoes in the field. The village is never completely deserted, however; a few women always spend the day in the village pounding rice, and one or two people are likely to be sick. These spend the day resting quietly in their houses or in the warm sun that falls on their verandas, and if anyone is sick enough to need a sacrifice, several people stay to help with that. Occasionally people take a day off and rest in the village, or do a few odd jobs. When a house is being built or thatched, many people must stay in the village to help, and at the village festivals almost everybody stays.

Garos work at a relaxed pace, and rest occasionally during the day; but they work steadily for long hours at often arduous tasks. When several people work together, they chat pleasantly through most of the day. They rest for as much as an hour around noon when they eat, but other rests are briefer. People were willing to stop their work to talk to me when I came to their fields, but after ten or fifteen minutes they were always anxious to get back to their labors.

By five o'clock or so people start to drift back into the village from the fields, or back to their own houses if they had been working elsewhere in the village. The wife again cooks rice and curry for her family. People often sit around and chat with friends and neighbors in the evening. If it is warm, it may be pleasant on the veranda, but on chilly winter evenings it is much more comfortable around the fire in the house. By nine o'clock most people are settling down to sleep, and one by one the fires, whose light flickers through the chinks in the bamboo walls, die down and the village is again silent until morning.

This routine is varied by market day, which comes once a week, by the varied agricultural tasks which change from month to month, and by ceremonies which enliven the village at intervals throughout the year. While the ceremonies are more flamboyant and more exciting than mundane farming, the largest part of every Garo's life is spent patiently working in his fields, scratching out enough food for himself and the members of his household.

# ❧ VI ❧

## The A'kim Bond

MARRIAGE ESTABLISHES OR PERPETUATES not only a household but also an enduring relationship between the lineages of the husband and wife. The mutual rights and duties which accompany marriage and which bind together the two lineages are known to the Garos as *a'kim*. This single term expresses the Garo concept so much better than any possible English paraphrase that the Garo word will be used here. A non-heir marriage establishes a new *a'kim* relationship, while the marriage of heirs allows an old *a'kim* relationship to be renewed. An heir marriage, that is, in a sense repeats a previous marriage, since husband and wife come from the same respective lineages as the wife's father and mother. Some of the most distinctive of the mutual obligations of the lineages which are connected by *a'kim* appear at the death of one of the married persons. At that time a series of practices are carried out which can collectively be called "replacement." These serve to perpetuate the *a'kim* relationship even in the face of death. Replacement, then, supplements heirship and the two together serve to maintain *a'kim*.

### MAINTENANCE OF THE A'KIM BOND: REPLACEMENT

Death leaves a gap in the family and the village, and every culture must make some provisions for helping its members to adapt to the new situation. The Garo techniques for readjusting

personal relationships after a death are focused on the attempt
to maintain the household as a continuing point of contact
between the same two lineages which it had always connected,
that is, to maintain *a'kim*. Since in any household the husband
must belong to one lineage while his wife and children belong to
another, the two lineages of these people each have responsibilities toward the particular household. Important among these
responsibilities is the guarantee that a dead member of their
lineage will be succeeded or "replaced" by another member of
the same lineage. This allows the perpetuation of the household
after the death of the members. Procedures differ, depending
upon whether a man or woman dies, whether or not the heir and
heiress have been chosen, and whether the deceased is the first
of a couple to die or was already widowed. In each case, however, if the procedures are carried out consistently—and for
the most part they are—the household will be maintained. The
following pages describe the various possibilities.

The death of a child, or even of an unmarried youth, entails
fewer complications than the death of a married person. Before
marriage the rules of *a'kim* are not yet established for that particular person, and so the lineage of a dead child does not have
to provide any replacement for him. Ceremonials are performed for children as for any dead person, but the social
complications are fewer. However, if a girl dies who has been
chosen as heiress, another girl must be chosen in her place—
either an unmarried sister or a related girl who can become the
adopted heiress. A married sister cannot be made heiress except
in the unlikely event that she happens to be married to a man
from the correct lineage who agrees to become heir. Finding a
new heiress involves a sort of replacement for the dead girl even
though she is not actually married, since her choice as heiress
gives her *a'kim* responsibilities. When a person has been
married, more complex adjustments must always be made.

Among married people the simplest adjustments follow the
death of old people who have already chosen their heirs and

heiresses. In a sense the very choice of heir and heiress amounts
to an arrangement for the time of death, before the death occurs,
since the younger couple, coming from the same respective
lineages as the older couple, will stay to carry on the household.
If a man dies after he already has a resident heir, then the heir
simply takes over as the responsible man of the household. If
the older man had already been weakened with age, then much
of the responsibility would already be upon the shoulders of the
younger man, and the death of the father-in-law only signals the
final step in the transfer of responsibility. If the dead man in
such a case is survived by a widow, then she remains in the
family of her daughter and son-in-law. After this time the Garos
refer to this woman as an additional 'wife' of the heir, or, more
precisely, they refer to her by the same term (*jik*) that they use
to refer to his wife. This terminology helped to persuade earlier
observers that the Garos had the custom of marrying their
widowed mothers-in-law, and they have been established in the
anthropological literature in this way.[1] The Garos, too, usually
maintain that this is their custom, and only close inquiry can
elicit the admission that the widow rarely, if ever, has sexual
relations with her son-in-law. Generally, they say, she will
suggest that her heir simply feed her and take care of her, but
that he continue to sleep exclusively with her daughter, his
original wife. In every case that I could learn anything about
this seems to have been the arrangement, and I would be most
surprised to find a man who actually engaged in sexual relations
with a woman who was the mother of his first wife. However, a
man and his mother-in-law do maintain all the *economic* relations appropriate to married people, and they therefore can be
called by the Garo terms that are otherwise properly translated
as "husband" (*se*) and "wife." The widowed mother-in-law
continues to live in the household that has always been hers, and
which is now occupied by her heiress and son-in-law as well.
She continues to participate in the woman's work of the household so long as and to the extent that her strength permits. She

goes to the fields and helps with the food preparation, and so assists in some of the essential work that the man could not appropriately do. Similarly, the man carries out the work that women cannot do, and is thereby able to give economic support to his widowed mother-in-law, just as he supports his wife. Nine households in Rengsanggri included not only a married couple and their children, but also the widowed mother of the wife; and a few of these also included some of the older woman's unmarried children. Women survive their husbands regularly enough to make this a common family pattern.

From all that is known of widespread mother-in-law avoidance, sexual relations with this woman would seem extremely unlikely, and it therefore clears the air to dispose of this formerly presumed case. The Garos share vigorously in the discomfort which so many people feel in the relations between mother-in-law and son-in-law. To change from the hesitation and avoidance that govern the behavior of Garo men toward their mothers-in-law to the intimacy of sexual relations would seem to defy the stability which we expect to find in human relationships, and the Garos do not attempt it. If the rules of *a'kim* were to be carried out with complete consistency, however, it would indeed be appropriate for the son-in-law actually to marry his mother-in-law. This would be a neat way of maintaining the tie between the two lineages upon which so much emphasis is placed. Here, then, seems to be a case in which the logic of the rules has gone beyond the psychological possibilities. Logic impels Garos to speak as if an heir married his mother-in-law when her husband dies. The difficulty of so radically altering the roles of the people concerned prevents this from ever actually happening.

A widow continues to live with her daughter as long as she lives. When she too eventually dies, little formal adjustment remains necessary. Her heiress can simply take over full responsibility from her, if the age of the mother had not effectively placed the daughter in this position already. Brothers and sisters of the heiress may continue to live in her house until their marriage, but then, one by one, all of them move away. The death of a surviving widow most often leaves the house occupied by a single married couple and their children. Such houses are not distinguished in their composition from new houses set up by daughters who move out of the parental home at the time of their marriage, nor, once the parents are dead, are there any particular responsibilities devolving upon their heirs. In spite of the absence of explicit symbols by which heirs and non-heirs can be distinguished, the difference is so important that it is generally remembered by everybody for as much as several generations.

If a woman dies before her husband, the arrangements may be slightly different. Not even the logic of the situation can lead the Garos to suggest that a man should marry his heiress (i.e. his daughter) when his wife dies, in the way that a widow should 'marry' her heir. Even rather old men dislike being without a wife, however, and Garos feel that widowers, whatever their age, have a legal right to demand a new wife. It becomes the responsibility of the dead wife's lineage to supply one. The search for a new or "replacement" wife for a man is much like the search for an adoptive heiress, except that since the person to be replaced (the former wife) is dead, the search must be carried out entirely by other family members. In this case the male members of the woman's lineage take the responsibility, and they are expected to find among the women of their lineage one who is free to marry the widower and to take the place of his former wife. As in all such cases the closest relatives take the first responsibility, looking among their 'sisters' and 'nieces,' but if no suitable person can be found near at hand, wider circles of kinsmen are consulted. For elderly men there is one additional possibility. Sometimes young unwed mothers are given to them, thus simultaneously disposing of the difficulty of finding husbands for such girls.

Since replacement wives are often given to elderly widowers, widowed men are rarer than single widowed women. Naban was the only single widowed man living in Rengsanggri when I was there, and he remained in the household with his daughter and her husband. He was an old and somewhat senile man; but the failure to give him a new wife was not due entirely to his great age, as I have known men from other villages who were by no means senile but who were persuaded to remain as widowers. Younger people sometimes joke about the demands of elderly men for new wives and sometimes complain about the difficulty of satisfying their desires, but for the most part they comply with an old man's wishes if it is at all possible to do so. The new wife may be much younger than her husband and the household may already include his heiress and her husband. Miman and Wajang each had a young wife living in his house along with a married heiress, the daughter of an earlier marriage. This arrangement, though logically reasonable for the requirements of *a'kim*, puts the in-marrying wife in an unusual position. She may be younger than the heiress of her husband, and there is little precedent to define her position. It is not surprising, therefore, that the Garos say that such a woman seldom remains with this family once her elderly husband dies. After his death her tie with the family is gone, and though in theory she is supposed to be allowed to stay, to live permanently and become the 'wife' of her former husband's heir, most women find the situation too difficult. Such women, it is said, quarrel with the rest of the family and other arrangements must be made for them. I did not happen to encounter actual examples of this, but apparently the widows move out and generally manage to marry again.

If a man is very old and can be persuaded to remain a widower, he may continue living in the house of his heir and heiress, and he should be able to rely on their support as long as he lives. When he dies, he leaves behind a single nuclear family to retain his house.

When people die who have not yet acquired heirs, the

arrangements are necessarily somewhat different. The mutual obligation of the families of a married couple to supply replacements in case one or the other should die is one of the principal reasons given for the *a'kim* relation. Since any widowed person wants a new spouse, it is a convenient rule for the two families to agree mutually to supply a replacement for their own member if he should die. Heirs amount to replacements chosen during the lifetime of the people from whom they inherit, but if a person should die before choosing an heir, his lineage mates must take over this responsibility. A dead woman's relatives must supply her husband with a replacement, and he cannot possibly be left alone if he has no married heiress. If the wife has an unmarried younger sister, she is an entirely appropriate choice, but only the closest of a range of relatives who may fill the position. An older sister or any older relative, however, is not suitable. In the absence of actual sisters the men of the lineage will have to look a bit further. Exactly as in the case of an old man who already had chosen an heir, the wife's relatives search among wider and wider kinship groups until a suitable person is found. The arrangements are usually made quickly. Sometimes a new marriage takes place within a few days of the death, and every effort is made not to leave the man alone for any great length of time.

In Rengsanggri seven of the 78 married women were originally married to their husbands as substitutes for a previous wife, and had moved to his home when they married. The replacement marriages must be thought of as localized around the original home of the first wife rather than that of the husband, since originally he may have moved from elsewhere. This home is retained by the husband after the first wife's death, though he is then joined by his new wife. A residence shift is required of the woman; this the Garos recognize as a rather divergent form of marriage, and the practices which initiate it are slightly different from the ordinary first marriage. It is not appropriate for the boys to go to capture a woman as they would a man, so a few women go and bring her back in what amounts to an imitation of the much more usual bridegroom capture. In the cases I heard about, younger female relatives of the dead woman went to "lead back" the new wife. The arrangements for these marriages were made earlier and agreed to by all sides before the actual wedding, so there was less uncertainty about the outcome than in the usual wedding, where the boy may flee at any moment. The usual marriage ceremony of killing the birds is performed for this couple, but it is done in the man's home, the place where the couple will live, and not in the girl's house, as in the more usual marriage.

The most complex arrangements follow the death of a man who has not yet chosen his heir. Widows are sometimes allowed to live for some time without either a husband or a resident heir, and they seem to be able to get along a bit more easily without a husband than a man can without a wife. Three women in Rengsanggri had neither a husband nor a male heir, though two of them had mature but still unmarried sons, who were able to do most of the work that a man should do. One of these was Nemnem, the woman who had neglected her duties as heiress. She maintained to me that she was able to take care of herself and live without a husband; but her youngest child, a son, was within a few years of the age of marriage, and many of the villagers predicted disaster for Nemnem when he left home. Since she herself had not been a responsible heiress, few people felt inclined to help her. Another woman had mature sons living with her, and since her heiress had already been chosen, it was expected that a new husband would be brought in soon. The third widow, Nata, had no mature sons, and lived alone with a young boy, the illegitimate son of her daughter, who was supposed to have served as Nata's heiress. In spite of repeated efforts, no boy had been persuaded to become the husband of this unattractive girl, and she finally married a widower, as a replacement for his first wife. Thereupon the old lady became partially dependent upon her daughter's family, but not a full member of her household as she would have been if her daughter had been married as a proper heiress.

In order to get a widow remarried, special arrangements must be made. The first move is similar to obtaining a usual heir, except that the man's surviving male lineage mates must assume the entire responsibility now that the man himself is dead. Just as the relatives of a woman must find a replacement to marry her widower, the relatives of a man must find somebody to marry the surviving widow. The younger brother of the dead man is an appropriate replacement, but the younger brother is only the closest of possible relatives and any younger member of the dead man's lineage will do. When a likely candidate is found, he is captured and brought in just like any other prospective husband, and with the same uncertainty of outcome. This man is married to the widow and, if he decides to stay, will form a real marriage with her, in which they will maintain sexual relations. Though replacement husbands are frequently a good deal younger than the widows they marry, and though they are admittedly somewhat similar to 'heirs' of the first husbands, it is still possible for them to become the real husbands of the widow, since they had not previously established a conflicting type of relationship that is difficult to overcome. The unique feature of this marriage stems from the feeling of Garos that it is unfair to expect a young man to marry a widow unless he is also given a younger wife who has never been married, or at least promised another wife at some time in the future. Every Garo man, that is, deserves one new wife, so a widow alone is not enough. If the widow has a daughter, however young, it is usual for the man to be married to both mother and daughter simultaneously. If the daughter is immature at the time, he may have to wait many years for her maturation before initiating sexual relations with her, but in the meantime he can maintain them with the older woman. If a widow does not have a daughter, then she, like a woman who passes the child-bearing age without a daughter, must adopt a girl. Like other adopted daughters, these girls sometimes move into the houses of their adoptive mothers when still very young, while others shift residence only when mature. A young wife of this sort, whether the adopted or true daughter, is called *jikgite* rather than *jik*, which is the term used for other wives. She is destined to become the wife of her mother's husband when she matures, though the only evidence villagers can give for the initiation of sexual relations is the girl's pregnancy. The *jikgite* should be considerably younger than the older wife. They say the two women are likely to quarrel if they are too close to the same age. If a *jikgite* must be adopted owing to the first wife's having no daughters, it is best to make the adoption while the girl is still young. To adopt a mature girl as *jikgite* is to invite quarreling between her and the older woman. Cases are readily cited where this was attempted, only to be followed by one or the other woman's having to leave. The best combination is certainly mother and daughter, since they will quarrel least of all. The older wife has a senior position, and villagers say that a man will not have sexual relations with the *jikgite* until the older wife specifically permits him to do so, but that she knows that she must eventually give permission or lose the support of the *jikgite*, who cares for the older wife just as an heiress does. However, as the first wife grows older, some men are reported to cease having sexual relations with her, and to shift entirely to the *jikgite*.

In Rengsanggri nine men were married to women who had previously had another husband. Three of these women had been divorced rather than widowed, but the same requirements hold for providing a *jikgite* to a man who marries a divorcee as for one who marries a widow. All but one had been assigned younger wives, though in two cases the girls were still immature. This left six men who had two potential sexual partners.

In some of these families there was no doubt that men simultaneously maintained sexual relations with both women. Jing-nang had children of about the same age by both a mother and her daughter from a previous marriage. In those cases where the younger wife grows up in the household where her future husband is already living, it would appear that there might be a very real difficulty in shifting from a relation that must inevitably be similar to that of father and daughter to that of husband and wife. That the shift in relationship can be made is evident from the case of Singgat. Singgat married Wilwil, who had divorced her previous husband. Both her children had died, so a young girl, Rangsi, the daughter of Wajang, was brought into her house as future *jikgite* for Singgat, and Wilwil raised her as her own child. Wilwil had no more children, but Rangsi grew up and recently she had a baby of whose paternity there seems to be no doubt. Families such as those of Singgat and Jingnang are pointed out by the villagers with approval, since everybody is carrying out his duty peacefully and without quarreling. Unfortunately people are not always so well-behaved. A case in point is that of Kam, who married Chan'mi after her previous husband had abandoned her. It was agreed that Chan'mi's daughter Dijak would become the *jikgite* of Kam when she matured. When I knew them, Dijak was a girl of about eighteen, clearly mature but not yet pregnant, and in the opinion of the people of Rengsanggri, who presumably knew, not yet engaging in sexual relations with her mother's husband as she should have been by that time. This was a matter of considerable worry to the people, since they felt that unless Kam did his duty by her, she would sooner or later commit adultery and manage to get pregnant by somebody else, or even run off with some other man. Either of these results would cause complications, and if Kam should lose his young wife, it would be his own fault. The blame of this situation was placed by the villagers on Kam, who was not having sexual relations with his first wife's daughter. Kam had been married to Chan'mi for about ten years and must have regarded his wife's daughter much as though she were his own. Apparently he found it difficult to transform his relations with her into those of a husband.

That such problems are not unique is indicated by the difficulties of the family of Jengram. His *jikgite* was Salchi, the daughter of his first wife. Two of Salchi's three children were reported to have fathers other than Jengram, her legitimate husband. I did not discover the paternity of the third child, and it was even suggested to me that it might have been Jengram. Nevertheless, this is apparently a case of exactly what is feared may happen to Dijak, if Kam is not able to initiate sexual relations with her.

While the logic of the system which requires a man to marry both a mother and daughter does entail certain practical difficulties, it is carried out some of the time, and many men, both those living today and those who show up in genealogical histories, have managed to have children by both women. Families in which a man is married in this way to both mother and daughter at once look superficially like those other households, in which an heir and his wife continue to live with the wife's mother after the father-in-law dies. The composition of the families is the same: mother and daughter and one man. In both cases the man is *called* 'husband' of both women and the women are the man's 'wives.' This has probably helped to perpetuate the idea both in the minds of Garos and in the writing of earlier observers of their customs that Garos actually "marry" their widowed mothers-in-law. In actual fact, all cases of real marriage to both mother and daughter are those in which a man marries the mother first, after her former husband dies or after she is divorced, and then a second wife is given to the husband in addition. Terminology does distinguish the cases, since when a man marries a girl before her father dies, she is never called *jikgite* but simply *jik*, and she is always considered the main wife.

There is one other way of providing for widows and widowers. It happens frequently, though not in accordance with any formal requirement, that lineages in the same area are united to each other by several marriages, so that several *a'kim* bonds join

them. It can easily happen that two men of one lineage (it may
be a fairly large lineage in which the two men are not closely
related) are married to two women of a second lineage (again
not necessarily close relatives). If the woman of one marriage
and the man of the other should both be widowed, then it can
be arranged to have the surviving spouses marry each other.
This is a recognized procedure, and the resulting marriage is
spoken of as one in which the two former houses have merged to
become one. The *a'kim* relationship is preserved, but after this
consists of a single marriage bond where there had formerly
been two. The real requirements of the system are met, in that
everybody is living in a family which includes both men and
women and everybody belongs to a functioning and complete
household. The marriage of Kaljing to Jiring was of this sort.
Kaljing, who was a member of the Manda sib from Misimagri,
had earlier been married to Chimchim, who was a Chambigong
of the village of Rengsanggri. When Chimchim died, the
Chambigongs had to find a replacement for her to give to
Kaljing. It happened that there was a widow, Jiring, of a closely
related lineage of the proper sib (Chambigong) living in Misimagri. She had formerly been married to a man of the Manda
sib, also of that village and therefore of the same village lineage
that Kaljing had come from, but he had died about three years
earlier. The family had brought in one young man in the hope
that he would marry Jiring if they promised him a younger wife
as well, but this young man had declined the match, and so she
was still without a husband when Kaljing's wife died. It therefore became possible to bring Jiring to Rengsanggri; she moved
into Kaljing's house as his wife, and the two houses were thereby merged into one.


### DEATH AND INHERITANCE

Besides requiring these rather complex rules of replacement,
death is also marked ceremonially, and at death, unlike the time

of marriage, gifts are transferred which symbolize the bond of *a'kim* which the marriage had formed between two groups of relatives.

As soon as they hear the news of a death, relatives and friends collect at the house of the deceased person. Visiting groups frequently come from other villages where relatives live, and particularly from the village where a man lived before his marriage. These visiting groups are rather formally conducted. They are organized by a close relative of the dead man, and may include from half a dozen to twenty or more people. They always carry with them the 'headman's' ceremonial drum, as well as two or three metal gongs, and they beat these and blow a horn as they walk single file to the other village. Such a party therefore announces its mission very clearly. The main ceremony is held in the village of the dead man. Generally at any death, except that of a small child, everybody in the village refrains from going to the fields for one day and most people take an active part in the funeral. Except for the closest kin, who are said to be too sad to help, one woman from each household of the village is expected to come to the dead person's house carrying a contribution of cotton and rice beer, which are used in the rituals, and a bunch of feathers which are waved over the corpse but are later taken back home again. Similarly one man from each household must cut a wooden pole and contribute it to the funeral pyre. The most closely related people work around the house of the dead person, preparing the body and helping with sacrifices. The women stay around the corpse, which is kept through the day in the back of the house. They wail from time to time in a highly stylized manner. Some women are recognized as being especially skillful at wailing, but most people show little evidence of genuine grief at a funeral. The most affluent villagers invite the men to a series of drinking parties, which are supposed to cheer up the relatives. I have stumbled upon these gatherings and have been gaily welcomed and urged to drink, and would never have recognized the occasion without being told that they were making the relatives of a dead man happy. The men who assemble with wood and who help build the pyre chat as pleasantly as at other times. In the evening some of the closest male relatives carry the body to the funeral pyre, where it is burned to the accompaniment of the beating of drums and gongs, and the ghost is sped on its way to the after-world. A few of the charred bones must be collected, wrapped in a cloth, and carried back to the house. The next day some of the closer friends and relatives of the family, but not all of the villagers, assemble in front of the dead person's house and assist in the building of a structure into which considerable amounts of grain are poured, and on which are hung pots, baskets, gourds, and other articles useful in the spirit world. The bones are buried in a small hole beneath this structure. Usually a man who is skilled at woodwork carves a rough head on the end of a wooden pole. The pole is decorated with some of the dead man's clothes or other characteristic objects. A rice-beer bottle or a replica of a man's gun may be hung from it, or the face may be decorated with a mustache. This crude image of the dead person announces to visitors that someone has died and, as one man explained to me, "that they should cry." The man who carves the post is supposed to be paid one leg of a cow which is killed. The bones are left buried for six months or so, until one of the major village ceremonies. At this time the deceased person's family takes the opportunity to hold a post-funeral ceremony (*delangsoa*), at which the structure is burned and if possible a cow is sacrificed and eaten by those friends and relatives who come to help. This ceremony ends the formal remembrance of the dead person.

At the time of the funeral of any married person, the relatives assemble and try to settle the formal questions which are raised by the death. If heirs have already been chosen, major decisions may be unnecessary. The relatives simply advise the young people who inherit the house to continue to live there peacefully and to take care of each other. If no heir or heiress has been chosen, the funeral provides a convenient opportunity to discuss who is available as a replacement, and sometimes, though not always, the question can be settled immediately, even before the relatives separate.

A ceremonial gift called *magual*, the nearest Garo parallel to bride price, is also made at funerals. When a man dies, the surviving members of the household—his heir if one has been chosen—must present *magual* to the household into whch he was born. By the time of a man's death, of course, his mother is likely to have died, but she should be succeeded by one of her daughters, a sister of the dead person, and even if the sister has also died, she should in her turn have been succeeded by one of her daughters. At any event, the household from which the dead person originally came will still exist if the provisions of heirship and replacement have been carried out consistently, and it is to this household that the main *magual* gift is to be made. Less expensive items are sometimes given to other households of closely related women of the dead man's lineage. Any heirloom may be given, but the most appropriate gift is a fine brass gong of the sort which Garos prize above all their other heirlooms. This gong is first used to hold the water for washing the body—the bottom of a gourd if no gong is available, providing an unsatisfactory substitute. One of the members of a visiting group of relatives later carries this gong from the house of the dead person back to the house of his mother. It is carried tied to the back by a carrying cloth of the sort that is otherwise used only for carrying small children. This symbolizes explicitly the idea that the gong is sent in return for the man who lived and worked as an adult in the house of his wife. It is said that the ghost of the dead man will see the gong and by that means will be able to find its way back to its mother's house so that it may be born there once again. If the man had been rich in life, his household is able to send a gong of considerable value, but if he had been poor, they may be able to send only an inexpensive one, or they may have to send some less precious heirloom. Whatever is sent, however, comes from the household and the economy where the dead man worked, and can be considered as much his own gift to his mother's house as the gift of his wife and her relatives. If the man has already chosen his heir, the heir will be instrumental in seeing that the *magual* is presented to the man's relatives, who, after all, should be close relatives of the heir as well. If no heir has been chosen, it is particularly important that the women of the household, with the cooperation of their male relatives, expedite the presentation of the gift, since this symbolizes their willingness to maintain their side of the *a'kim* relationship. Unless they send *magual*, the relatives of the man are not likely to feel that they should send another man to act as a replacement for the dead person. So the *magual*, though formally given in return for one man, becomes a prerequisite for obtaining the next man. *Magual* with a value of several hundred rupees is occasionally given, but it need not be so valuable to discharge the obligation. In fact, people seldom hesitate to offer some *magual*, but they may be embarrassed that they cannot give a more valuable piece.

When a woman dies who had set up a separate household at her marriage, *magual* is given to the house of her birth just as it is for a man. But a girl who marries as an heiress and never moves out of her parental home requires no *magual* since she never shifts residence.

The recipients of *magual* frequently, though not invariably, kill a cow in honor of the dead person after returning to their own village. Another type of gift made at funerals is called *kokam*, and this obligates the recipients to kill a cow. *Kokam* is discussed in Chapter VIII.

If the rules of replacement, combined with the rules of heirship, are carried out consistently, people will always be left in the house to carry it on. Occasions hardly arise without a provision existing which will allow the household to continue. Together, these rules provide for long-term continuity and for long-term association of the two lineages which are linked together in a particular household. Whatever happens, each of the two lineages should go on supplying members of the proper sex so that the household can be perpetuated. With great consistency, the system is actually carried out as indicated by the formal rules. Houses do continue for many generations. Successive men and women from two respective lineages do follow each other as the occupants of a single household, and property and status do descend in the household from mother to daughter and from father-in-law to son-in-law.

The rules of inheritance have been mentioned in a number of places, but it seems well to state them a bit more explicitly and fully at this point. Boys, at the time of their marriage, are allowed to take personal clothing and few small possessions with them, and if they earn money while single, it is generally considered theirs to take with them as well. Girls who marry as non-heiresses can also take a few personal possessions, but are less likely to have substantial savings of their own. However, girls are more likely to live near their families, and gain the labor of their parents and other relatives in the building of their first house. They may also receive a few casual donations of basketry and tools with which they can set up housekeeping; but these do not amount to much, and non-heir couples begin married life in modest circumstances.

Property is never divided at death. The only formal transfers of goods are *magual* and *kokam*, which are of a ceremonial nature or a payment for a service but in no way a division of property among survivors. The heir and heiress simply continue to use the family possessions. The property may be of considerable value, although the method of land tenure is such that no permanent source of income and no important capital goods are inherited privately, and non-heirs have as much access to village land as heirs. Heirs retain the house (except that the house of a woman who dies in pregnancy is abandoned), any associated outbuildings, wood sheds, pig sties, granaries and the grain stored in them, and any animals belonging to the household. Standing crops may represent considerable value, and all tools, articles of clothing, basketry, and other small movable property are also automatically retained by the chosen daughter and her husband. Finally, heirlooms, which may be of great value, but may also be almost nonexistent, are inherited by them.

Besides objects and wealth, social status is also inherited by the heir and heiress. When an older member of a household dies, the Garos view his heir as stepping into the social position of the dead person—a woman into the position of her mother and a man into the position of his 'uncle' and father-in-law. The clearest symbolic expression of this is the assumption by the heir of kinship terms formerly appropriate to his father-in-law. After the old man's death, other sons-in-law call the heir by the term which is more generally used for "father-in-law," and are in turn called "son-in-law" by the heir. It has been pointed out that Garos also speak as if the son-in-law inherited his mother-in-law when her husband dies, since after this she is regarded as a 'wife' of the younger man. Moreover, the wife's siblings call him by a term that otherwise means father's younger brother. This terminology is analyzed more fully in Appendix C. Beyond this somewhat superficial terminological matter, the occupants of the family house are considered to be the living incumbents in the role of man and woman of that particular house. Households continue, though their members come and go. The most striking example of this is the title of *nokma* or 'headman' which, as will be explained in Chapter IX, adheres to the senior household of the village. The man who happens to be married to the heiress of that household is considered to be the 'headman' of the village.

## THE A'KIM BOND

The *a'kim* bond is usually an asymmetrical relationship, women coming from one lineage, men from another. Occasionally men from two households marry each other's sisters and trade residences, but the Garos recognize this as a special relationship to which they give the name *paping-deping*, "father and son to each other." Properly speaking the term applies only if both men marry as heirs, in which case each inherits the position of the other's father, and so in a sense they become symbolic fathers to each other, but it is loosely applied even if the men are not heirs. Such exchanges are not usually arranged together. Rather, one man marries first, and the kinship ties which he establishes help to facilitate the arrangement of a subsequent marriage between his wife's younger brother and his own sister. The first man married helps to make the arrangements for the second to return to the house from which the first man had come. After possibly eight years of marriage, Gajang, the *nokma* of Rengsanggri, sent his wife's younger brother, Polsing, back to Songmagri to become the heir of his (Gajang's) father. In this case, I was told, Gajang's father was unable to find a close 'nephew' from his own village to become his heir, and took Polsing as the most desirable person in the absence of a closer 'nephew'. Even so, Polsing was a member of a closely related lineage, being a Chambigong of Rengsanggri, while his father-in-law was a Chambigong of Songmagri.

Once the brother exchange is begun, it may be perpetuated for two or three generations, as each man tries to bring an heir from his own household. If he must accept an heir from a closely related household, of course, it will be a case of classificatory brother exchange instead. In the case of genuine *paping-deping*, the children of the marriages will, of course, be simultaneously both matrilateral and patrilateral cross-cousins. As my analysis of cross-cousins marriage in Chapter III and in Appendix B shows, any man and woman of opposite moieties can be considered as classificatory cross-cousins of both kinds, and the children of *paping-deping* marriages are simply the most closely related in both directions of the many possibilities.

Although the two marriages of *paping-deping* are not simultaneously arranged, their symmetry is clearly recognized. This is
most strikingly illustrated by the modification of the *magual*
gift at the death of the men in the relationship. *Magual* is
ordinarily given to the man's original home as a sort of delayed
payment. It is usually a strict rule that it can never be returned
to its house of origin. In the case of *paping-deping*, however, the
gift given at the death of the first man to die *can* be returned
when the second man dies. This is in such sharp contrast with
the usual practice that the gift in this case is ordinarily not even
referred to as *magual*. There is, indeed, some feeling that the
two men are given in exchange for each other, and that the
*magual* payment is thus unnecessary. No particular advantage
arises from having a *paping-deping* partner, and usually no
strong effort is made to arrange these relationships. Certainly
the possibility of receiving back the death gift is not the kind of
inducement that would encourage it. Most people, in fact, seem
to feel that it is a mildly awkward arrangement. It places people
in a rather ambiguous relationship, for how can a man be
father and son to the same person? If quarrels should arise in
the family, some people might blame it on the *paping-deping*
arrangement; but if people manage to live amicably, then no
one worries about it. No question arises about its propriety.
Among the seventy married men in Rengsanggri, no true
*paping-deping* pair existed. Manchok and Kandok had married
each other's sisters, but Manchok was not an heir. Two Rengsanggri men, however, were in true *paping-deping* relation with
men in other villages, and a number of other pairs turned up in
genealogies of former generations or of other villages. Marriage
of two men to each other's classificatory 'sisters' was, as might
be expected, a good deal more common.[2]

I have stressed the permanence of the *a'kim* bond. It is inconceivable, however, that a society could be ordered so perfectly that such a relationship would be indestructible, and
certainly ways exist in Garo society by which the bond can be

broken. None of these are felt to be desirable, and none can happen automatically or simply through lapse of observance, however; and whenever the *a'kim* bond is broken, some formal recognition of the break is required. The ways in which the break can come about will be considered along with divorce, in Chapter X. Suffice it to say here that *a'kim* is not casually broken, but that if everybody involved dies in rapid succession there is no need to reconstitute a household, and it can be allowed to end. Since the primary purpose both of heirship and of replacement is to provide the mutual assistance that people require, the obligations can be readily allowed to lapse if both husband and wife die at nearly the same time.

Marriage and *a'kim* are supposed to last. People display a quiet satisfaction in a long, unbroken succession of marriages between the same two lineages. Furthermore, lineages acquire reputations for the promptness with which they provide replacements. The more readily a lineage fulfills its own obligations, the more eager others will be to contract marriages with it, and so there is considerable motivation to keep the bonds intact. The continuity provided by the systems of heirship and replacement gives a permanence to the structure of the society around which can be built the more inclusive groupings of the lineage and village.

The *a'kim* relationship is in some ways remarkably similar to the relationship of lineages among the Kachin of Burma, which has been analyzed by E. R. Leach.[3] The Kachin have patrilineal lineages which are associated with one another in long-term relationships in which women from one particular lineage marry men from another particular lineage. Like Garo *a'kim*, this relationship implies classificatory matrilateral cross-cousin marriage, though in this patrilineal society men marry a woman from their mother's lineage (classificatory MoBrDa) rather than a woman marrying a man from her father's lineage (classificatory FaSiSo), as among the Garos.

Among the Kachin the lineages are ranked with respect to

each other. Men consistently take women from higher lineages, or to put it another way, women marry down and men marry up. The relationship between the two intermarrying lineages is asymmetrical both in rank and in method of intermarriage (since a man never takes his wife from a lineage into which his sister may marry), and Leach shows that the lineage relation has other asymmetrical aspects as well. He demonstrates, in fact, that matrilateral cross-cousin marriage can appropriately form one feature of a widely ramifying system of ranked lineages in which rights to women are only one of a large number of associated rights that are distributed and exchanged unequally among the lineages. I can imagine a historical process in which lineages which are ranked, for whatever reasons, gradually acquire the habit of specifying repetitive marriages between them. Once people get used to thinking of women "marrying up" or "marrying down," the logic of the situation would readily lead to explicit recognition of marriage to the mother's brother's daughter as simply the closest possible marriage within the general rule.[4]

While ranked lineages fit well with matrilateral cross-cousin marriage, it is clearly possible for this marriage to take place with considerable frequency but without any associated ranking of lineages. The Garos have rules which result in about half of the first marriages being between classificatory matrilateral cross-cousins, though their lineages are not ranked. It is easy to specify the point at which the system described by Leach breaks down for the Garos. Only one of a group of sisters need undertake the particular type of marriage which is governed by lineage principles, and no rule requires *all* the women of a single lineage to marry into one or a restricted number of other lineages. The empirical situation among the Garos is not unlike that found among a society such as the Hopi, where the women of any one lineage contract marriages with men from many others.[5] The Garos have a large number of lineages which in rank and other respects are equal to one another. The bonds of marriage tie these lineages together in all directions, except that they all fall into one or the other of two large exogamous groups, so that any single lineage can contract marriages with only one half of the others. Lineage ties are extremely important, and for any one particular household they are asymmetrical and long-lasting in a way reminiscent of the Kachin system; but what holds for a single household does not hold as a general picture for the relationship of whole corporate lineages of a group of neighboring villages or of the whole society.

# ❧VII❧

# *Extended Kinship*

## THE FAMILIES OF SISTERS

WHEN A NON-HEIRESS daughter marries and sets up an independent household, the Garos say that the new house "comes out" of the parental home. The parental home remains intact and only loses one of its members. Though "coming out" disrupts and changes the residential and economic bonds that had formerly joined the members of the family, it does not, of course, sever their ties completely. Rather, the households of two sisters are likely to cooperate more closely with each other than with any other households. Most often a sister who "comes out" sets up her new home in the same village where her mother and her mother's heiress live. If space is available, she may build her house in the same part of the village, even right beside her mother's house. In spite of periodic rebuilding of houses, the spatial arrangement of families is rather stable, since they most often rebuild in their old location, tearing down the old house before erecting the new. Since even non-heiress daughters frequently build near to their mother's homes, the villagers tend to be spatially arranged according to kinship, so that close relatives often live near to each other. This cannot be a firm rule, for if one section of the village becomes too crowded to build new houses conveniently, even real sisters may live at opposite ends of the village. Certain circumstances can even cause a woman to move to an entirely different village.

So long as the families of two sisters remain together in the same village, they ordinarily remain closely associated, and the members help each other on many occasions. Adult sisters are less circumspect with each other than brothers, and cooperate more often. They move freely into each other's households, exchange small favors, and lend household articles to one another. Of two equally close neighbors, for instance, people are most likely to choose a sister's house at which to light a bundle of sticks in order to save the effort of kindling a fire. Children are said to feel less shy in entering their mother's sister's house than that of their mother's brother or of less closely related people. The husbands of sisters are expected to cooperate closely and to treat each other with respect and courtesy, but also with friendliness and without any strong reserve. In this society where husbands are often related to the people of the village primarily through their wives, the husbands of two sisters are likely to be as closely associated as any two male neighbors can be. Usually the husbands of sisters are not closely related except through their wives—that is, they are unlikely to be close lineage relatives of each other. Fewer complicating problems of authority intrude between them than between brothers, and one of the few self-reciprocal kinship terms used by Garos is used between them so long as neither has inherited the position of their father-in-law. The activities in which the husbands of sisters must cooperate are not likely to throw them into conflict. There are no built-in factors likely to make theirs a difficult relationship. As a result they are generally able to maintain a friendly informality, and seldom have difficulty in helping each other out when help is needed. They often join in the same work activities and find it possible to conform closely to the ideal behavior.

The children of sisters call each other by the same kinship terms as they use for real siblings, and regard each other as only slightly less closely related. They run freely into each other's houses when they are small, and since sisters are likely to cooperate quite consistently in taking care of each other's children, a mother's sister, whether younger or older, is regarded quite explicitly as "like a mother." Children may be close and intimate with her without hesitation or any shyness. Similarly the mother's sister's husband is considered as "like a father." Separate residence, however, ensures that the distinction between the people living in the same house and those in the house of the mother's sister is never lost. Children of sisters lack, for instance, some of the circumspection of real siblings. Sons of sisters are not as careful as real brothers to keep apart when they sleep in the bachelors' house. A boy might have a little less hesitation in joking with a parallel cousin than with his own sister. Since the terms for siblings are used for a wide group of relatives, and in their most extended sense for everybody in one's own moiety who is near one's own age, the distinction between siblings and first parallel cousins is only the first step in a gradual weakening of the "sibling" tie which becomes ever feebler the more distantly the two people are related. People of the same sib name who are of about the same age, refer to each other by the terms used for siblings; but unless they can trace their relationship to each other, there is little specific coloring of kinship to their personal relations.

The families of two sisters are not completely equivalent to one another. If one of the sisters and her husband are heirs of the sisters' parents, and especially if the parents have died, there are a few formal differences. Inheritance may give the heirs a head start in maintaining or accumulating wealth and thereby in maintaining a respected position in the village. The heir of a rich man may lose his wealth, and even a non-heir may be able to attain wealth by hard work and good luck, so that the advantage of heirship is far from absolute; but the non-heir family is always spoken of as having "come out" of the house of the sister who was heir. However, the few formal ways in which the difference is shown, in the inheritance of kinship terms by the heir and heiress, and in the order of rice-beer drinking, only slightly upset the near equivalence of the families of sisters.

## BROTHERS AND SISTERS AND THEIR FAMILIES

Although men always leave their parents' house at marriage, not all of them move to a different village. In fact, a few men must remain in the village of their mother and of their lineage, and a few of these men even bring their wives from another village and with them set up new households in their own village. This is because men hold the positions of authority and make most of the important decisions. Since the lineage is an organization within which authority is exercised, it would be difficult or impossible to have a residence group built around the lineage without having some responsible male members of that lineage actually in residence. The Garos put it this way: "No woman wants to live in a village unless at least one of her 'brothers' or 'uncles' is present in that village." All or even a majority of the men cannot be required to live in the village of their lineage, since this would require their sisters to move elsewhere and defeat the purpose of keeping some men at home; but it must somehow be arranged that a certain proportion of them stays. As will be seen later, this only rarely requires that a woman actually shift from the village she was raised in to the village of her husband. It does make it impossible to regard the Garo village as exclusively built around a co-resident group of either men or women of a lineage. It must include both.

The particular circumstances which persuade men to move their wives to their own villages are varied. In most of the instances I investigated, the man first lived for a time in his wife's village, and only later returned, bringing his wife to his own village. Some of the men said rather vaguely that they were not happy in their wife's village but wanted to be near their own relatives. Tanggeng said that he wanted to grow cotton as he had been accustomed to do as a bachelor, but that it was not customary to grow cotton in his wife's village. Whatever the motives, the move is not to be taken lightly, for it requires the agreement of the wife and approval and permission of her relatives, specifically of her male lineage mates. Moreover, an underlying motive for the move is almost always the feeling that a man of that lineage is needed to keep an eye on the affairs of his 'sisters.' If the woman is willing, and particularly if she has reasonably close male relatives who have already moved to her husband's village to marry his lineage 'sisters,' the woman's lineage mates will probably recognize the needs of the husband's relatives and agree to the move. Some men certainly feel, however, that they would not like to take a wife away from her own relatives. One man told me, "She might get sick and my relatives wouldn't take such good care of her as her own relatives would." Furthermore, some men may actually prefer to escape from their own village, where one must deal with close relatives with whom relations can be strained. In another village one has less authority and less responsibility, and so life in some ways is simpler.

Even if a man does bring his wife to his own parents' village, in subsistence matters he is always completely separate from his parents' household. Unless he is divorced, he will not join that household again. Gifts are seldom exchanged between an out-married son and his family, and except for the mutual freedom of hospitality and occasional contributions or shares in compensations following legal disputes, the economic relationship of a son and his parents ends with his marriage. Emotional and legal ties remain throughout the man's life, and these are eventually symbolized by the ceremonial gifts given by his heirs to the mother's household when he dies. Men generally look back on the mother's house with fondness, and like to take their children back to see the grandparents on occasional informal visits. Sons and brothers are always welcomed back and freely entertained. Since most men marry within six or eight miles of their homes, such visits are not rare; and these are times of amicable conversation and a source of pleasure to everyone, though men are said to miss their original village less as the years go by and as they become more firmly settled with their wives.

Important legal responsibilities continue to tie a brother to the households of his mother and sisters. A woman and her husband speak of her male lineage mates as their *chratang*, and these *chratang* have definite responsibilities toward their 'mothers,' their 'sisters', and their 'sisters' children' and their families. Each household has several *chratang* who may take responsibility toward it, but they are recognized as having varying degrees of responsibility according to the intimacy of their kinship ties to the household, the proximity of their residence, their age, and such personal characteristics as wealth and prestige in the community. Ordinarily a man interferes very little in the daily life of his 'sisters' ' families, and everyone recognizes the appropriateness of a 'sister' and her husband's trying to solve their problems by themselves. Nevertheless, a woman's *chratang*, as a male representative of the lineage to which she and her children belong, acts as a sort of umpire for his 'sister's' family. If for any reason there is real quarreling within that family, whether the 'sister' and her husband are not getting on or the children are grossly disobedient, then the *chratang* will be called in to attempt to quiet things down or arbitrate the argument in some way. Either a woman or her husband may complain to the *chratang* if it is believed that the other is not properly fulfilling his or her duties. If a complaint is made, the *chratang* is expected to give impartial help in straightening out problems, but he does not interfere unless called upon to do so. In the extreme case where it is determined that his 'sister' has committed adultery, he will be expected to help punish her, though he will also have to contribute to any fine which she has to pay. He has responsibility for the acts of his 'sister' and has the corresponding right to try to dissuade her from doing wrong. In less serious cases, he may occasionally lecture his 'sister,' telling her to be a good wife and to take proper care of her husband. On the other hand, if the 'sister' feels that her husband is not behaving properly toward her, she may also complain to her *chratang*, and he will be expected to defend her, to do what he can to urge the husband to mend his ways, and ultimately to take his 'sister's' side in any legal dispute with him. In any domestic difficulty, then, the wife's *chratang* become a source of pressure toward settlement and peace.

Similarly, if the children get out of hand and the parents feel that they cannot cope with them, they may call in the *chratang* to administer punishment in the form of moral lectures or even, if the matter is serious enough, in the form of a beating. This authority of the 'uncle' is more often held out as a potential threat than actually exercised. If the family gets along without serious quarrels between husband and wife and without gross indiscipline on the part of the children, the 'uncle' may never be called in; but both the women and their husbands like to have at least one of the wife's *chratang* resident in the same village, since they feel that his proximity is an insurance against conflict within their own family.

It is easy to speak of the 'mother's brother' as if he were a specific person like the father, or as if the brother-sister relationship were a uniquely individual one like that of husband and wife. Actually a boy or girl may have several 'uncles,' a woman several 'brothers,' and her husband several *chratang*; and if classificatory relatives are included, this is certain to be the case. This dilutes the personal aspects of the relationship. All 'brothers' share the legal responsibility towards all of their 'sisters,' and while the relationship is more intense with true sisters, the responsibilities of a man toward classificatory 'sisters' and 'nieces' are of the same sort. A man has responsibilities toward his wife on the one hand and toward his 'sisters,' the women of his lineage, on the other. He lives and works and spends the largest part of his time with his wife in the household they share. They generally develop an intimate, uniquely personal bond which transcends others in intensity. The responsibilities toward a 'sister' and her family are much more formal and less continuous, though still important. A man fulfills his duty toward his 'sister' but he spends his life with his wife.

When a couple live in the husband's village, they inevitably have more to do with the husband's 'sisters' and their families than if they stay in the wife's village; but this does not alter the pattern of whatever contact they have. The husband and brother of a woman have a relation not unlike that of the husbands of two sisters. There is less constraint between them than between real brothers, but like all close male relatives, they tend to avoid extreme intimacy. Even though the wife's brother has a potential authority over his sister and her children, a husband is by no means under his control. Brothers-in-law should help each other and maintain friendly relations. It is not a point of great conflict.

The wife of a man and his sister have few barriers between them which might prevent companionship and cooperation, although residence does not usually bring them together. Apparently the fact that authority largely adheres to the men is enough to make the relationship of women to each other less difficult than that of men. Without the intervention of complicating authority, sisters-in-law have little cause for restraint; but since they lack the common upbringing that unites sisters, they are less likely to be intimate.

Children look upon the households of their father's 'sisters' quite differently from those of their mother's 'sisters.' Father's sister is terminologically equated with mother's brother's wife, and the same term (*mani*) may even be used for one's mother-in-law. All are women of the opposite moiety, and a man must behave much more circumspectly with them than with women of their age who belong to his own moiety. The husbands of these *mani* are all *mama*, classificatory 'mother's brother' (or 'father's sister's husband'), and they must also be dealt with cautiously. From a child's point of view each household is either composed of people in the same moiety as his own parents, or else the moiety positions of the husband and wife are reversed. He learns at an early age to recognize the distinction.

Male cross-cousins refer to each other by the same terms as

are used for brothers-in-law (*boning*, man of the opposite moiety
of one's own generation), but in the absence of the complications of authority that may inhibit the relationship of brothers-
in-law, male cross-cousins may be the most intimate of friends,
and this relationship may persist into adulthood as long as
neither marries the other's sister. They may joke, tease, and
while young and if so inclined, roughhouse with each other.
Female cross-cousins call each other by the same term as
sisters-in-law (*sari*) and may also be intimate with one another.
Though intimacy may develop between cross-cousins of the
same sex, it cannot be called a relationship of licensed freedom.
It simply lacks any restraining factors, and the same intimate
relationship may develop between any unrelated people who
find each other compatible.

The relationship of close cross-cousins of the opposite sex is
entirely different. It is recognized that these are uniquely suitable marriage partners, but rather than implying a particular
intimacy, this makes the cousins reluctant to associate beyond
the absolutely necessary minimum. To visit unnecessarily with
a cross-cousin of the opposite sex would be to invite the teasing
of everyone else in the village. Cross-cousins are such eligible
partners that people will laugh if they engage in anything
remotely resembling a flirtation. This is particularly true of a
boy and the daughter of his mother's brother, since everyone
thinks that he might be taken to be his uncle's heir, and it would
be most immodest to appear eager for this job. Boys are wary
enough of their uncles to keep away from their daughters, and
they fear the universal ridicule that would engulf them if they
did not.

The restrictions which make boys hesitate to associate with
their female cross-cousins are in striking contrast to the restrictions which prevent intimacy between a boy and his sister. No
one raises an eyebrow at the companionship of a brother and
sister. They may be alone together and sit and chat informally,
and a brother is considered a proper escort for an adult but

unmarried sister. Nobody thinks of incest because a brother and sister pass the time of day together. Garos do not joke broadly with their sisters and certainly do not have close physical contact with them; to do so would make them feel profoundly uncomfortable. Somehow Garo men learn to feel restrained in their relations with their sisters without any need for formal rules or external sanctions. With cross-cousins the situation is reversed. One has little hesitation on one's own part about joking, teasing, or even physical contact with cross-cousins, but one dreads the ridicule of everyone else. If others are present, a cross-cousin is a suitable person to dance with at village ceremonies, but one would hate to be caught alone with her. Anyone who defied the ridicule and went ahead with a flirtation would warrant nothing more drastic than still more laughter, but laughter is enough to make even the most determined boy desist.

With less closely related girls the feelings fall between these two extremes of sisters and first cross-cousins. Parallel cousins are treated like sisters, except that the restrictions are a bit less strong. Distant classificatory cross-cousins can be approached without everybody's immediate laughter. This means that it is the remotely related or unrelated girls with whom one can most easily strike up a flirtation. Once people are married, the fear of being laughed at for association with a cross-cousin disappears, as does a man's hesitation at becoming involved with the girl's father, his maternal uncle. Being safely married, he may associate with other cross-cousins without subjecting himself to anyone's ridicule.

### AUTHORITY AND CROSS-COUSIN MARRIAGE

Garos place a considerable emphasis on avuncular authority, and there is also a high proportion of marriages to the classificatory mother's brother's daughter. This is a combination of traits which has been believed unlikely, because it has been felt that a boy would not normally care to marry the daughter of that figure of authority, the mother's brother.[1] Such an assumption is indeed in harmony with the usual inclination of Garo boys, but it is irrelevant to the choice of spouse since it is the girl's father and not the nephew who initiates the marriage negotiations. The authority that the nephew dislikes is precisely what makes the relationship attractive to his uncle. While the nephew may fear being under the jurisdiction of his uncle, the latter may be delighted to have a son-in-law whom he can control by virtue of their lineage relationship.

A man once recited for me in somewhat stylized fashion the words a man might use to persuade his daughter not to marry the wrong man: "What pain I have. Someone else's 'nephew' (*gritang*) will not support me, only my own 'nephew' will support me. Someone else's nephew would not take care of us when sick. My own 'nephew' alone would care for us even when in pain. He would provide clothing as another would not. He will not lose the family property. Another would not stay with us, another would not support us even though he inherited our property." There could hardly be a more explicit statement of a man's reasons for wanting a lineage mate to become his son-in-law.

Undoubtedly the factors determining the choice of marriage partners are quite different in contractual marriages, where most arrangements are made by members of the older generation, from those in marriages in which the young people take direct initiative. Interestingly, both kinds occur among the Garos. Girls who are not chosen as heiresses have relatively few restrictions on their choice of a husband, so long as they observe the rules of exogamy. For these girls, and for the boys chosen by them, the question of whether they are close-cross-cousins is largely irrelevant. But heiresses have arrangements made for them, and the forces determining the choice of their spouses are to be found in the interests and desires of the older generation.

## BROTHERS AND THEIR FAMILIES

Two brothers are not particularly likely to marry into the same village, but even if they do, unless they happen to marry closely related girls, they will be associated with different groups of affinal relatives. Correspondingly, brothers and their families have much less to do with each other than sisters and their families. Brothers cooperate in a formal way when disputes must be settled, but they rarely help each other in the daily subsistence tasks. A good deal of the circumspection with which young brothers treat each other holds over into adulthood. The relationship is always colored by a consciousness of authority and the possibility of punishment of one by the other. A man's close companions are more likely to be his brothers-in-law or the husbands of his wife's sisters than his own brothers. The wives and children of brothers are not likely to be intimate, or if they are, they may reckon their kinship by other routes than this one. The children are parallel cousins and they call each other by the sibling terms, but if their mothers are not closely related, the children are hardly reckoned as close relatives either, and they rarely take each other into consideration in family affairs. Rengsanggri men can associate freely with a younger brother's wife without hesitation or criticism from others, but an older brother's wife tends to be thought of as like the wife of the maternal uncle, and men tend to be quite shy with them.

## COOPERATIVE ACTIVITIES

A single household cannot always act independently, but must often cooperate with others. Kinship helps to determine participation in many of the cooperative activities; thus the kinship relations of those who cooperate and the occasions on which they work together must be described. It is convenient to distinguish two types of extended kinship groups. On the one hand, there are matrilineal descent groups, the lineages, sibs, and moieties. Children are automatically assigned to the matrilineal descent groups of their mother, and since one must always marry some-one from a different descent group, all the members of a descent group can never live together. Other kinship groups are resi-dential, and include some of the members of a matrilineal descent group together with their spouses and children. The core of these residential groups is always a matrilineal descent group, but those which are larger than the household always include a few of the men of the matrilineal descent group as well as most of the women, together with their spouses. Before describing these residential kin groups, it is necessary to specify the matrilineal descent groups more precisely.[2]

Since Garos reckon descent in the matriline, individuals measure the degree of their relationship to one another by the distance of their collateral matrilineages. Real siblings are the closest of lineage relatives. Children of sisters are considered slightly less close, while children of the daughters of sisters are still more distant. Counting out this way, a point is soon reached beyond which literal kinship can no longer be traced. All those matrilineal kinsmen who can trace their real kinship ties with one another can be said to form a "minimal lineage," but since the old people can generally remember more distant kinship ties than can the young, the minimal lineage is broader for the elderly and its boundaries can never be precise. While the group within which real kinship can be traced is dimly recog-nized by the Garos and is important for some purposes, the reckoning of matrilineal kinship does not stop at this point. A single village may include a half dozen minimal lineages, and in a village such as Rengsanggri, these are all felt to be related to each other in a more inclusive matrilineal descent group that can be called the "village lineage." In these villages one or the other member of each married couple belongs to the village lineage, though no one is likely to be able to give all the genea-logical ties connecting them. Even beyond the village, some village lineages are considered more closely related to each other than to those in other villages, and eventually many groups of village lineages pyramid together into named sibs and moieties.

In certain affairs, formal membership in a descent group is a prerequisite. The least ambiguous of these is the search for heirs and for replacements, which has been discussed in earlier chapters. When a man wishes to provide himself with an heir and wants a 'nephew' to marry his daughter, he starts his search within approximately the range of kinsmen that I have called his minimal lineage. If, because of the absence of boys, unreasonable age differences, or mutual dislike, a man fails to find a suitable 'nephew' within the minimal lineage, he will look among a wider descent group, first among closely related minimal lineages, then throughout the whole village, and then in villages considered to be closely related. A man simply looks as far as necessary. When the younger man is related within the bounds of approximately the minimal lineage, the older man will call him his 'real nephew,' (*gritang*). If they are more distantly related—if they come from the same village, for instance, but not from the same minimal lineage—the uncle still calls him 'nephew' but on questioning may admit that he is a "rather distant 'nephew'". Although the lineages have no precise boundaries, common lineage membership is absolutely necessary in an heir and, other things being equal, a closer 'nephew' is more desirable than a distant one. The authority wielded within the lineage appears most clearly when disputes become serious enough to come under formal arbitration. These disputes are seen as conflicts between two opposing sides, with the relatives of each of the principals forming their respective parties. The procedure for dealing with legal disputes will be considered in more detail in Chapter X.

The authority within a lineage is exercised according to age, the older member always being allowed to direct and punish the younger members. The age differences are otherwise symbolized

in only one way—the order in which rice beer is served.
When beer is first passed out at a gathering, the people should
be served in order of formal seniority. A maternal uncle should
be served before his nephew, and an older brother before a
younger one. Even an older sister may precede a younger
brother, though generally men and women do not drink together. Of husbands married to two sisters, the man married to
the older should drink first. This arrangement can be upset,
however, if the younger girl's husband is the heir of their
father-in-law, since once a man dies, the heir is served in the
order formerly appropriate to his father-in-law. Men may be
related to each other in more than one way, of course, and this
sometimes leads to situations where one man is alternately
senior or junior to another, depending upon which kinship
connection is followed. Absolute age is likely to be the final
determinant in such a case, but the matter need not lead to
quarrels. Nobody actually memorizes a precise order of drinking and still less jockeys for position. Those serving the beer
offer it first to those present who seem to be senior. It is good
form for each man as he is served to glance around and make
sure he is not drinking before someone who is his senior. It is
also polite to suggest that such a person be served first and send
the server to him. This frequently leads to polite little arguments, in which men say in effect "Please, after you" until one,
generally the one to whom the drink was first offered, admits to
his seniority and drinks. In spite of this formal deference, older
people do not monopolize positions of power, and an old person
cannot exercise authority outside his lineage simply because of
his age. One defers to one's lineage seniors, but not to old
people in general.

    In many activities the residential kin groups are more in
evidence than those defined strictly by membership in the
matrilineal line. The residential kin groups include a core of
matrilineally related people together with their spouses. Their
residential contiguity inevitably brings them together for

many of life's mundane activities. The household is really the smallest of these groups. Like the larger ones it is composed of a unilineally related core, in this case all women, together with their spouses. The larger groups can be considered as being formed from a number of related households.

The system by which the households of non-heirs are considered to "come out" of the household of the heir results in a formal structure that unites the households of a village. An actual example should make this clearer than an abstract discussion. The chart found on page 180 gives a schematic representation of the genealogical relationship of the households of Rengsanggri to one another. The households are arranged in such a way that a house which has "come out" from another is shown as branching out above the ancestral household. Thus, #2 and #3 recently "came out" of #1, while #4 "came out" a generation earlier; #10 recently "came out" of #9, which in turn had "come out" of #7, which in its turn had "come out" of #1 even earlier. For the most part, the relationship of the houses to one another is unambiguous, and there is no difficulty in placing them in the proper order; but a few complications do arise. The greatest difficulty is the placing of sons and brothers of the main village lineage (*chratang*) who have remained in Rengsanggri after marriage. As will be explained in Chapter IX, their households can sometimes be considered as related simultaneously to two or occasionally even more kinship groups, according to the relationship of the several men of the household. These households have simply been assigned to the place where they seemed to be most intimately associated at the time I was in the village; but to indicate the lesser precision of the location of the households in which the man rather than his wife belongs to the main Rengsanggri lineage, they are joined to the rest of the diagram by dotted lines. The household of Jengnon, #33, is felt to be the second most senior in the village and is said to have "come out" of #1 many generations ago, even before these households

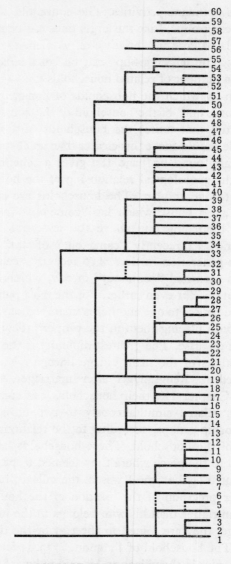

LINEAGE SEGMENTATION
Leading to the
HOUSEHOLDS OF RENGSANGGRI

moved to Rengsanggri. More recently a daughter from #1 was adopted by #33 as heiress, when the latter failed to have a daughter of its own. This adopted heiress is said to have been a sister of several other girls who moved out of #1 and who with their husbands founded the households now occupied by Bano (#13), Chondu (#19), and Singron (#30). These are all old households, but since the sister who became ancestress to #33 had moved into an already established and older household, it is still considered to be older than the others. The households emerging from #44 and all related to each other and thought in some way to have "come out" of #1, but nobody can remember the exact connections. Households #56-#60 cannot be precisely related to any other households, though all are considered somehow derived from #1. Most people can give the genealogies within the major blocks of households—#1-#12, #13-#18, #33-#43, etc.—but only a few of the older and more interested people can offer precise genealogical data as to how these are connected to one another. The numbers on this chart are the serial numbers assigned to the households of the village, and are the same as those used in the Appendix. A comparison with the village map which is on page 26 will show that there is a tendency, but no fixed rule, for houses which are closely related genealogically to be close to each other geographically as well.

It is evident from the chart that there are several stages of segmentation which divide the households into related groups. Households #1 to #12, for instance, form a group set off quite clearly from other households in the village. It includes all the households in the village that have "come out" of #1 in the last three generations, as well as four households of men of the lineage who live with their wives in Rengsanggri rather than in the wife's own village. Since exact genealogical relationship within this set of households is pretty generally known, it can be considered as the residential counterpart of the inevitably dispersed minimal lineage. As the Garos describe such groups of households, they have a somewhat more concrete existence than the minimal lineages. All of the households are seen as belonging together because they have all "come out" of the same household within the last few generations, and that household is the most senior. However, the only way this group is ever referred to by Garos is by calling it by the name of the present man of the oldest household—as "Chondu's relatives" or "Maljing's relatives."

Groups of this sort generally involve from six to twelve households and a depth of approximately five generations, three still living and two deceased. Garos feel that every group of this size should include at least one household in which the man is a member of the main lineage, so that he can look after the women of the other households. It will be noticed from the dotted lines on the segmentation diagram that each major block of households except #13-#18 contains one or more households of this sort. Even #13-#18 were not alone, however, since—as will be explained fully in Chapter IX—Anat was the son of #17, and though he had married into #6, he was able to look after his mother's group of households. Since its members help each other in many activities, a block of households such as this can be called the "cooperating group," but like the minimal lineage, it is only one point on a continuum of kinship groups. Segmentation goes on below this level so that some houses within the cooperating group are felt to be especially closely related to each other, while several cooperating groups in turn join together to form the village.

The importance of the relationship of households to one another within the village appears in the numerous cooperative work groups which include people from more than one household. Labor is exchanged between the households of the village in many ways. These are described in some detail in the next chapter, but it can be pointed out here that kinship is the most important single factor determining which households help each other. Residential proximity and friendship may bias this pattern, but it is kinsmen above all who come to each other's assistance in the fields, at house-building, and at the time of sickness.

Neither the minimal lineage nor the cooperating group is more than vaguely recognized by the Garos themselves. They rarely verbalize their existence and have no terms by which to label them clearly, but when they are questioned closely, it is evident that they do in fact recognize their presence and if started off in the right direction, can even list the houses in their village and assign them to specific cooperating groups. Ordinarily they have no reason to do such a thing.

In no case do all the members of a precisely defined group of relatives have to assemble for any purpose. For each activity there are better- and worse-qualified people who may take part. The better one is qualified, the more likely one is to participate in a given activity, but there is never complete assurance that any particular person will help on a given occasion, and there are always individuals around the borders of the relevant group who may or may not take part, depending upon more or less chance factors. According to the importance or seriousness of the activity, the size of the relevant group will expand or contract. This means that it is impossible to assign everybody in a village or group of villages to one specific "cooperating group" or minimal lineage with complete assurance and say that he will act as a member of this group on all occasions. The Garos do not recognize any such rigid boundaries. The size and range of a group is defined temporarily for each particular activity as it arises.

# ❧VIII❧

# Transactions
# Between Households

THE PEOPLE OF RENGSANGGRI are close enough to nature
to understand, as few men in the industrialized West can, the
processes by which wealth is extracted from the soil and converted into the goods they want. In the first instance a man may
use those things which he himself produces. Each man has the
main responsibility for his own patch of land, and enjoys the
results of his own work upon it. Each man can gather wild crops
from fallow land and use them. Each can fish and use his catch
to feed his family. But there is more to the organization of labor
than this, for a Garo does not always use the products of his
own industry. Labor and goods are exchanged in so many ways
that everyone spends a significant portion of his time growing
crops, erecting buildings, and performing sacrifices that are
destined to benefit someone else.

Many of the relationships between households can be readily
defined as exchanges or "transactions" of goods and services. It
is possible to think of these as "economic" transactions, for they
include those subsistence and material goods which have loosely
been called "economic" by anthropologists. However, they also
include services at rituals or in connection with the treatment of
disease, and even such things as prestige and power, which are
remote from those situations which have been traditionally
labeled as "economic." The man who can accumulate wealth

and use it to entertain generously can gain prestige and power. The result of many of these transactions, then, is not so much differential consumption of goods as differential prestige, with high status going to the man who can skillfully manage his resources and manipulate the traditional techniques of exchange. None of these transactions involve the use of money. This situation contrasts sharply with that of the market, where money is always used. The rare occasions when money is used within the village are direct reflections of the market, and will be considered in Chapter XI.

This chapter will describe the non-monetary transactions of the village in some detail. Rather than categorize them according to any such traditional but ill-defined concepts as economic and non-economic, it is more useful to consider them according to their general significance for Garo social organization. In some cases the goods or services given and received by the two parties to the transaction are of the same kind and of approximately equivalent amount, as in simple labor exchange, while in others the items are quite different, as in prestige acquired for giving a feast. These can be called, respectively, symmetrical and asymmetrical transactions. The social implications of the two types are very different. Symmetrical transactions cannot lead to any fundamental redistribution of the goods in the society, but are entered into for one of two different motives: first, simply for the sake of companionship, so that two or more people can work or celebrate together rather than by themselves; second, so that the labor of many people can be concentrated in one place at one time. Certain technological operations, such as house-building and most ceremonials, require more labor than one man or one household could possibly supply, whereas by exchanging labor with one's neighbors it is possible to draw on the resources of many other households. A symmetrical transaction made for companionship is soon completed and can be called "short-term," but if made to concentrate labor, it may not be completed for many months or years,

and can be called "long-term." Asymmetrical transactions
are not completed with the same goods, and thus lead to
a real redistribution of the goods produced by the community, with the result that some families become rich, others
poor.

Underlying any system of exchange is a system of property
rights, and at least a degree of mutual respect for the property
rights of each other. This does not imply that there are no disagreements over property, or that generally accepted rights are
never infringed upon; but it does mean that members of the
society can predict, within limits, that other members will act
in accordance with the property rules. Garo families each have
rights to particular patches of land for cultivation which are not
to be molested by others. The man who plants a fruit tree is
recognized to have first rights to its fruit, which he alone may
pick to sell, though others may pick it to eat themselves. All are
free to collect wild jungle crops from land during its fallow
period. Houses belong to individual families, but the courtyards and paths between them are for public use. The system
of exchanges to be described here presupposes mutual understanding of these property rights.


### SHORT-TERM SYMMETRICAL TRANSACTIONS

*Women's Chores.* Village women often work together without
exchanging anything more than each other's companionship.
One may bring her paddy for pounding and winnowing to the
front of her neighbor's house. She may use her neighbor's
mortar, but except for their steady conversation, the women
work independently. Even more often, at the cotton ginning
season, two or more women sit together, each with her own gin
and supply of cotton, relieving the tedium by chatting with
friends. These jobs can also be done alone by the woman at her
own house.

*Fishing Groups.* The usual arrangement of most fishing

parties is only slightly more formalized than that of women's chores. A pair of men often fish together, each using his own net which he throws and hauls in by himself; less frequently, they fish with hook and line. The men work near to each other, but neither requires the other's labor. Nevertheless, the custom is for each to take half of their combined catch. Trap fishing, on the other hand, is an entirely individual matter, and each man claims the fish caught in his own trap. Other methods of fishing, such as poisoning, require cooperative labor for technological reasons, not simply for companionship; here, appropriately, the fish are divided equally when the members of the party come from different households.

*Butchering.* The manner in which cattle are butchered does not precisely constitute an exchange between households, but it does frequently require cooperation between them. One household cannot eat an entire cow before the meat spoils, so beef is almost always cooked as part of a feast to which many are invited. At festivals when each household is expected to serve some beef, several households generally cooperate to purchase a cow from the market. Each contributes a number of rupees, though not everyone need contribute the same number. The cow is then butchered by several men, sometimes including even non-contributers who help out freely. The flesh of the animal is weighed out into one-seer portions, which are distributed according to the contribution of each family. Bones, blood, tripe, intestines, liver, and lungs are each divided into as many portions as the original price in rupees; then each contributor takes away the number of portions to which his share in the total investment entitles him. The cow is originally purchased from the market with cash and with all the haggling of any market transaction, but the division of meat is carried on with absolutely no haggling at all. One or two men may weigh out all the flesh, another divide the lungs and liver, and still another apportion the bones, but it would be unthinkable to question another's honesty. Butchering and the division of meat are carried on in an atmosphere of complete mutual trust, very different from that of the market.

Fishing, companionable work of women in the village, and even butchering are of little importance compared to the types of labor exchange that take place in the fields and on ceremonial occasions.

*Kamka'grima* (*kamka'a* 'work,' -*grim*- 'together, in common'). At certain peak agricultural periods, particularly at rice planting or rice harvest, two or three households whose members are close friends, or more often relatives, sometimes agree to pool their labor. The members of the households all work together for one day on the plot of a single household. The second day they work on another plot and then continue in rotation until the job is completed everywhere. The plots differ in size and the numbers in the households vary, and thus the amount of labor exchanged may be quite uneven. No accurate accounting is kept of the labor in this arrangement, though the exchange is felt to be roughly equal.

A clearer picture of just how *kamka'grima* works can be gained from a single detailed example. At rice planting three Rengsanggri households cooperated—those of Singron, his wife's married brother Ranjeng, and Seng'jan, who was a neighbor of Singron but was not closely related to the others. At this time Singron's household could marshal the unusual number of six working adults, while from Ranjeng's household came only himself and his wife. Seng'jan's house had four working members, one of whom however, was a rather old lady, and another a not fully mature youth, both of whom probably worked at a slightly slower pace than the others. Not everybody worked every day. Other pressing jobs, such as pounding rice and taking care of a sick child, kept individuals from helping for one or more days; and a few days were skipped entirely, to allow the participants either to go to market or to join the rest of the village in burning and planting the new fields—a task which had to be attended to before this group had quite finished their rice planting. The exact record of number of days spent by each household is as follows:

| | Workers from each household | | |
| | Singron's | Ranjeng's | Seng'jan's |
| --- | --- | --- | --- |
| March 15, Singron's field | 6 | 1 | 1 |
| March 16, Market day, no planting | | | |
| March 17, Singron's field | 5 | 2 | 4 |
| March 18, Seng'jan's field | 5 | 1 | 2 |
| March 19, Ranjeng's field | 6 | 2 | 3 |
| March 20, Singron's field | 6 | 2 | 4 |
| March 21, Seng'jan's field | 6 | 2 | 4 |
| March 22, Ranjeng's field | 5 | 1 | 2 |
| March 23, market day, no planting | | | |
| March 24, no planting, all preparing seeds for the new fields | | | |
| March 25, Singron's field | 5 | 2 | 3 |
| Planting in the new fields intervened, and the rice planting was not completed until: | | | |
| March 31, Ranjeng's field | 5 | 2 | 3 |

The inequality in amounts of labor given and gained by the households is marked. Singron's household gave 27 man-days of labor to others, and received only 19; Seng'jan's household gave 20 and received 14; while Ranjeng's gave only 10 but received no less than 24 man-days of labor from the others. The imbalance is slightly, though by no means entirely, corrected by the fact that the two workers from Ranjeng's house were both able and strong, while two of those from Seng'jan's were probably slightly slower in their work. Moreover, the members of Singron's household may have felt little concern since Ranjeng was the son of Mebeson, Singron's mother-in-law, though he maintained a separate household. Some of the discrepancy might be made up at another time, such as the harvest, but some of it, as a result of imprecise book-keeping, is simply ignored and indeed hardly realized. No one demands that the amounts of labor given and received be exactly equivalent, though the exchange is not expected to allow any household to gain an advantage over any other. If the imbalance is too great, any household is free to withdraw, or at least to decline to participate in a similar arrangement at another time.

Not everybody joins a group such as this, even at planting or harvest. Many households prefer to plant alone, and are entirely free to do so. Cooperation often takes place repeatedly between the same households over the years, but the arrangements are not truly permanent and can be broken by any party whenever it wishes. If the amounts of labor given and received are approximately equal, the only advantage that anyone gains is the pleasure that some people feel in working in a large and sociable group.

*Baraa.* More careful accounting is kept when labor is exchanged in the fields according to a system known as *baraa.* This is generally a short-term arrangement in which one or more people each give a day's labor to another household, and then, usually on the following day, the same number of workers give the same in return. If a single man works one day, his labor should be repaid by the labor of another man, while a single woman's labor is repaid by a woman. If several people work, the composition of the returning work party need not be identical, but the number of workers is always the same and in this *baraa* is sharply distinguished from *kamka'grima.* Garos described *baraa* as being "just like money," since it is calculated so closely. *Baraa* is commonly engaged in by men when they first cut the forest and when they build field houses, and by women at maize planting. Both men and women may *baraa* at times of general cultivation, and at both the planting and the harvesting of cotton. The motive for *baraa* is generally companionship. The labor exchanged is so nearly equal that neither side should profit. The worker even brings his own rice to the fields for his midday meal. Garos say that they get less tired when working with friends, and so *baraa* is very common. Close friends often *baraa* repeatedly with each other, but each day's labor requires a new agreement and is carefully paid back.

*Village Levies.*    Another method by which labor is organized is not an exchange between households, even though each household gives labor and is helped by the labor of others. Large work parties are occasionally required for jobs that benefit the village as a whole but no single family more than any other. Today, at least in the Rengsanggri area, most of these are organized by the local government magistrate (known as the *loskor*), for he has the power to levy work groups to keep the paths cleared. On one occasion, however, the villagers themselves organize a work party in the same way. Just before the fields are burned, a crew must circle the fields and clear the brush away from the edge of the forest, to make sure that the forest does not burn. For these tasks one member from each household (or occasionally two for road clearing) joins the work party. Exceptions are virtually never made to this rule, and it gives the larger households a slight advantage over the smaller ones, since a smaller percentage of their work force must be spared. The total amount levied under this system is not great, totaling perhaps half a dozen days of work per household per year. A man, a woman, or an adolescent may equally well take part in this labor.

Labor is mustered in the same manner for the benefit of one particular household when, after a death, one man from each household must cut a pole for the funeral pyre. Strictly speaking, this assistance at funerals is a long-term, symmetrical transaction, since repayment will come only after another death, but the method of organizing the labor is the same as for the village levies in which road clearing or fire protection immediately benefits everyone.

*Hospitality at Feasts.*   One other transaction between Garo households is in part symmetrical. This occurs at the four annual village ceremonies, in which each household in the village plays host to everyone else. On each such occasion, every household must provide rice beer, rice, and some form of curry to everyone who comes. The expense is great as special foods are appropriate for each festival. These may be more expensive than the ordinary daily foods and must certainly be served in larger amounts; but, of course, everybody can also eat well in each of the other houses. Since the rich people provide more opulent feasts than their poorer neighbors, and very rarely an extremely poor house is skipped entirely, this type of exchange has an asymmetrical aspect; but since almost everyone does do some entertaining, it is in part symmetrical as well.

## LONG-TERM SYMMETRICAL TRANSACTIONS

The other symmetrical transactions between households of a Garo village do more than provide for companionship or merrymaking. Some jobs demand that more labor be concentrated at one time than a single house could ever provide. This implies a long delay between the giving of labor and its return, and makes impossible any close balancing of the amount of labor exchanged. Rather, Garos feel that all people owe their friends, neighbors, and relatives certain kinds of assistance whenever this is needed. They keep no precise account of how much help a household gives on these occasions, but each man knows that in the future his own household will need similar help, and he must then be able to count on others. The symmetry of these transactions then is a long-term one only. In the short run they may be quite one-sided.

*Informal Favors.*   The simplest long-term but symmetrical

transactions range from such neighborly favors as the loan of a basket or cooking pot to the mobilization of half a dozen or more people for temporary jobs. A man who happens to be walking back from the market may be willing to help his neighbor carry his purchases with no specific compensation, though in other contexts similar porterage is done for money wages or with the hope of a monetary profit. Several men in Rengsanggri who did not have enough rice from their own fields, purchased rather large quantities of rice from people in another village who had a surplus. These men were able to recruit enough of their neighbors to fetch it in a single trip. No wages were paid to the neighbors, though they were served a meal after their return. The cost of the meal was far less than wages for the same work would have been, and the real reciprocity of these arrangements came with the knowledge that at some other time one might be called upon for similar favors to that day's helpers. Occasionally neighbors and relatives even work in the fields for a household that has been smitten by an unusual amount of sickness, or for a widow who has no man in her house, and they expect no direct compensation.

*House-Building.* Garo houses are large and well-made, and great care is lavished upon their construction. Once built they last for ten years or so, until the bamboo rots too thoroughly for comfort. House-building requires far more labor than a single household can provide in one year. The only way houses can be built is by organizing labor in such a way that everyone participates in building a few houses each year. With no tradition of compensating fellow villagers with money, no precise payment for labor can be made. Instead, labor is provided on the basis of long-term reciprocity. It is the responsibility of all men to help others build their houses, though the responsibility is strongest for close neighbors and especially for relatives.

The magnitude of the task of house-building can best be grasped by actual example. Jurang built a new house while I was there (house 38a on the village map), and by combining my

own estimates with his, a fairly full picture of the required
labor can be given. His house was a bit smaller than most, but it
was well-made and the amount of labor required was probably
not far from average. Fourteen days of labor were required to
cut bamboo before building even began. Jurang himself worked
eight days and Aling, his father-in-law, two days, while
Rongsin, Ajeng, Gurang, and Rangjan worked one day each
before enough bamboo was accumulated. Jurang worked three
days by himself cutting small wooden posts, but was fortunate
in not having to cut larger ones because he already had some
serviceable posts left from a house he had occupied some years
before. Cutting large posts would have required many additional days of labor. Jurang estimated the number who worked
on the actual construction as 30 on the first day and 32 on the
second, two days being enough to complete all but the thatching. These are larger work parties than is typical, but the
number of days worked is smaller, and the total of 62 man-days
of labor is reasonable for the actual building. Jurang estimated
the number thatching the next day at 100; I did not count the
number at this time myself, but the figure is probably high. A
smaller house required 28 men to thatch, while 16 women
helped cook food for the feast which followed; whereas a bigger
house required 53 men and 28 women. A total of 60 people
seems a reasonable estimate for Jurang's thatching. Since
thatching does not take all day, this does not mean 60 full days
of labor. Jurang used bamboo leaves rather than thatching
grass for his roof. This saved time, though grass provides a
more durable roof. If thatching grass is used, it must be cut
ahead of time, like the bamboo, and tied in bundles for the final
day of thatching, whereas bamboo leaves are ordinarily cut the
same day as the thatching. If thatchers are counted as working
a half day each, a total of 109 days of labor is a reasonable
estimate for the amount of time spent preparing for and building this house. A larger house, on which thatching grass rather
than bamboo leaves was used, and for which the major wooden

posts needed to be cut new, might easily take twice as much labor. On the other hand, Jusin built a tiny house with a mere 29 man-days of labor. This is just about the bare minimum, and the finished building hardly met the minimum standards of good housing in Rengsanggri.

Houses are not the only structures Rengsanggri men must build. Every year each household builds at least one field house, sometimes two. These are much smaller and less elaborate than the village houses; but since they must be built every year, a significant amount of labor must be expended in their construction. The cutting of the bamboo, wooden posts, and thatch preparatory to building a field house takes up to ten man-days of labor, and the actual work of construction usually requires another ten, so that twenty days every year must be spent by most households in building field houses. Those households with two plots of land often build two field houses; thus, in one year the 60 households of Rengsanggri managed to construct 74 field houses. Most of the households which built two included more than one adult man, of course. Most of the work of building field houses is done by the men of the household, with occasional help from their wives. Sometimes labor is exchanged by *baraa*—or particularly in the case of thatching by *kamka-grima*, in which several men thatch together in turn. Since everyone must build field houses at the same time each year, there is no need, and indeed no possibility, for the same kinds of labor exchange as are used for building the much bigger village houses.

Most households had at least one granary somewhere in the village, though the number per household varied from none to four. The village had a total of 85 granaries for its 60 households. Granaries are solidly built but last a shorter time than houses. The Garos maintain that this is due to the absence of fires, the smoke from which reduces decay and insect damage in the houses. A small group of men, typically six or eight, help the owner to build his granary, a job which generally takes two days with this number of workers. The owner must put in a few preliminary days of work to prepare the bamboo that will be used. Smaller buildings—wood sheds and pig sties—are generally built by the owner without outside help.

All told, it is reasonable to estimate that most households provide thirty or more man-days of labor every year for building projects of one sort or another. It is true that house-building is a pleasant and convivial job, enjoyed by all the workers, but buildings are clearly important to the Garos to rate so great an expenditure of effort; and indeed the results of their labors are houses of grace and comfort.

Only when a large house is thatched do anything like a majority of the villagers participate, and even at a thatching many people are always missing. For some of the preparatory jobs the house owner works alone or with a small number of other men. The actual construction may be attended by ten of more men each day, but the composition of the crew varies from day to day. Many men apparently feel that by working one day they have fulfilled their obligation, and are then free to pursue some other task on the next. If two houses are being built simultaneously in the village, a man may work one day on one and on the other the next. As in so many jobs, the most closely related people are most apt to help each other, or to help each other most often. Thus a man may work for several days on the house of a close relative, while a more distant relative will put in only a single day, and a remote relative (nobody in the village is completely unrelated to anybody else) may not help at all. The pattern is modified by neighborhood and friendship, but kinship is the most important single determinant of assistance.

Considerable skill is required in house construction, and several distinct jobs must be done; nevertheless, the work is organized without any formalized leadership. There are no specialized carpenters, and even the owner never directs others in their work. The owner does not, in fact, come right out and ask others to help, but simply lets it be known that he will be building a house; he relies on the others to volunteer, knowing that those who have no other more pressing business will be willing to help. On the job, each helps where he sees the need. Houses are built according to a standard pattern, which the workers know well, so nobody needs to make any decisions or direct the work. The older men mostly sit to one side shaping pieces of bamboo, while the younger men do the actual construction.

The owner of the house has a few duties toward his workers other than the obligation to work on their houses at some other time. He must provide a steady supply of rice beer. Men building a house do not drink heavily, but just enough to cause an already sociable task to take on a slightly festive air. The owner must also provide tobacco for the water pipes which are passed around regularly. He often, though not always, provides a midday meal of rice and curry. His duties are greatest on the day of the thatching, and it is on this day that the largest number of people assemble. After the thatching is completed, a sacrifice is held to drive undesirable spirits from the house, and the house itself acts as the altar on which the blood of the sacrificial animal is smeared. The host must supply a meal, as well as some rice beer, and men like to be able to supply enough beer for a party that will last through the afternoon and early evening, after the thatching is finished. The ability to provide a lavish feast and large amounts of rice beer enables some men to command larger amounts of labor and thereby to build bigger houses than others. This, however, lends to the transaction of housebuilding an asymmetrical aspect, whose implications will be considered more fully in the next section.

*Sacrifices for Disease.* Another symmetrical transaction is assistance given during times of illness. Like house-building, though for different reasons, sickness demands the help of more people than a single household can supply, and this labor must be concentrated at the right moment. Unlike those for housebuilding, the requirements for this labor cannot be predicted, since disease strikes without warning; but the period between the giving of help by one household and the time when it can be paid back is likely to be so long that close accounting and exact repayment are out of the question. Rather, as in the case of house-building, everyone has a general obligation to friends, neighbors, and relatives to come and to help when sickness strikes. Reasonably enough, no sacrifice is performed for an ordinary cold or other minor ailment, and occasionally a man may conduct a sacrifice both for and by himself. But for anything serious, several people must assist. If a woman becomes ill, for instance, her husband may mention to her neighbors that he plans a sacrifice. A number of friends and relatives, knowing of the woman's sickness, and in the back of their minds knowing that at any unpredictable moment it may be they who will require help, offer their services. The more closely related the sick person is, the stronger is the obligation to help; but as with house-building, even remotely related friends also help each other regardless of kinship. It seems that often a miserable night of disease and discomfort resolves people to take action as soon as possible the next day, for many sacrifices are performed in the morning. Helpers at sacrifices are always men, and they gather at the house of the sick person. Building the altar is the major contribution of most of the helpers. It is not onerous work, but even rather pleasant and sociable; and since the patient usually gets well following a sacrifice, it gives people considerable satisfaction to know that they are doing something concrete for him. If a man in the sick person's house is skillful, he may perform the ritual himself, but otherwise another of the helpers must do it. At every sacrifice one of the men who helps to build the altar should be skillful enough to perform the actual ceremony. This priest (*kamal*) receives no special reward for his work, and no man spends more than a small fraction of his time performing sacrifices. Every man can carry out a few simple sacrifices, and all have the opportunity to learn more by observing them as they are done by others. Some men become more interested than others, and a degree of prestige

and social recognition go to any man who is skillful at performing these rituals. The household of the sick person must provide
the animal, either from their own possessions or buying it. The
ensuing meal gives a partial compensation to the participants,
but the food eaten is not regarded so much a payment for the
work of sacrificing as continued participation in the event.
Besides the satisfaction of knowing that one has helped a friend,
the participant also knows that when his turn comes, he will
have willing helpers.

*Kokam.* The final long-term but symmetrical exchange
between households is more carefully measured than those mentioned previously. It also differs from the rest in that it frequently takes place between households in different villages
rather than those in the same village, and it is always between
kinsmen. One category of gifts which the household of the dead
person distributes at funerals is called *kokam*. (The other category, *magual*, was considered in Chapter VI.) *Kokam* is a payment given to those who slaughter a cow in honor of the deceased. Slaughtering may be done by a son, but also by a more
distant relative, whether a member of the same lineage or not,
and it is frequently done by the man who leads a party from
another village to attend a funeral. Killing a cow brings honor
both to the deceased and to the man who organizes the killing,
and the occasion provides a fine meal to the friends and relatives
who help. The organizer receives the *kokam* from the household of the dead man, and like *magual* this is most appropriately
a brass heirloom gong, though something else may be substituted if no gongs are available. The gong is carried back to the
organizer's village, where the cow is killed and a slender
wooden post erected to advertise the event. The gong thus
acquired can be used for nothing other than to be returned to
the original family when somebody in the acquiring family dies.
At that time the original family must sacrifice a cow in return.
In other words, the *kokam* gifts form a symbolic record of the
obligations that are set up for returning the honor of killing a

cow, and in this way households bestow honor upon one another. One man may be followed in death by several cows. A rich man who has many gongs which can be distributed, and who in the past has collected gongs in return for having killed cows in other people's honor, will have more killed for him than a poor man; and, moreover, people are more likely to want to give honor to a rich man. When Tuak, the father-in-law of Anat, died, ten cows were killed in his honor; but Tuak was a very wealthy and respected man in Rengsanggri. Others die in humbler circumstances, and a few have no cow killed for them at all. *Kokam* may be distributed and cows slaughtered for both men and women, but the amounts tend to be a good deal larger for men.

## ASYMMETRICAL TRANSACTIONS

The relationships that have been considered so far are, at least in the long run, roughly symmetrical, since both parties give and receive approximately the same thing. The initial contribution may not be paid back for many years and the amounts may be hardly counted, let alone balanced; or, on the other hand, labor may be repaid the next day in closely measured quantities. Ultimately, however, the amounts given and received should be more or less equal. Other transactions take place between the various households of a village which are not even in the long run symmetrical, but in which the goods or services exchanged are quite different. Inevitably some households do slightly better than others in agriculture. Some have a larger percentage of able-bodied workers, more industrious or ambitious members, or less sickness; or by good fortune they acquire better land one year. These fortunate households obtain the larger crops. This advantage can, by skillful manipulation, be translated into reasonably enduring differences in wealth and prestige. It is the purpose of the following pages to show how this comes about.

*Meat Payment for Services.*    The man who carves a memorial post to be erected before the house of a dead man receives the leg of a cow in return for his labors. The midwife and the priest who sacrifices at a birth may also each be compensated with a leg of a cow. These legs are the closest approach to a wage in the traditional village exchange system, but they involve only a relatively small resource and are regarded more as a traditional gift than as a real payment. The other asymmetrical transactions are more important in their over-all effect on the distribution of wealth.

*A'jak.*    When people find themselves short of food before the harvest, they may be forced to ask a richer neighbor to advance some grain in return for the promise of labor. In the usual arrangement, one full winnowing basket of paddy is given in return for the promise of the work of six people for a day in the fields. The debt may be repaid soon after the paddy is given, but it may be delayed for a month or more until the man who advances the grain requires the labor. The workers are given their midday meal of rice and curry, but they are not otherwise compensated, since they have received the paddy earlier. Since most households are unable to supply six workers from their own numbers, they must often obtain the assistance of friends from other households, and the friends must then be repaid by *baraa*, as described above. Thus if household A can supply four workers, it may get two more people from household B to join them on the appropriate day when they work together on the land of the man who had advanced paddy to A. Then, on the next day or soon afterward, two people from household A will go to work on B's land to return their help.

Garos realize that *a'jak* brings a profit to the lender. The amount of labor he receives is worth more than the cost of the paddy he gives, and indeed wage labor when it is available brings pay two or three times as high as *a'jak*; but wage labor is not widely available. The only justification for the small amount of grain given in *a'jak* is that it is the borrower who comes to ask

for it rather than the supplier who looks for labor. The poor
man, of course, is hungry and hardly in a position to bargain.
*A'jak* enables a man who one year has large stocks of paddy in
his possession to clear a large amount of land, counting on
requests for *a'jak* to furnish labor to keep it cultivated and even
to help at planting and harvesting. This enables him to reap a
better harvest the following year, and thus to maintain his
wealth. Poor people, on the other hand, are forced to accept
*a'jak* from others, so that during the season when they should
be attending to their own fields they may have to spend an in-
convenient number of days working in other men's fields; thus
they in turn get a small crop of their own and once again, the
next year, are in the awkward situation of having to accept
*a'jak*. In this way differences in wealth, once established, can be
perpetuated over many years, and even over generations,
regardless of the absence of permanent land ownership. The
inequality should not be exaggerated. Poor families who tighten
their belts and work hard in their fields can and sometimes do
extricate themselves, and rich people can lose their wealth if
they do not manage their crops carefully. Wealth differentials
are not as marked or as permanent as they can be where land is
permanently and privately owned. Gajang, the 'headman' of
Rengsanggri, is reputed to have given about twenty winnowing
baskets of paddy before the 1956 harvest, and eight other households were said to have given amounts ranging from this down
to as little as a basket or two. The total amount given was somewhat less than usual that year because the availability of wage
labor on a new road that was being built near by cut down the
demand for *a'jak*.

*Dena.*    Some people with large supplies of grain loan it to
others with the agreement that instead of being paid back in
labor, they will be paid back double the amount of grain at the
time of the harvest. This is not as common as *a'jak*, but its
effect is much the same, since it allows differences in wealth to
be perpetuated. Occasionally rice is loaned, but in much smaller

amounts and with the agreement only to pay back the same amount. Such a loan is called *srua*, and is made only where claims such as kinship can be invoked. It is a friendly helping gesture, not a business deal like *a'jak* or *dena*. Grain in Rengsanggri is never loaned at intermediate rates; the interest charge is 100 per cent or nothing. In other parts of the Garo Hills repayment at the rate of one and one-half times the original amount is sometimes agreed upon.

*Entertainment as a Means to Prestige.* *A'jak* and *dena* seem to be weighted in a lop-sided manner to the advantage of the rich members of the community, but the wealth they bring has only limited uses. Wealthy people can buy a few better clothes, eat a little more meat, command larger work parties, and therefore build bigger houses; but all this does not set them off in any sharp way from the poorer people. Rich people spend most of their time working in the fields like everyone else. The main use of wealth is to entertain on a comparatively lavish scale. This converts wealth into prestige and power, while materially the wealth is again distributed throughout the community, since everyone shares in the consumption of the goods that rich men accumulate. Feasts are not given in the Rengsanggri area on occasions designed specifically to validate or establish prestige, though such feasts do occur in some parts of the hills. The Rengsanggri custom is for ambitious men to seize as times for particularly lavish entertainment those numerous occasions when hospitality is appropriate. During the ceremonies, when the villagers are entertained in every house in turn, the richer houses entertain abundantly. The poorest houses seldom fail to offer something; but fewer people visit them, partly to avoid embarassing the householders and partly because there is less expectation of a bountiful spread. It is hardly reasonable for any single person to visit every one of the sixty households in the village, but most do assemble at the richer houses, where they can confidently expect to be greeted with copious amounts of rice beer and liberal quantities of rice and curry.

Entertaining is appropriate on many other occasions. When a death occurs in the community, the wealthy villagers invite others in for a consolation drink. A few relatives may kill a cow, which they say they do to honor the dead person, but which actually brings as much honor to the man who offers the cow. At the post-funeral ceremony the dead man's household has the opportunity to kill a cow and entertain. Beer and sometimes food are distributed by participants in legal disputes. Lunch may be served to house-builders, while thatchers in particular are supposed to be rewarded with food and beer. A few households offer feasts to others out in the fields at the *Asiroka* ceremony, before rice planting. Even the sacrifices to banish disease may be more liberal if the family is wealthy, and thus may provide a larger feast for the helpers. A son or a daughter who has moved away from his or her parents to marry, and who is wealthy enough, may slaughter a cow, ostensibly to honor the parents. Usually the time of one of the major village festivals is chosen for this, and most of the animal is sent to the parents' home. One leg is retained by the son's or daughter's family, however, and there is meat enough for two feasts, one at each house. The feast is described as one of giving thanks to the parents for their help to the child, but honor comes not only to the parents but to the child as well. The greatest hospitality and greatest prestige derive from killing a cow, and a record of the number killed is made public by decorating the front of the killer's house with the horns and frontal bones of the animals. Wealthy houses may be hung with two or three dozen sets.

One of these feasts may serve simultaneously to validate the right of a household to use its own gongs for beating at village festivals. A house must have about fifteen gongs before it is considered decent to use them, and houses which do not own enough must borrow them from a richer neighbor when they are needed. But just to accumulate and own enough gongs is not sufficient; the household must kill a cow for some occasion, such as to honor a parent, before the gongs can be used. After this the household will be expected to entertain regularly and on a larger than average scale, and so to maintain its prestigeful position. In Rengsanggri eight households owned enough gongs to be used in festivals: those of Gajang, Jengnon, Nanggan, Anat, Kakan, Chondu, Rongsin, and Gurang. Many other households had a few gongs but used those from one of these eight households and carried them to their houses when it was their turn to entertain during village festivals. Feasts are frequent enough for poor people to eat significantly better than they would if they relied entirely on their own gardens. Wealth differences lead to greater differences in prestige than in standards of consumption. Prestige and social standing go to the industrious and skillful.

The Garos have a clear conception of the relation between rich and poor. They recognize that it is the poor who create wealth for the rich, and even summarize this in the saying *Mane chagipa rasong; dilgipa Saljong*: "The rich people have luck, the poor people are like Saljong!" That is, like the God Saljong, the poor people create wealth for others. But this does not seem wrong to the Garos, and those who are forced to take *a'jak*, or to borrow grain at 100 per cent interest, are rarely resentful at the terms of the bargain. Rather they feel that it is fortunate that rich people exist because, as they say, "If there were no rich people, who would feed us at hungry times of the year?" The rich regularly feed the poor, whether through providing them with grain, serving them a meal when they work on their fields, or in lavish entertainment in the village. This ability and willingness to feed others is considered ample justification for the position of wealthy villagers.

*Heirlooms.* If wealth differences rested only upon stocks of grain that could be loaned at a profit, they would be less stable than they are. A bad harvest, or even an elephant in the granaries, might obliterate the differences in wealth. But grain and other crops can be sold and the money used to purchase jewelry, heirlooms, and even land titles. (Land titles are discussed in the next chapter.) Heirlooms bring no income or interest, but they provide a way of hoarding wealth. They contribute to inertia in wealth differences, since after a bad year a few heirlooms can be sold and supplies purchased as a continued foundation for wealth. A man who can count on the labor of others to plant large fields obtains not only large harvests of grain, but also larger than average supplies of cotton and ginger, which can be sold for cash. Some of this money can be used to purchase little luxuries for the family, fancy clothes for special occasions, or cheap toys for the children; but some of it is converted into heirlooms. These are stored in chests in the back of the house, but are occasionally displayed publicly. The most prized heirlooms are the gongs.

Gongs vary according to metal and workmanship, and range in price from cheap ones worth only a few rupees to elegant ones worth several hundred. Garos recognize more than a dozen kinds, measuring anywhere from perhaps a yard in diameter down to no more than a few inches, and variously made of iron, brass, or bell metal. Some of the finest gongs are decorated with engraved outlines of elephants, tigers, snakes, and other animals. No one seems to know the origin of these gongs, and the Garos consider them to have been handed down from antiquity. Most of them, including the ordinary ones that are beaten at festivals, are more or less basin-shaped and can be held by one rim and struck on the bottom. The most valuable gongs are never beaten but only displayed at the *Wangala* festival. A gong worth several hundred rupees is an extremely valuable piece of property to a Garo, who can hardly hope by wage labor to earn more than two rupees in one day. Like other heirlooms they can be sold for money, and so they represent a saving which can be cashed in if the family runs into difficulties, but heirlooms are sold only at infrequent intervals and with great reluctance. Garos reckon the rise and fall of families by the number of gongs they are able to buy or are forced to sell.

Personal jewelry ranks second only to gongs as a repository of value. Its sale brings less cash than most gongs, but jewelry can be sold a little more freely and is displayed on more occasions. Silver jewelry of several kinds, some of it hung with silver coins, is worn by both men and women, especially at village festivals; but jewelry is much more than a thing of beauty, since it can always be sold if necessary. Once when I was negotiating the purchase of a silver neckpiece, my friends speculated as to whether I would be able to sell it after returning home to America. Only when they finally decided that I would be able to sell it there were they reassured that it would not be an extravagant purchase.

## WEALTH AND POWER

As a result of the transactions which have been described in this chapter, wealth differences can be perpetuated over many years and even over generations, since all of the goods upon which wealth depends are inherited without division by the heir and heiress of the household. Any villager can point out which households are the wealthiest in the village, and even in a rough way grade them in relation to one another; and he can also point out which households are increasing their status by hard work, and which are losing their wealth through poor management of resources. Wealth is by no means permanent.

People admire the rich men, but they do not defer to them in any formal manner, and an observer could not possibly tell from watching a group of men in ordinary daily pursuits which of them were rich and which poor. If one looked at the size of their houses or measured the size of their fields, however, the relative position of the men would become fairly clear, and the more one observed the details of personal relations, the clearer it would become. Village life is so organized that few important village-wide decisions must be made, but when problems do arise people are usually willing to go along with the decisions of

the elite. The *nokma* must formally designate the day for ceremonies, but before doing so he informally samples the opinions
of other wealthy men. If disagreements arise about the distribution of plots for cultivation, the wealthy men can usually
carry along public opinion toward some solution. I once
watched villagers buying a cow for a ceremony. Every household had contributed money toward the price of the cow, but it
was four or five wealthy men who put their heads together and
decided whether or not to try to make the seller come down in
price. These are not profound questions; but somebody must
decide them, and most villagers are happy to leave them to the
wealthy men. After all, they "feed" the poorer people, and their
very wealth is evidence of their ability. My own judgment of the
ability of the various men in the village was close to the consensus of the villagers. I agreed with them that the wealthy
people were often more able and intelligent than the others. It
does take more than ordinary ability to accumulate or hold on
to wealth.

# ℨIX℈

## The Village

THE PEOPLE OF RENGSANGGRI said that their village had originally been settled by the grandparents of some of the oldest people still living. The village had prospered, and many daughters were born to the original families; and so, as they brought in their husbands, the village grew rapidly to its present sixty households. It seems entirely reasonable to suppose that the seven or eight groups of households which are found today in Rengsanggri, and which I have called cooperating groups, are the product of several stages of expansion and division of the kinship groups, a process that is still in operation. In every case most of the women and a few of the men of the various cooperating groups call themselves by the same sib name, Chambigong, and they all regard themselves as a good deal more closely related to one another than to people from other villages, even if these also have the same sib name. It is believed, in other words, that the people who belong to what may be called the village lineage (consisting of several minimal lineages) are more closely related to each other than to others of the same sib who live elsewhere. Even though the actual kin ties are forgotten or almost forgotten, there seems no reason to doubt their validity. With one exception, one or the other member of every married couple in Rengsanggri was a member of the Chambigong sib. Except for two replacement wives from a closely related village,

all these Chambigongs were considered to be members of the
Rengsanggri branch (village lineage) of that sib. About three-
quarters of the wives were members of the Chambigong sib
while their husbands belonged to sibs of the opposite moiety;
but some married Chambigong men had to live there as well.
All Chambigong women had fairly close male relatives living in
the village. This led to some interesting if complicating
arrangements.

If a man brings his wife to live in his village because the
women of his own lineage need to have a male relative present,
his children will be members of the sib and moiety of their
mother, and of a lineage that is based in her village rather than
in the one in which they are actually raised. Their displaced
residence is well recognized, and people who grow up in the
village of their fathers generally refer to their mother's village
as their "real" village, even though they may never have been
there except for short visits. Their "own" village is the village
of their mother's lineage, even though they actually reside in
the village of their father. In a village like Rengsanggri, where
such "reversed" marriages are distinctly a minority, these
children inevitably belong to the opposite moiety from the
majority of their contemporaries. For this reason they have an
unusually good chance to find a spouse within the same village.
It has come about in this way that several adult men who are
married to Rengsanggri women have lived in Rengsanggri since
birth, although they belong to lineages associated with other
villages. These men do not differ in their formal status from
other men who have moved in from a different village only upon
marriage. Like them, they live in this village by virtue of having
married a Rengsanggri woman. It is simply propinquity that
gives a locally raised boy a good chance of being taken as a
husband to a local girl. These men, when casually asked, often
give the name of their mother's village as their own, even though
they have never lived there. Still, they are members of the
village lineage and sib that is based in that other village. They

retain the right to go back and share in the use of its land, and they retain obligations to the people who live there. The only way that such men can stay in their fathers' village after marriage is by marrying a local girl, though since men ordinarily change residence at marriage there is no great difficulty in marrying a girl from another village and moving there. I have even heard of cases in which a boy who belongs to one lineage and village by right of descent, but is brought up in a different village—that of his father—then marries a girl from a third village and takes her back to live in the village of his own and his mother's lineage. This typical avunculocal pattern is entirely possible within the approved residence rules of the society, but it is not common.

The daughter of a man who brings his wife from another village must also marry a local boy if she is to remain living there as an adult. Since boys belonging to the opposite moiety are likely to be plentiful locally, this may not be too difficult. Sometimes a girl who is brought up in her father's village marries a boy from a different village and then sets up housekeeping with him in the village of her lineage, the village from which her mother originally came. However, the system of heirs and heiresses assures that at least some of the girls raised in their father's village will continue to live there after their marriage. A man who brings his wife to his own village is as anxious as anyone else to provide himself with an heir who can join the household as a son-in-law. Since such a man already lives in the village of his own lineage, he is not likely to have to go far to find a 'nephew,' and can ordinarily find a boy within the same village who will become his son-in-law. When this marriage occurs, it is in one sense an atypical marriage, since like the girl's parents, the couple will be one of the minority of those in the village in which the boy is a member of the main village lineage, while the girl is from another village. This boy, like his father-in-law, will reside in the place where most of the women of his lineage reside and will, like the father-in-law, be able to take some of the responsibility for the affairs of his 'sisters' ' and eventually his 'nieces' ' households. He will be a local 'maternal uncle' to the children of his 'sisters,' and thus one of the more accessible sources of lineage discipline. Considered from a different point of view, the marriage is a typical uxorilocal one. The boy moves from the house of his mother to that of his wife, and joins in all the household activities with her. The girl continues to live in the place where she has lived all her life, though it is not really her own village.

This couple in its turn may have children and be succeeded by a daughter who once again marries a boy from the same village. In this way households in which the man belongs to the village lineage and the woman to an outside one are perpetuated indefinitely. Even after several generations the women of the household, and the children of these women, give the village of their matrilineage as their own proper village, and they do not lose their right to go back to that village and live. They can, in fact, only continue to live in the village of their birth so long as they continue to marry local men. Still, once a woman is brought in from another village, the village to which she moves will have acquired a more or less permanent resident lineage man. Even after the first man dies, his successor will be there to take lineage responsibility. Although sixteen of the seventy married men in Rengsanggri were members of the Rengsanggri lineage and married to non-Rengsanggri women, only nine of their wives had to shift residence. The other seven were raised in Rengsanggri, the village of their fathers.

The rules of residence have been sufficiently described to make a few general observations. It is clear that the residence rules of the Garos appear entirely different depending upon whether one considers locality from the point of view of the individual household or from that of the village as a whole. From the point of view of the households, heir marriages are uxorilocal and at the same time avunculocal, since a man lives with both his wife and his maternal uncle; non-heir marriages are neolocal, since the couple always establishes a new and separate household; and replacement marriages are localized at the residence which was occupied by the previous spouse before he or she died. From the point of view of the village, the most common marriage requires that the man move to his wife's village, but as has been explained, some wives move instead and the resulting "reversed" marriages lead to a number of other patterns. The distinction between village residence and household residence has rarely been made clear in the anthropological literature, but it is an essential distinction for the Garos and undoubtedly for many other people. The residence of each married couple can be considered in both ways. It frequently happens, for instance, that a boy moves to his wife's village at his marriage but sets up a new household with her there. Such a marriage is uxorilocal with respect to the village but neolocal with respect to the household. The data for the seventy marriages in Rengsanggri (not including second wives) are summarized in Table 1. More detailed data on each of these marriages are given in Appendix B. Residence with respect to the household can best be categorized according to the type of marriage, whether of heirs, non-heirs, or replacements. Replacement-female can describe those marriages in which the woman has married a widower and moved to his house, and replacement-male the opposite case. Residence with respect to the village must take into account both the lineage membership of the spouses and the village where they were actually raised. Thus a man or woman may be "foreign" in the sense of belonging to a lineage which is based in a village other than Rengsanggri, but still have lived in Rengsanggri since birth. Most Rengsanggri marriages follow one of four patterns: 1) A man belonging to a non-Rengsanggri lineage, and raised in another village, moves into Rengsanggri when he marries a Rengsanggri Chambigong woman. 2) A Rengsanggri Chambigong man brings his wife from another village and lineage. 3) A Rengsanggri Chambigong man marries a woman who belongs to a

## TABLE I
## RESIDENCE OF RENGSANGGRI MARRIED COUPLES

| (by village) | by household | | | | | Total |
|---|---|---|---|---|---|---|
| | Heir | Non-Heir | Replacement Female | Replacement Male | Joining | |
| (1) "Foreign" man marries a local woman | 19 | 14 | 4 | 9 | | 46 |
| (2) Local man marries "foreign" woman but lives locally | 5 | 2 | 2 | | | 9 |
| (3) Local man marries locally raised woman of "foreign" lineage | 4 | 3 | | | | 7 |
| (4) Locally raised man of "foreign" lineage marries local woman | | 3 | 1 | | | 4 |
| (5) "Foreign" man marries woman of local lineage who was raised elsewhere | | 1 | | | | 1 |
| (6) Both are from other villages | | | 1 | | 1 | 2 |
| (7) "Foreign" man marries locally raised "foreign" woman | | 1 | | | | 1 |
| Total | 28 | 24 | 8 | 9 | 1 | 70 |

different lineage but who was raised in Rengsanggri, her father being a Rengsanggri Chambigong. 4) A man of a "foreign" lineage, who was raised in Rengsanggri—his father being a Rengsanggri Chambigong—marries a Rengsanggri Chambigong woman. Patterns 2) and 3) both produce "reversed" marriages, in that the man rather than the woman is a member of the Rengsanggri lineage. Patterns 3) and 4) are endogamous, in the sense that both husband and wife were raised in Rengsanggri, but they are not of course members of the same lineage. Three other possibilities occur more rarely: 5) One woman of the Rengsanggri lineage who had been raised away from the village moved back to Rengsanggri when she married. 6) Two women from closely allied lineages were given as replacements for deceased Rengsanggri Chambigong women. 7) There was one exceptional couple which did not fit the pattern at all. The woman was brought up in Rengsanggri, her father having been a Chambigong, but she belonged to a lineage of another village. She married a Nepali, which is an unusual thing for a Garo to do, and they lived away from the village until a few months before my final census; then they moved in with the woman's sister's heiress, who still lived in Rengsanggri appropriately married to a local Chambigong. When I left, they were living separately in a field house. While it seemed doubtful that they would remain permanently in the village, unfortunately for the perfection of my data, they still lived there when my final census was taken.

It is immediately apparent from Table 1 that a great deal of variation exists. Variations of this sort have often been interpreted in one of two ways: (1) as giving evidence that the society is shifting its residence pattern from one type to another, or (2) as an indication of "loose structuring," implying that there is wide latitude left for individual choice. Neither of the explanations has any relevance in the case of the Garos. All the residence patterns are necessary to Garo kinship structure as it exists today. Some men must move in with their wives' families, while others must set up new households. Some men must move to their wives' villages, while others must bring their wives to their own villages. The diversity of residence patterns is no more indicative of change than the presence of both horizontal and vertical girders in skyscraper construction is an indication of changing architectural techniques. All residence patterns have their essential part in Garo social structure.

Moreover, the decision as to where any particular couple is to live is not simply a matter of individual preference, but must be made with reference to the residences of other people and to strict kinship requirements. These hardly represent free individual alternatives such as could justify the interpretation that this is a loosely structured society. Rather, these different modes of residence are more comparable to the kind of specialization which has always been looked for in economic organization but which has not been expected in the realm of kinship. The varied residence patterns are just as necessary to the Garos as varied economic specializations are in many societies, and are no more an indication of change or of loose structuring than these. Since it is not possible to say that any particular residence pattern is "preferred," it is unreasonable to demand that their custom be summed up by any such simple term as "matrilocal." It would seem inherently futile to force any simple typology of even such a superficially simple phenomenon as residence upon the societies of the world.

Since women dislike living in a village unless some male members of their lineage are present, it may be difficult to bring a woman from another village to live with her husband; but, of course, many men from other villages always move in as husbands. If a woman is chosen from a village which has already sent one or preferably several husbands, then her situation will be made easier. She can rely on these in-marrying men from her own village and lineage to give her the same support that her husband gives to the women of the main village lineage. This means that the more people of an outside lineage are present in a village, the easier it is to bring in still another one. Of the many villages which have sent spouses to Rengsanggri, the single village of Waramgri and its lineage of Agidok Sangma is represented by thirteen of the 62 in-married men, and by nine of the nineteen women, some of whom were born in Rengsanggri, even if they still belong to the lineage from Waramgri. There are enough Waramgri people present in Rengsanggri to give each other plenty of support, if it is needed, and an additional Waramgri person has little hesitation about moving in. Garo villages are small enough that it is difficult for more than one outside lineage to get established in this way, and apparently it has repeatedly come to be regarded as appropriate for a particular village and its lineage to send spouses to another particular village. Rengsanggri has reached this point; the people in the village recognize their rather special position in regard to Waramgri, and readily point out what a large number of Waramgri people live in Rengsanggri. Although both men and women from Waramgri have moved to Rengsanggri, this does not imply that it is equally easy for Rengsanggri people to live in Waramgri, and few have made this move. People regard it as appropriate for one village to send many people to another as spouses, but I was never able to get any Garo to admit to the possibility that by remaining there long enough they might become genuine members of the second village. It is not felt possible that the Waramgri people could ever be regarded as true people of Rengsanggri.

One must also try to explain the initially somewhat puzzling occurrence of many villages which have two lineages instead of only one—always lineages which belong to sibs of opposite moieties. Garos simply say that this is the way the villages have always been, that the original founders included people from two different sibs, and as a result descendants of both can still live there. These villages never, to my knowledge, have lineages which belong to two sibs of the same moiety, such as would be expected occasionally if the distribution were the result of

chance initial settlement. Rather it seems likely that villages
with two sibs actually develop by some such gradual process as
the following: First a number of outside women are brought
into a village. Slowly it becomes easier and more appropriate to
bring in people from one particular village, and then eventually
these people whose lineage origins stem from another village
became so well established in their new village that they are
considered to belong there by lineage right and not by right of
marriage alone. At this point it even becomes possible for them

## TABLE 2

### Residence of the Married Couples of Songmagri

| | |
|---|---|
| 1. "Foreign" man of Sangma moiety marries a local Chambigong (Marak) woman      ...      ...      ... | 11 |
| 2. "Foreign" man of Marak moiety marries a local Manda (Sangma) woman      ...      ...      ...      ...      ... | 22 |
| 3. Local Manda (Sangma) man marries local Chambigong (Marak) woman      ...      ...      ...      ... | 10 |
| 4. Local Chambigong (Marak) man marries local Manda (Sangma) woman      ...      ...      ...      ...      ... | 10 |
| 5. Local Manda man marries a locally raised "foreign" (though Marak) woman      ...      ...      ...      ... | 1 |
| 6. Local Chambigong man marries a locally raised "foreign" (though Sangma) woman      ...      ... | 2 |
| 7. Local Manda (Sangma) man marries a "foreign" (though Marak) woman but lives locally      ...      ... | 1 |
| 8. Locally raised "foreign" (though Sangma) man marries a local Chambigong (Marak) woman      ...      ... | 1 |
| 9. Entirely "foreign" couple      ...      ...      ...      ... | 1 |
| 10. Local Chambigong Marak man marries local Chambigong Marak woman in disapproved moiety endogamy | 1 |
| Total      ... | 60 |

to bring in spouses from outside and go on living there; and the result is a two-lineage village. The fact that the village now has both men and women of the two opposite moieties makes it possible for more people to find spouses locally. The tendency is for a higher proportion of marriages to occur within the village between members of the different lineages.

The village of Songmagri, only about a mile away from Rengsanggri, and the one from which the Rengsanggri people say they are derived, is a village in which two lineages are considered to be native. One is a lineage of Chambigong in the Marak moiety, a sister lineage to that of Rengsanggri, while the other is a lineage of the Manda sib of the Sangma moiety. This village has 51 households and 60 married couples, not including second wives. The varying residence patterns which have brought these couples to Songmagri are shown in Table 2, categorized according to lineage membership.

Quite different categories from those applicable to Rengsanggri are required for an understanding of the Songmagri residence pattern. The latter village had a total of 32 couples in which the woman belonged to the local Manda lineage, 23 in which she was a local Chambigong, and only five (rows 5, 6, 7, 9 of Table 2) in which she was a member of some other lineage not considered as properly belonging to Songmagri. This compares with nineteen couples out of Rengsanggri's 70 in which the woman did not belong to the main Chambigong lineage (rows 2, 3, 6, 7 of Table 1). Even more striking is the fact that only two of the married women in Songmagri were raised in other villages, while nine women moved in to live with Rengsanggri men. Exactly one-third of the marriages in Songmagri are between members of the two main lineages. Clearly, in a village such as Songmagri the problem of keeping both men and women of a single lineage together in the same village has been neatly solved. A matrilineal lineage cannot afford to alienate either its male or female members, since women are needed to reproduce and supply new members, while men are

needed to fill positions of authority. In Songmagri both sexes
are available in the same spot. It is no longer necessary to move
women in order to keep a few men at home. Nevertheless, the
possibilities available to people who marry are not so different
from the possibilities in Rengsanggri. One should still marry a
member of the opposite moiety. Heirs are still incorporated into
the father-in-law's household, and non-heir households continue to separate from it. If both husband and wife belong to
the same village, they will have no alternative but to live in that
village. This limitation of choice can never happen to Rengsanggri people, since they must always marry someone from a
lineage based in another village.

Some situations inherent in the marriage pattern cause
periodic readjustment of the lineages and cooperating groups
within the villages. One such situation is well illustrated by the
household of Tuak (household #6). Tuak was a Chambigong
man of Rengsanggri, a son of the household which holds the
headmanship. He, unlike most men, lived in his own village
after marriage, so that he was able to take considerable responsibility for the affairs of his 'sisters' ' households, and notably for
the household to which the 'headman' belonged. Tuak's household was considered generally to be a member of the same
cooperating group as that of the 'headman' and of the several
women whose households had recently "come out" from it. His
house was even built in the same part of the village as most of
their houses. As Tuak grew older he looked for a 'nephew' to
come to be his son-in-law. The only boy in the 'headman's'
household was too young and Tuak was not even able to find
any boy from any of the households of this cooperating group.
However, by looking slightly further he was able to find a man
of the same village (from household #17) from a closely allied
minimal lineage. This man, Anat, married Tuak's daughter and
moved to Tuak's house from his mother's, which was in a
different part of the village. Anat was able to look after his own
close relatives, since he lived in the same village, even though in

a slightly different neighborhood. Eventually Tuak died and Anat succeeded to his position. Everybody remembers that it is still Tuak's house which he maintains, and he is still considered to have responsibility toward the houses of the women of the 'headman's' minimal lineage, just as Tuak had. This has not meant that he has lost his connection with his own family. They, too, consider him to be a close relative and rely on him in the same way. Anat's household has therefore been placed in such a position that its head has responsibility toward two sets of households, the one inherited from his father-in-law and the one consisting of his own close kin. Depending upon the circumstances, the household can cooperate with either set of relatives, and Anat can take responsibility in kinship matters toward both groups. By degrees—particularly if Anat eventually obtains an heir who is a member of his own minimal lineage—the household will probably be considered more and more a part of the cooperating group of Anat's own mother's house. If other men of the 'headman's' minimal lineage who live locally assume more responsibility toward the 'headman's' cooperating group, Anat's responsibility could be more rapidly reduced. Real kinship would take precedence over heirship as a determinant of cooperation and responsibility. The shift in responsibility would take place only gradually over the course of many years.

Households in which the woman is a member of the village lineage may also be gradually reoriented toward a new set of related households. An example is provided by the case of Ringin, who was an old lady when I knew her. As a girl she had been taken as adopted heiress by a fairly close relative of her mother. Whether or not her real mother and her adopted mother were at that time considered members of the same cooperating group, their descendants today certainly are not. Ringin moved into her adopted mother's house, and her husband came to live with her there. For a time this household was naturally considered to be part of the group of the adopted mother. Eventually the older woman died, however, and gradually everybody began to think of the house as actually belonging with the houses of Ringin's own biological sisters, two of whom are still living in the village. At the present time only the older people remember that Ringin was originally an adopted daughter who had inherited her household from somebody else. Most younger people believe that she established her own household by "coming out" of the house of her sister Nuri, who is the heiress of their mother, and everybody, young and old, speaks as if this were the case. It is unreasonable to consider these houses as belonging to anything other than the same cooperating group.

Ringin had no children who lived to adulthood, and so no new households have branched off from hers. This is probably one reason, along with the partial dying out of the lineage from which Ringin's adopted mother came, that her house is usually spoken of as having "come out" of her real sister's house. Few other relatives are present, and since it is convenient to assign her to some group, her own relatives form a natural place. Her childlessness has also meant that she in her turn had to adopt an heiress. The girl she chose also came from a somewhat different though not distantly related minimal lineage. It seems likely that in another generation this household will be considered to be part of the cooperating group from which Ringin's heiress came. Real kinship gradually tends to take precedence over adoptive relationships. The mere fact that a girl is adopted does not mean that she loses her ties with her own mother and her mother's household.

It should not be concluded from these examples that adoptive kinship ties are unimportant. The ancestry of Jengnon's house has already been described. It is considered to be the second oldest in the village, and the fact that only a few generations ago an heiress had to be adopted in order to perpetuate this household in no way reduces its seniority. If the people calculated according to actual kinship ties, the house of Jengnon would be no more senior than the households descended from the adopted heiress's sisters. Since she was adopted into a household that was already an old one, the household retained that seniority without interruption, regardless of the adoption. No doubt the fact that this was an old and important household has encouraged the recognition of ties which tend to maintain its seniority, whereas the rather shallow genealogical depth of Ringin's household, and the absence of households which have branched off from it, have meant that the older ties could be ignored and actual kinship alone remembered.

### 'HEADMANSHIP'

I have referred in a number of places to 'headmanship,' and it is at last possible to explain the nature, duties, and privileges of a 'headman.' In any village at least one man—and often two, three, or occasionally even more—is referred to by the term *nokma*, which is generally—though badly—translated as 'headman.' These *nokma*s wear no symbol of their position which would permit a stranger to recognize them, but any villager can name and point out the individuals in his village who rate this title.

To explain how a man becomes *nokma*, it is first necessary to refer once more to the lineage structure of the village. It is simplest to consider villages with a single main lineage first. Just as one household of each cooperating group is considered to be senior by virtue of the fact that all the other households have "come out" from it, one household is the most senior of the whole village, since all of the houses ultimately "came out" from it. The process may, of course, have involved many stages, but the senior household is ordinarily considered to be that of the first *nokma*. Normally the *nokma*, like any other man, looks for a 'nephew,' that is, a younger man from his own lineage, to come and be his son-in-law and heir. In this case, the 'nephew' not only becomes the heir to the house and property but also succeeds to the 'headmanship' when his father-in-law dies. Inevitably the *nokma*s of many villages have grown up in a different village, and belong to a different sib and to the opposite moiety from the people of the main village lineage. A *nokma* should, however, be a member of the same lineage and from the same village as the previous *nokma*, so generally a succession of 'headmen' are members of one village and lineage by descent but hold the status of 'headman' in another village by virtue of being married to the women who are successively chosen as heiress in the senior house of the village.

The 'headmanship' is thought of as adhering more closely to the house than to any individual person. All the symbols of office go with the house and not with the man. The most important of the symbols is a particular kind of drum so heavily endowed with supernatural power that no one else in the village dares to keep it in his house. It is not necessarily dangerous to use, for at village festivals the drum is carried from house to house and then anybody may beat it. Funeral parties will even carry it to another village if they should go to pay condolences after a death in that village, but it can only be kept permanently in the *nokma*'s house. The house itself is constructed with specially carved posts which are flattened on two sides instead of being left round as in all other houses; and when a house of a *nokma* is thatched, special little straw animals decorate the roof. Even the term *nokma* is etymologically related to that for 'house' or 'household'—i.e. *nok*; while *-ma* is a suffix which in some contexts means 'big' or 'large'; thus *nokma* literally means the 'big house,' though it is used to refer to the man of that house.

It has already been pointed out that a single village often has more than one *nokma*. If so, one of them is always considered to be the "first" *nokma* and the others are considered to be secondary to him. The ranking of *nokma*s may conceivably have been encouraged by the government's custom of recording only a single *nokma*'s name for certain official purposes. But while in some doubtful cases two *nokma*s of about equal stature may have been given inequality in this way, it seems more likely that the inequality of *nokma*s and the requirement that one be considered senior has been inherent in Garo social organization and is not simply a response to foreign rule. If two lineages are found in the same village, each always has its own *nokma*, the man of its senior house. Since the *nokma*ship is acquired by marrying into a lineage, the *nokma* can never belong to the lineage of which he is *nokma*. So in Songmagri, where there are two lineages, the first *nokma* is the Chambigong *nokma* and is himself a Manda Sangma, but like his father-in-law he comes from another village. The Manda *nokma*, on the other hand, is a Chambigong of the Songmagri lineage of Chambigong. Even if a *nokma* comes from the opposite lineage of a two-lineage village, he is *nokma* only because of his marriage and never simply because of his own lineage affiliation.

Even villages with only one lineage may have two or more *nokma*s. In Rengsanggri the second *nokma* is Jengnon, who is himself an Agidok from Waramgri, as were his father-in-law and his grandfather-in-law before him. He is married to the woman who is heiress in the house that is considered the second oldest in the village. Jengnon is explicitly considered a *nokma*, but he is unquestionably second to Gajang, the first *nokma*, who is himself a Manda from Songmagri. Jengnon's house does not happen to have all the symbols of *nokma*ship, such as the specially carved house posts or the special drum, though in other villages more than one house is sometimes equipped with these things.

Perhaps the most important single characteristic of a *nokma* is the possession of titles to land. The land which surrounds a village is divided into numerous patches, and titles to these patches are typically distributed among a few of the richest households of the village, including those of the *nokma*s. A plot of land to which a man holds title is known as *a'king*, and a *nokma* who holds a title is known as an *a'king nokma*. Titles to *a'king* can be bought and sold among members of the village;

however, at the present time sale is unusual, and land titles often stay in the same family for generations, always being inherited intact by the heir and heiress of the last title-holders. Prices in the past have varied from 25 to 75 rupees for the amount of land suitable for one family's cultivation; on the other hand, titles even today are sometimes purchased with brass gongs instead of money.

Holding a title brings almost no direct benefit, for the title-holder has no more right to use the land than anyone else in the village. Nevertheless it confers great prestige, and titles like, heirlooms and jewelry, can be an important repository of savings. They can be converted into other forms of wealth and used to tide the household over poor years, as well as to give stability to its position of wealth in the village. Titles are considered even safer than ownership of heirlooms, since heirlooms can be stolen or destroyed. Moreover, title to some land is a necessary prerequisite for being considered a *nokma*, though land title alone is not enough. Four men in Rengsanggri had title to some land: Gajang, Jengnon, Nanggan, and Bano; but the first two of these held the most, and only they were considered *nokma*s. Bano was not a wealthy man, though the household he inherited had formerly been much wealthier. He performed no cere-monies appropriate to *nokma*ship, and people suggested that he might soon be forced to sell some of his land titles. Nanggan was much richer. He held title to more land than Bano, but still not as much as either Jengnon or Gajang. Nanggan did not perform the ceremonies of a *nokma* or possess any of the sym-bols of one; but the main obstacle to his being considered a *nokma* was that his household had such little genealogical depth. Nanggan purchased some of his title from one Rojang, who was from a family that had formerly been very wealthy, but who was gradually forced to sell some of his land to fellow villagers, and eventually moved away from Rengsanggri. Nanggan himself was an heir, but his father-in-law had been a non-heir who had married a girl from what is now Jengnon's household and lived separately. In another generation or two, if Nanggan's heir and his heir's heir continue to maintain the wealth of the household, they will be obvious candidates for *nokma*ship, and may assume the symbols and obligations of the office.

Jengnon and Gajang have title to more land than anyone else in the village and are both occupants of ancient households. Jengnon, however, performs few of the *nokma*'s ceremonies and does not maintain the symbols of office, such as the drum. I was told the following grim story to explain his reasons for not keeping a drum. Several generations ago one of Jengnon's predecessors, Songnat, had considered acquiring one, and finally announced that he would obtain it the following day; but before he had the chance he was bitten by a tiger and died. Later another man of this house, Tonga (Jengnon's wife's mother's mother's father), also made up his mind to obtain the drum, but a bear bit him. Tonga did not die, but he was badly hurt and made no more moves to acquire the drum. Tonga's heir Banjang in his turn announced that he would try for a drum, but he was killed by an elephant; and understandably no one in that house has since attempted to assume this powerful symbol of office. Nevertheless, in view of the land titles held and the great age of the household, Jengnon, the present heir of these unfortunate men, is universally considered to be the second *nokma* of the village.

It is more usual for each *nokma* to keep a sacred drum, and ordinarily all those who do so perform the ceremony of *satsatsoa* at the *Wangala* festival. Before a household first acquires the drum, the man should have a dream indicating that it is appropriate, otherwise he will die. Once acquired, however, the drum, like all aspects of *nokma*ship, may be inherited by the heir without any additional dreams. Gajang, who held title to the most land of all, successfully kept the drum and was the undisputed first *nokma* of Rengsanggri. He was regarded as holding his land by inheritance from long ago, even from the first settlement of the land. Every other household in Rengsanggri was regarded as having originally "come out" of Gajang's household, or as the people often phrased it, Gajang was 'father-in-law' (*obite*) to all the people of the village.

To be considered a *nokma* one must first of all be the occupant of a house with great genealogical depth, from which many other households have "come out," and also possess substantial land titles. One ought to be at least wealthy enough to own sufficient gongs to be played at feasts. Ideally one should also assume at least some of the symbols of the office and perform some of its duties. Titles, responsibilities, and symbols of office all descend to the son-in-law of the former *nokma*.

Superficially, marriage to a particular girl seems to be an extraordinarily poor way of recruitment to the 'headmanship.' The *nokma* himself is the man with the most direct voice in choosing his successor, just as any man chooses his own heir. It is true that kinsmen take a slightly greater interest in helping to choose the boy who is destined to become *nokma*, but this is only a degree greater than the interest they show in the case of any important or wealthy household. The village as a whole has no real voice in the selection of its prospective *nokma*. This matters very little, however, because the *nokma*ship does not in reality confer much authority. The *nokma* does not direct the villagers in their work or make many more decisions than other men, and the duties and burdens of *nokma*ship may even loom larger to the candidate than the prerogatives. The duties consist primarily of playing a ceremonial role to mark important points in the annual cycle, such as planting, harvest, and the time when the villagers begin to clear the jungle. Then the *nokma* must act as ceremonial leader, performing sacrifices and reciting incantations to ensure vigor for the crops and prosperity for the village. These are important duties, but not such as require much in the way of authority or ability to make important decisions. At many of the sacrifices the *nokma* is expected to provide the sacrificial animal himself. This brings a degree of prestige, but may also be a considerable burden on the household economy. If a *nokma* is really unable to furnish the animal, other villagers may assist him, but it is always preferable for the *nokma* to provide it himself. In Rengsanggri the two *nokma*s sacrificed at the *den'birsia* ceremony in alternate years. This alternation was viewed mainly as a sharing of the burdens rather than the privileges of office. The other sacrifices were performed by the first *nokma* only.

Garos maintain that most bachelors do not welcome the prospect of being chosen as a *nokma*. When brought in as an heir to a *nokma*, a boy may appear as reluctant as any prospective son-in-law; but since his relatives all urge him to accept, and his lineage mates and the men of the village to which he is taken encourage him, assuring him that he is capable enough, sooner or later it is possible to find a boy to undertake the job. Later, when his father-in-law dies, he will have to perform the village ceremonies himself. Gajang said that he did not know how at first, but that everybody helped him and taught him and so he was gradually learning.

A *nokma* who performs sacrifices should belong to a wealthy household; and if he has title to considerable tracts of land, this implies wealth. Land titles alone do not provide mobile wealth that can readily be converted into sacrificial animals, and to sell titles for such purposes would rapidly undermine one of the bases for the *nokma*ship. Still, in many villages the first *nokma* has the wealthiest household of all. A bit of extra effort is made on the part of all concerned to ensure that the heir of a *nokma*, the prospective successor to that position, is an able and responsible individual, capable of the hard work necessary to maintain the household and fulfill his duties—though Garos admit that they cannot always predict from the qualities of a young man what his status as an adult will be. The astute choice of able youths does not provide a sufficient explanation for the reasonably consistent wealth of *nokma*s; and there are moreover, ways in which an inpecunious *nokma* can escape his duties.

Occasionally a man who is *nokma* finds himself unable to

carry out the duties of his office. He may feel that he does not have the financial resources to provide the sacrificial animals or the personal qualifications for the job. He may also feel that for some reason the supernatural powers of the drum he keeps in his house are too strong for him and may be the cause of a run of bad luck or a series of deaths in his family. For a time the villagers are likely to help him and encourage him to continue his duties, but if circumstances overwhelm him, he may abandon the drum and cease to perform the rituals. Since the welfare of the village demands that somebody carry out the sacrifices, another man must assume the responsibility. No well-defined procedure for choosing a new *nokma* exists, for a shift in *nokma*ship is hardly likely to be required more than once in several generations. Probably a second *nokma*, if there is one, can take over the responsibilities without difficulty. For a time, perhaps for several generations, the villagers will remember that the household of the former *nokma* was considered to be older than that of the present one, but given the expectation that the *nokma*'s house should properly be the house in the village from which all the other houses have "come out," sufficient time will ensure that the new *nokma*'s house will come to be regarded as the oldest and the genealogical claims of the people will be rearranged. I did not witness the actual transfer of any *nokma*ship but I did know of a few villages where the present *nokma*'s house was known to be the junior of another house, which had given up its title to *nokma*ship within the last generation or two. In Songmagri Changjan had given up the title of the Manda *nokma* because of a combination of poverty and misfortune. It was still remembered that this house had once been the house of a *nokma*, and there were even suggestions that its present occupant might once more assume the duties of the office, though nothing concrete was being done about the matter. Donen, the man of an only slightly less ancient house, had come to be considered the most important Manda *nokma* (he being a Chambigong), and performed the required rituals. The other case of a switch of *nokma*ship with which I was well acquainted was a modern one in which the man who should rightfully have been *nokma* of the village had become a Christian and so could no longer participate in the old ceremonial life of the village. Since there were many non-Christians remaining in the village, somebody had to perform the ceremonies, and the man from one of the senior households in the village took over the job. He described his position as "like a *nokma*" but modestly refused to give himself the actual title.

It is easy for me to imagine that under certain circumstances Nanggan could take over the duties of *nokma* in Rengsanggri. If for some reason both Gajang and Jengnon felt unable to continue, the villagers would surely accept ceremonials performed by Nanggan. True, Nanggan's house is not an ancient one, but he is a wealthy man, holds some land title, and is respected by everyone. After a few generations people would probably begin to talk as if their households had "come out" of Nanggan's and eventually, even if they were not aware of what they were doing, they would probably rearrange their genealogies accordingly.

Since a certain amount of prestige is connected with the *nokma*ship, it is by no means a completely unattractive position, though the office has no obvious privileges. One must have a big house so that the villagers can be entertained at the times of sacrifice; but most of the cost of building it falls upon the *nokma* himself, and a large house brings few advantages to the family. A *nokma* must sacrifice more often and feed more people than others. No proportionate compensation balances these economically burdensome duties, but providing food always brings prestige. All rich people justify their wealth by sharing it with others in the form of feasts. The *nokma* is likely to be the greatest feast-giver of all and consequently may have the greatest prestige, and it is perhaps chiefly for this reason that men can be found who are willing to be *nokma*. Some men may even be delighted to become *nokma*, and to use its opportunities as a

means for gaining status and prestige; but the ideals of the
society would never permit them to admit this openly or
explicitly.

The only way in which ambition for office ever becomes mani-
fest is in disputes over land titles. These may occur in a
scrambled way so that each holder has title to many small
patches scattered among the others; indeed, a village can
expand if its *nokma* purchases title to what had formerly
belonged to the *nokma* of a neighboring village. Except in
extreme circumstances, however, villagers would object to their
*nokma*'s selling land to another village, since this would alienate
the land on which they depend. Even the district courts appear
generally to have held that land title could not be sold without
the consent of the villagers. Since men ordinarily cultivate land
whose title is held by one of their fellow villagers, there is
clearly an opportunity for quarreling, and land titles have
occasionally been the subject of acrimonious disputes. The
quarrels are described as being between the *nokma*s, but the
*nokma*s are to some extent only the symbolic figureheads in the
persons of which opposing villages press their claims. In recent
years, when land has been purchased by the *nokma* of one
village from a title-holder in another village, the villagers have
all contributed to the purchase price. In such a case the *nokma*
may still be cited as the title-holder, the man in whose name the
purchase is made; but the villagers understandably feel that
they all have a common right to its use and to a part in any
decision concerning its resale. Land sales are so uncommon that
it is impossible to say how typical such contributions are, or
whether the Garos have any sound basis for their claims that
formerly the *nokma*s themselves paid the price. Possibly in pre-
British times land disputes were a principal cause of inter-
village warfare; but if so this has been forgotten, and the picture
has been hopelessly muddled today by the failure of the government to recognize more than one *nokma* in each village. The
outline maps which have been drawn by the government gener-

ally show the boundaries between villages fairly well, but they never show the individual plots within the village. Even most villagers are quite uncertain about some of the boundaries. No less a person than Gajang, the first *nokma*, had to confer with his mother-in-law on a few points when I asked him about them. In the absence of written records there is plenty of opportunity for quarreling over the boundaries. No serious quarrels had arisen for a number of years in the areas I knew, but villagers did recognize disagreements over land title as a possible source of dispute—unlike the division of land into plots for cultivation, about which quarrels seemed quite inconceivable.

It is possible that aggressive individuals have sometimes used the position of *nokma* as a means to power. The office does contain possibilities for the acquisition of great prestige through feast-giving, and this in turn grants influence in local decision-making, but the potentialities of the office for either constant quarrels or large-scale aggrandizement should not be exaggerated. The title-holder receives only one direct benefit from his title, and this is financially insignificant. If an outsider wants to cultivate land within the village's territory, he is supposed to pay an annual fee (*a'wil*) usually said to be one rupee per plot, to the title-holder. This is at best little more than a token payment, and it is rarely paid since few people cultivate outside their own villages. Nepalis who have settled in the hills and who wish to obtain grazing privileges for their cattle may pay the *nokma* some money which the Garo interpret as *a'wil*, but the amounts are not large.

The first *nokma* is described as the man who apportions the scrub land among the families so that it can be cleared and eventually cultivated by them. Plots must somehow be distributed each year, and if this were literally the *nokma*'s job it could be an important one; but the apportioning is done more on the basis of tradition than by reassignment. Which plot a man cultivated eight or ten years ago counts heavily, and he can generally claim the same plot again. Although there must always be a few readjustments, I never heard of a single dispute about the apportioning of fields, in marked contrast to the quarrels over titles. The *nokma* therefore does not really make many decisions about the distribution of the land among the villagers, although this is formally defined as his job. It is firmly denied that title to the land gives the *nokma* the right to apportion it. Where several *nokmas* have title to different parts of a village's lands, such title never gives them individual rights to apportion their own. Each may have a voice in the division of all the land, as do all prestigeful men, whether *nokmas* or not, but no man has sole authority.

Land used by the villagers does not even correspond precisely to that to which its *nokmas* hold title, for between closely associated villages the plots of the *nokmas* of the various villages may be somewhat scrambled. For instance, the *nokma* of Songmagri had title to part of the land used by the Rengsanggri people, while the first *nokma* of Rengsanggri held title to some land which was used by Misimagri people. These three villages are all considered to be closely related, however, having branched from a common parent village, and such scrambling of land titles and use would not occur among unrelated villages.

The *nokma* also has the responsibility of designating the day for village ceremonies, but in this he cannot depart from the technical requirements of the agricultural cycle. He generally waits to make sure everyone's work has advanced to the proper point, and he also listens to the suggestions of other men.

Beyond these responsibilities, the *nokma* does not have any formal duties or privileges. The subsistence activities of the village are carried on by the household. Larger work groups are organized traditionally, with jobs apportioned almost exclusively according to sex and age, so that no one needs to direct work activities. Since the organization of the village requires little concentration of authority, its ceremonial leadership can be assigned according to the unusual method of inheritance by a son-in-law.

Physically the village is unambiguously distinct from its neighbors, and it certainly is an important unit of the society. It is, in the first place, a kinship group since residence in the village must, except in rare cases, be based either upon descent, in a particular matrilineal lineage, or upon marriage to somebody in that group. Like the smaller cooperating group, a Garo village *must* include both some of the men and most of the women of the core lineage (or lineages, if it has two) together with their spouses and children. People feel a strong tie to their village, and when strangers meet, one of their first questions is likely to be, "What is your village?" In this case a man gives the village where he lives at the time, the village generally of his wife, and not necessarily of his lineage. While the burning of the fields is the only activity demanding coordinated action, the various households of the village synchronize their entire agricultural cycle by means of the many village ceremonies. Some tasks must be finished and others may not be begun before one of the ceremonies. The 'headman' performs some of the ceremonial rituals, and while others are carried out individually by the households, all agree beforehand to do so on the same day. The village is more easily defined than either the lineage or the cooperating group. It has visible boundaries and is given a name by the people. Men and women can be unambiguously assigned to membership in a particular village, as they cannot always be assigned to the smaller groups.

## VILLAGE CLUSTERS, SIBS, AND MOIETIES

In Garo society the village is the largest group of which all the members regularly join in cooperative activities, but more extensive organizations are also recognized. First, several neighboring villages may be considered to be related. One of these is usually believed to have been the original village from which the founders of the other "daughter" villages moved. In many cases there seems no reason to doubt that the tradition corresponds with historical events. To judge by their genealogies, the original founders of Rengsanggri may have come from Songmagri around 1880, soon after the British first occupied the district. The peace which the British imposed on the hills may have made it possible to live in smaller and more scattered villages than the people had formerly done. Perhaps most of the groups of linked villages that are now to be found have resulted from the splitting of larger villages during the period of British rule. The difficulty of access to the fields would make more dispersed settlement desirable so long as enemies did not threaten. Nowadays villages only rarely move, split up, or die out. I saw just one village in the process of being moved. This was an undertaking that was destined to last for three years, since the villagers could not muster sufficient labor to rebuild more than a third of their houses in a single year. The move was being made solely for the sake of the water supply, which was failing at the old site.

Splitting up of villages is also a slow process. Just a few years before my visit several households moved out of Rengsanggri to the opposite end of the land that was considered to belong to that village. The reasons for this shift were of modern origin. A few of the people were considering adopting Christianity and wished to live separately, while others wished to practice new techniques of agriculture and to live in a place accessible to land suitable for wet rice and for pineapple groves. But the way in which they left seems likely to have been similar to earlier village divisions. A few households shifted their residence and were considered for a time simply as an outlying part of Rengsanggri. Already when I was there, however, this location was known by a different village name, Asonanggri, and seemed destined to become a fully separate village. Nevertheless, in spite of occasional shifts and splits, most village sites are essentially permanent. People may be born, spend their whole lives, and die in the same village location.

The various components of a "village cluster," as these

groups of related and neighboring villages can be called, generally include a few lineages which belong to the same sib. Thus Rengsanggri and Songmagri both have lineages of the Chambigong sib, and the Rengsanggri Chambigongs are considered to be ultimately derived from the Songmagri Chambigongs. Songmagri, however, also includes a lineage belonging to the Manda Sangma sib. Many Manda men from Songmagri, including the first *nokma*, have married into Rengsanggri, but few women of that sib live there and Rengsanggri is not considered to have a lineage of the Manda sib associated with it, even though this village is still closely associated with the mother village. The people of Rengsanggri simply say that it happened that households with Chambigong women settled first in the location of Rengsanggri and so that is still the village's only legitimate lineage.

The village cluster has little except sentimental importance. Its constituent villages are close enough to make visiting easy, so the people are apt to know each other fairly well. Kinship unites the villages to each other more closely than to completely unrelated neighbors. If a man is unable to find an heir from his own village, he will accept a boy from a different village of the same village cluster so long as he belongs to the proper sib. People occasionally, but not commonly, move back and forth between such related villages.

More important than these somewhat minor matters is the fact that the government, in attempting to define 'headmanship' and to draw the boundaries of villages, has often paid more attention to the village cluster than to the single village. Government sketch maps officially define the boundaries between the village clusters, but the boundaries between the component villages are often simply a matter of understanding among the people of the villages. Even more important, the government may recognize just one main first *nokma* of the whole village cluster. This is the man with whom the government deals if it hopes to have something done, but the arrangement has little

relation to the feelings of the villagers about their own leadership.

The sib is a much larger group than the village lineage or
even than the associated lineages of a village cluster. A sib is
most realistically referred to as a name group, since giving of a
name is its only real function. Each Garo has three names, and
for complete identification gives his personal name first, his sib
name second, and his moiety name last. The personal name may
be changed after a spell of bad luck, but sib and moiety names
are never changed. Second and more specific names are occasionally appended to the sib name. The members of the main
lineage of Rengsanggri said that they were Chambigong-anil,
and while they could mention many other village lineages that
were also Chambigong-anil, other Chambigongs fell into other
subgroups. These appended names are used only rarely and are
little more than nicknames. A few sibs have the same name as
villages, but it is not clear whether the sibs were named for the
villages or vice versa, and only a few of the names have any
recognizable meaning. Although marriage within both the sib
and moiety is considered improper, people feel much stronger
about marriage within a sib, and common sib membership is
thought to confer a remote kinship tie. A person from a distant
village with whom no real kinship can be traced can be naturally
and rapidly assigned a place by virtue of his sib name, so long as
this name occurs locally as well. Two men whose wives have the
same sib name, for instance, may refer to each other by the same
term used by the husbands of two sisters. In the rare case when
a man cannot find an heir in his own village cluster, he may
prefer a man with the same sib name to somebody with an
entirely different name. However, many thousands of people
with the same sib name are scattered over many miles of territory and they cannot possibly all act in any cooperative way.

In all the Garo Hills several hundred sib names occur, and in
some parts of the district more are found in a single village than
is true in the area around Rengsanggri or in the whole western

portion of the hills. Most of the sibs are more or less localized, however, being found in a good many villages in one section of the hills but being rare or absent in other regions. Some of the sibs of the Rengsanggri area, including Chambigong—which may be the most widespread single sib among the Garos—are found throughout the western third of the district, but others are more localized. Rengsanggri itself includes people with only four sib names: Chambigong, which belongs to the Marak moiety; and Agidok, Manda, and Tigite, which all belong to the Sangma moiety. Many nearby villages have two additional Marak sibs—Bolwari and Rangsa—but these six include almost everybody in the villages with which Rengsanggri has regular contact or from which marriage partners are likely to be taken.

Most of the sibs of the Garos, and all of those found in the area of Rengsanggri, fall into one or the other of the two exogamous groups which the Garos label as Sangma and Marak, respectively. All relatives therefore fall into one of two classes, which are systematically reflected in the kinship terminology. Mother's brother and father's sister's husband, for instance, fall into the same moiety and are called by the same term. Moiety exogamy implies that people in each kinship position must belong to the appropriate moiety, and terminological distinctions often parallel the personal relations between relatives. Men from opposite moieties occasionally tease each other. They sometimes say that the Maraks are stronger, but that the Sangmas are more intelligent. This is considered to be a good joke, but is never taken seriously. At some ceremonies men perform individual dances with a sword and shield, during which they must shout out the name of their own moiety. This mild joking rivalry is not much emphasized, and marriage regulation is the most important aspect of the moiety division.

Conservative Garos still feel strongly about moiety exogamy. Nobody in Rengsanggri had defied this rule, though there were couples in near-by villages who had, to the mixed amusement and mild disgust of the Rengsanggri people. It may be that among the more educated Garos the rule is relaxing, but even with them it is still followed in the great majority of cases. A council of Garo Baptists recently passed a motion to the effect that they would not consider marriage within the moiety as improper, but that marriage within the sib would continue to be so considered. There is no body among non-Christians who could pass such a judgment. Everyone can cite a few cases of breach of exogamous rules, and even of marriage, or what amounts to common-law marriage, within the sib. It is difficult to get explicit comments on why exogamy is desirable other than the vague "It is the custom." However, marriage within the moiety or sib would confuse the over-all kinship pattern, particularly the relation of lineages to one another. The Garos say that the replacement of spouses and the obtaining of heirs is impossible if one marries within the moiety. Marriage usually sets up the permament link which connects two lineages, presumably forever. This is felt to be impossible if marriage is within the moiety, and even worse if within the sib. As the individual sees this, it means that if his spouse dies, the lineage of his spouse will not provide him with a replacement, and a man will not be able to persuade a nephew to come to be his heir. These are serious matters, and the few couples who do marry within their own moiety or sib do so in defiance of these threats. If they are determined enough and can face down the disapproval of their neighbors, they will eventually be allowed to live together and may do so peacefully for many years; but they will never have the protection and support that their kinship system could provide if they had married according to its rules.

The Garos of Rengsanggri reckon kinship in ever widening circles—from the immediate family to the cooperating group and lineage, to the village and village cluster, to the sib and moiety. Ultimately, the system embraces everybody with whom the people have any regular contact, though this may be far beyond the boundary within which exact kinship can be traced.

At the outermost reaches of the system it is enough to know a person's moiety, sex, and approximate age relative to one's own in order to assign a kinship category to him, and though such people will not ordinarily address each other by kinship terms or refer to each other primarily as kinsmen, they will, if questioned, have no trouble in explaining what kinship terms are appropriate. There is no boundary beyond which kinship ceases; it simply grows gradually weaker as one deals with more remotely related individuals.

# X

# The Settlement of Disputes

PROCEDURE

THE EARLIER CHAPTERS MAY HAVE left the impression that obligations are met by Garos with exemplary regularity, and that each man peacefully plays his part in village life with little or no threat of force. So idyllic a picture would certainly be an oversimplification, for while Garo behavior has its regularities, variability exists as well. A degree of variability need not interfere with the ability of the members of the society to cooperate with each other, but variability must have its limits. Still, while everyone must be able to make some dependable predictions about the behavior of the people around him, no society ever succeeds in reducing the behavior of its members to complete uniformity or predictability—partly, no doubt, because of the inherent biological differences among men. In practice the limits of permitted behavior are difficult to draw. People continually step beyond the limit and every society provides means of punishing them, and thereby of pushing them back in the direction of acceptable behavior. A whole battery of sanctions can be mobilized with which to punish nonconforming behavior. Ridicule, social disapproval, threats of supernatural punishment, withdrawal of reciprocal services, or, ultimately, physical force all serve to keep people in line. Garos fear each other's ridicule enough to make laughter an effective sanction in some areas of behavior. It has been pointed out how certain relatives avoid each other because they know that others will laugh if they do not. Ridicule effectively enforces these rather formalized kinship relations, though no other sanction could be applied if people defied the rule. In countless other instances, significant or trivial, people behave in ways designed to avoid the ridicule or disapproval of their neighbors. The manner of dress, the etiquette of entertaining, the tempo of work in the fields, are all in part regulated according to standards enforceable by no other sanction. Sometimes, of course, other sanctions are built into the social organization. Garos must make sure that they will continue to receive the services of others. This encourages men to continue in cooperative work activities, for if a man does not cooperate he knows that he cannot expect help in return.

Occasionally more stringent measures must be applied, and the Garos have effective procedures for directing force when it must be used. We can consider legal sanctions to be those which are applied by legitimate authorities and which have the threat of force behind them. Such sanctions are applied to punish several types of illegal behavior. It is impossible today to determine with certainty the methods which the Garos used to settle disputes before they became incorporated into British India. In my final chapter I shall make some guesses as to what these may have been, but in the present discussion I will consider only the situation of recent years. The Garos have been incorporated into a larger governmental system for almost a century, and it is absurd to look upon them today as an independent tribe. Certainly their present legal system cannot be understood without reference to the larger political systems of which the Garos are a part.

For almost one hundred years there has existed in Assam a political division known as the Garo Hills District. Today its relation to the State of Assam and to the Indian nation are defined by the Indian constitution. The Deputy Commissioner's office established by the British continues as the chief local arm of the state administration, supervising state schools, roads, and forests. Certain legal problems, including such major crimes as murder and treason, remain under the jurisdiction of its court. In the time of British rule the Deputy Commissioner was always British; since then he has been a plains Indian, usually a member of the Indian Civil Service. The constitution, however, provided for the establishment of a new District Council, to be composed of about twenty members elected from several constituencies into which the district was divided. This council elects from among its members a "chief executive member" just as the parliament in New Delhi chooses the national prime minister. Jurisdiction of Garo customary law was transferred to the District Council, and courts were established to judge disputes covered by this law. The collection of various taxes, including the important house tax, was likewise transferred, and the District Council began to build roads, to open schools, and to administer forests. In 1956, the jurisdictional boundaries between it and the Deputy Commissioner's office had not yet become completely clear.

The Garo Hills District is divided into fifty-five administrative districts known as *eleka*s, each of which includes about twenty villages. A petty magistrate with the title of *loskor* is appointed for each *eleka*. Formerly the appointment was made by the Deputy Commissioner's office; but today, though many appointees of the Deputy Commissioner remain in power, the power of appointment has shifted to the District Council. Both departments have used the same method to choose a *loskor*. Since the higher levels of government have not been intimately acquainted with the local situation in the *eleka*, they have called a meeting of the governmentally recognized *nokma*s of the villages in the area, and these men have voted for the man that they would prefer as *loskor*. The decision of the *nokma*s has not been mandatory on the official responsible for the appointment, but in practice seems generally to have been followed. The *nokma*s, in turn, seem to have been guided principally by the bribes given by the aspirants to the office—an attractive one since it offers numerous possibilities for financial gain. Haphazard though this method seems, it has recruited some remarkably able men to the office of *loskor*. To bribe *nokmas* successfully requires considerable wealth, and wealth brings respect and influence. Bribing also implies skill at manipulating the levers of authority. By and large only a clever man would be likely to succeed, and he could hardly succeed without already possessing wealth and hence the respect of his neighbors. The office has attracted vigorous and intelligent, but not always high-principled men. Few *loskors* have been Christians, and this has meant that few have had much formal education. They have been virtually the only influential Garos who were not Christians. Whether or not the choice of non-Christians was a deliberate governmental policy I could not determine, but it has probably had the effect of slowing down the rate of change of certain laws, particularly those concerning family obligations. Many Christians look with little sympathy upon some of the older family customs, and a Christian *loskor* might have encouraged some innovations. Once appointed, the position of *loskor* has in practice been a permanent one.

The *loskor* has several duties. He collects the house tax within his district, keeping a fixed portion of this as his own payment, and he organizes work parties to keep the roads open. His most important duty, however, is to supervise and try to settle legal disputes. The *loskor* sometimes appoints one or more assistants called *sordars*, to whom the District Council pays an annual stipend of 100 Rupees, together with a shirt and a pair of short pants. Saljing, who lived in Rengsanggri, was a *sordar*; but not every village had one, and a *sordar* does not have jurisdiction over a particular village. As a general assistant to the *loskor* he may assist in collecting information about a dispute, and in petty matters a *sordar* may sit as representative of the *loskor* and preside at a trial. The *loskor*ship demands a large part of a man's time, but a *sordar* spends most of his time working in his fields like his neighbors.

In theory it is the *loskor* who, as presiding officer at a meeting to settle a dispute, passes judgment upon the rights and wrongs of the argument. Often the *loskor* is in no position to do more than guide the consensus of opinion among the men who meet, but he does put the government's stamp of approval on the decision. He must act well within the bounds of customary law; but if the evidence is contradictory or unusually complex, the *loskor* may exert considerable influence toward the settlement of the dispute in one way or another. Today the *loskor*s are powerful men. Any decision of the *loskor* may be appealed to the higher courts of the district, but the procedure of appeal is lengthy and expensive, and it is certainly more convenient to settle a case at the local level if that is possible. Decisions of both the District Council court and the Deputy Commissioner's court can be appealed to the high court of Assam, though for most Garos the procedure is prohibitively expensive.

### FALSE ACCUSATION

The pettiest trial I ever attended was in some ways the most illuminating. A Rengsanggri youth named Mingcheng was reported to have insulted a newly married husband named Wilson by asking him "Why did you marry an old wife?"— implying by this that he, Mingcheng, had had sexual relations with her before she was married. I was assured that if both of these youths had been unmarried, a similar comment would have been accepted as a joke; but Wilson did not take it as a joke, and actually believed Mingcheng's insinuation. Wilson went to his wife, Nengji, who when told of the accusation was also upset, and maintained that it had no basis in reality. The young husband and wife felt that this was a serious enough insult to require formal litigation, and so they reported it to Saljing, the *sordar* who lived in Rengsanggri.

Saljing called a meeting of the relatives both of Mingcheng and of Nengji and Wilson, and they all assembled in Nengji's house one evening. The men sat to the back of the fireplace, where men always sit on public occasions, while women crowded around the front. Everybody chatted amiably until Wilson began to tell his story, whereupon they all quieted down to listen attentively. Squatting beside the fireplace, Wilson told what Mingcheng had said and how it had temporarily caused misunderstanding between himself and his wife. Mingcheng then came back to the rear of the house and as Wilson had done, squatting down by the fireplace, calmly told his side of the story. He did not try to deny what he had said, but simply tried to make it clear that he intended it only as a joke. Next, and last, Nengji spoke. I never saw a Garo witness look nervous, and Nengji spoke out without apparent shyness or hesitation in spite of the fact that about twenty men, mostly a good deal older than she, were listening carefully to all that she said, and that her honor was to some extent at stake. Nengji corroborated Wilson's story, and when the *sordar* asked if Mingcheng's statement had angered her, she said yes. A rumble of assent arose from the men who were sitting about her, indicating their view that of course she would be upset by such a statement. The tenor of the meeting was entirely friendly. Relatives of both parties sat in the same circle, and far from assuming any threatening attitude, they seemed united in their desire to settle the dispute of these young people rationally and permanently. Everyone listened attentively, but one man or another occasionally interrupted to ask a question, and others would mutter agreement when a point was made. The *sordar* unmistakably presided. He did much of the questioning, and once or twice he even suggested that the others should quiet down so that the witnesses could be heard; but he was hardly autocratic, and several times he leaned toward people around him, saying "Don't you think so?" or "Would that be proper?" His role was to guide the discussion and encourage the group to reach a consensus, which he could then summarize as the decision of the court.

When Nengji finished, the *sordar* suggested that perhaps fifteen rupees should be paid as compensation and asked Nengji whether that would satisfy her, or whether she would hold out for more. Nengji agreed that the sum would be adequate. Following this, two of the older members of Mingcheng's lineage, both of whom had moved away from Rengsanggri to live with their wives but had come back for the trial, proceeded one after another, to beat Mingcheng. The first 'uncle' put on a vigorous display of being furious with the boy. He struck him hard on the back and shouted at him for several minutes, accusing him of ignoring elementary standards of decency. Mingcheng endured this blustering and beating without movement or outcry. He simply squatted by the fireplace and held on to one of its posts while receiving the blows on his back. Finally, other men stirred from their silence and at first quietly, but gradually more insistently, suggested that he had had enough, until the 'uncle,' still muttering deprecations, returned to his place. The other 'uncle' rose and beat him, but for a shorter time, and several of Mingcheng's other relatives made derisive comments to him about his bad behavior.

When his relatives had finished with him, several of them stepped outside to collect the fifteen rupees for his compensation. When after a short time they returned with the money, the *sordar* again asked the girl if she would take this money in full compensation for the insult. By this time she had consulted with her own relatives, and now she said no, she would not take it, that she would decline any monetary compensation and was satisfied with the knowledge that her honor had been publicly vindicated and that Mingcheng had been proved wrong. This precipitated the greatest turmoil of the evening. The relatives of the boy demanded that the relatives of the girl accept the money, but the latter, especially the girl's elderly grandfather, kept insisting that they would not take it. Clearly honor was more valuable than a few rupees. To me, sitting on the sidelines, it seemed clear from the beginning that the girl and her relatives could not be forced into accepting the money against their will, but the others had to demonstrate their willingness to fulfill their obligations. The argument was loud and vigorous, but tempers were never frayed, let alone lost. Arguers joked with each other even while disputing. After first trying to give ten rupees if they couldn't give fifteen, they gave in to the obduracy of the others and the argument died down. The honor of the girl's family was vindicated, while Mingcheng's family had demonstrated its own willingness to compensate for their member's error. Mingcheng had been beaten and publicly disgraced.

In the end one rupee was given to the *sordar* as an informal payment for his services, and the rest of the fifteen rupees were returned to the relatives of Mingcheng. The girl's own household had to bear the expense of providing rice beer and tobacco for the crowd. After no more than three-quarters of an hour the case was settled, and people returned to their own homes. Mingcheng went home temporarily subdued, but not permanently disgraced.

The attitudes displayed in this case are typical of many more significant Garo court cases. The attempt is always to find a formula that will satisfy the honor of all the parties and restore peace to the community. Of course in more serious cases feelings run higher, and divergent points of view may not be so easily reconciled. Some complex cases are appealed to the district courts. Very rarely disputes may leave such bitterness that resolution can come only if some people move away permanently from their village and in the past some of these disputes undoubtedly led to war; but litigation does not usually end in such extremes. Most trials do lead to the settlement that they are designed to achieve.

The *loskor*, or whoever presides at the hearing of a case, must act within the limits of customary law since he usually has to rely upon the kinship groups of the principals in the case for enforcing his decisions. This obliges him to find a solution

which both sides can accept. One of the most important obligations of members of a kinship group is to support each other in
legal cases and to punish each other when guilty. In any serious
quarrel which arises out of misbehaviour—such as divorce,
theft, or false accusation—the two principals, each with their
relatives, come together at a formal meeting such as that which
considered Mingcheng's behavior. This assembly constitutes
the lowest Garo court, and its sessions are always described by
the Garos as consisting of a meeting between two opposing
groups of relatives who are seen as representing the principals.
They defend and look out for the interests of their protégé if his
rights have been infringed upon, and they are considered to be
collectively responsible for any improper act of which he may
be guilty. Specifically they are responsible for cash contributions toward the compensation that is given to redress any
injury. Conversely, the relatives have the right, or even the
duty, to punish him, by either a physical beating or a verbal
denunciation or both. If a man behaves so badly that his relatives have to contribute their money to pay his compensation,
he deserves to be punished by them. Relatives also share in any
compensation that is received by an injured party, and thus gain
recognition of the support which they have given. The money
required for compensation is neither collected nor distributed
in a systematic fashion, and sometimes after a trial in which
compensation is given, different participants in a case give quite
different guesses as to how much the various relatives gave or
received. Garos were amused at my curiosity about these
amounts, since even the closest relatives did not feel this was
important enough to remember. One contributes in order to
uphold his own and his family's honor. It would be uncouth to
calculate such a contribution too closely, but the contribution is
the most explicit act of support that one can give to one's kinsmen, and it certainly does a man's reputation no harm to be
known as a vigorous supporter of his relatives at trials.

The greatest responsibility is held by the closely related

members of the lineages of the principals to a dispute, but the precise range of relatives is ill-defined and varies from case to case. More people will assemble to deal with a serious case than with a petty one. Relatives who live near by, and especially those living in the village of the principals, are more likely to assemble than those from elsewhere. Finally, while lineage mates are more likely to assemble than others, close relatives of other lineages also join them. A father will be considered on the side of his son, for instance, even though he is not his lineage mate. A father may even contribute to the compensation his son pays, or share in what he receives, though a father never takes part in beating or publicly denouncing his son.

The group that supports a disputant might be briefly characterized as a matrilineally skewed kindred, since all relatives can take part, but those related to one in the matrilineal direction are more likely to do so than others. The degree of relationship out to which kinsmen feel responsibility is in no way fixed, but depends upon the seriousness of the case and upon the availability or absence of other more closely related kinsmen who might more appropriately take charge. Since the lineages never split up in a precise manner, no boundaries can neatly distinguish those responsible from those who are not. Responsibility simply grows weaker as one becomes less closely related.

Criminal law as such does not exist for the Garos, since a suit is always brought by a private party, even though a government official supervises the court. But while all trials are seen as disputes between two opposing kinship groups, people at most ordinary trials do not obstinately back up their own relative and refuse to consider the opposite side. Quite the reverse is in fact the case. When it is evident that one's own relative is at fault, one does not try to minimize this fact; rather, by arranging compensation with dispatch and by vigorously punishing the culprit, one demonstrates to the other side and to the public at large that here is a group of men who know their responsibilities and are willing to live up to them. The actual tenor of the trials I attended was a firm intention to reach a consensus as to what action should be taken. There were well-defined procedures to be followed, and usually there was little question of fixing guilt since people knew each other's characters so intimately. Most cases could be disposed of by arranging compensation, which was set according to reasonably fixed standards. Members of the two "opposing" sides show no animosity toward each other, and never exhibit an unreasonable disposition to back up a relative at the expense of their reputation as reasonable and law-abiding citizens.

Ideally, and usually in practice as well, the compensation should end the dispute and clear the air. To pay compensation is to acknowledge guilt formally, and grant satisfaction to the other side. Afterward everyone should return to normal life, and not nurse injured feelings. The explicit purpose of the trial is to pacify people, to soothe their damaged reputations, or to compensate them for any loss. Every effort is made to find a solution which will be accepted so firmly by all sides that bickering will be avoided. Of course, not everyone is always satisfied. People sometimes feel that justice has miscarried and go away from a trial discontented; but ideally this should not happen, and usually there is enough agreement so that a man who feels unfairly treated will have little sympathy from his relatives and little choice but to accept the public consensus. Garo law has little in the way of moral overtone. Unlawful acts are felt to be wrong because they hurt some particular person, not because they violate an abstract moral precept. The injured party has legal means of redressing such an action, and Garos are more apt to cite the danger of legal action than abstract principles when explaining why some behavior must not be indulged in.

Though Mingcheng was tried for having made a false accusation, more often such cases grow out of a formal charge of illegal behavior, which may then be determined not to have taken place. To make a false accusation is to be guilty of one of the several categories of illegal behavior recognized among the Garos. Since false accusation is illegal, people may hesitate to accuse others of infringing upon their rights without having reasonable grounds for the charge.

Tangri once accused her husband, Gojing, of committing adultery with Singring, the wife of Gurang. The matter was brought to trial, but the evidence for her accusation was determined to be inadequate. Thus Tangri had to pay a compensation of fifteen rupees to Singring for having falsely accused her. If Tangri's accusation had proved to be justified, she could have collected compensation instead.

Since most legal cases begin with an accusation, either the accuser or the accused should eventually be found in the wrong. This neat device undoubtedly helps limit the amount of litigation. Garos are not free with their accusations, or at least not with public ones. The rule, however, has one serious defect. In some cases the evidence is simply not sufficient to decide whether the accuser or the accused is in the wrong. Until a generation or two ago arguments of this sort were resolved by resorting to ordeals, but ordeals are no longer practiced, and Garos say that people no longer believe in them. Many people still living remember them well and described them to me clearly.

One type of ordeal required the two opponents to dive under water, the last to come up thereby demonstrating his veracity. In another, boiling water was poured over the arm of the accused person; if it burned him, he was shown to be guilty. Other procedures had the same purpose, though they did not involve tests of personal strength. A favorite method was to heat a carefully measured amount of water with a carefully measured amount of wood. If the water boiled over, the accused man was shown to be indeed guilty. At other times, a chicken was tied outside at night. If it survived the night without being taken by a wild animal, the accused was shown to be innocent. In every case, the result was to show clearly that one person or the other was in the wrong. Most people accepted the outcome, compensations were paid, and the cases were settled. I was told of many cases in which even the man shown to be guilty admitted his guilt after the outcome of an ordeal. Sometimes a man would continue to protest his innocence, but it did him little good since even his relatives were by that time convinced that he was lying. In any case a compensation would have to be paid, and the dispute should then be at an end.

In this skeptical age, the teaching of missionaries and indirect exposure to new ideas from the rest of the world have destroyed the former faith in the reliability of these ordeals, and a new difficulty has arisen in the settlement of disputes. Today, when evidence is insufficient the case must simply be dismissed. This brings Garo practice into line with the Western belief that no man should be punished unless the evidence against him leaves no reasonable doubt of his guilt, but it also leaves cases dangling without final settlement. People may continue to believe in a person's guilt but have no way of winding up an argument. While I was in Rengsanggri, a prominent member of the village was accused by his wife of having committed adultery with another woman of the village. They both denied it, and the case was eventually dismissed for lack of evidence. Villagers with whom I talked were privately convinced that the accusation was justified. In earlier years they probably could have extracted compensation from the accused man and his relatives, or at least they would have been able to test him by an ordeal. Today, evidence is presented more formally than before, and the intimate knowledge villagers have of one another is less likely to be taken into account in reaching a decision. Since ordeals are no longer possible, denial of guilt has become more attractive. In this case charging adultery, since it ended without a decision, hard feelings were created which were never mollified; and some villagers predicted that these people would continue their adulterous relationship at every opportunity.

## VIOLENCE

Head-hunting is gone, but murder, suicide, and brawling all occur and are all dealt with at formal trials. Since the establishment of British power, murder has been punished by the district government, and for many years murderers have been punished by imprisonment. This kind of sentence does not fall within customary law, but is imposed entirely by the higher branches of the government. I was told that in a village one or two days' walk east of Rengsanggri a boy had a fight with his own father. The boy was not yet old enough to marry, but he was considered old enough to work and to be responsible for his own actions. His father had chastised him for being lazy and not working, and the boy lost his temper, grabbed a bush knife and struck his father with it several times. The father died, and at a trial held by the Deputy Commissioner in Tura the boy was found guilty of murder and sentenced to a prison term. This was not the only action taken, however, for the relatives of father and son all met together at another time in their village, and it was agreed that the relatives of the son should pay a compensation of 500 rupees to the relatives of the father.

This was a much larger compensation than is paid under any other circumstances. It seems to be paid only in limited parts of the district, for a few Garos, when I inquired about the matter, denied that they had ever heard of such a thing in their own areas. Murder is not, of course, an everyday occurrence, and I did not have the fortune to be present at any murder trial.

Garos describe suicide as if it were a punishable offense. One of the *loskor*s told me of a woman who had been very sick and in great pain, and who had finally cut her own throat. (Pain, disease, and crippling old age were the usual reasons given for suicide.) She did not die for a week and was taken to the hospital in Tura, where the *loskor* was able to question her. She denied that anyone else had done this, and so, as Rate explained it, he was unable to press the case because there was no complainant. Characteristically, he felt that even suicide required a complainant, in accordance with the Garo idea that the only wrong action is one that harms another, and that the injured person has the right to press for damages.

Fighting or beating may be a complicating factor in cases of divorce or in other disputes, but trials resulting from fighting alone are not very common. Beating itself is not rare, and if administered by the proper person it is entirely legal, and may even be an integral part of a punishment for some other legal infraction. It is occasionally possible, however, for an injured party to claim and to receive compensation from a person who has injured him. I was told of one case in which a woman claimed compensation from a man who had created a disturbance one night while drunk, by careening about the village, making a great deal of noise, and using offensive language. He apparently did no more to the woman than beat upon her house with a stick, which might, abstractly, be looked upon as disturbance of the peace; but as always, the complaint was made by an individual person who felt her rights had been violated. False accusation and violence constitute two categories of illegal behavior. The most frequent disputes, however, concern personal property and family rights.

## DISPUTES OVER PROPERTY

Except for various kinds of family quarrels, disagreements over personal property are, as might be expected, the most frequent subject of litigation. Outright theft is not a great problem. People often padlock a box or two in which they keep valuables, but they never lock their houses. I was sometimes warned to be careful to put my possessions in a safe place if I left the village for more than a few hours. People felt there was no danger from any of the villagers, but strangers did come through and were not always to be trusted. Money, other articles of value, animals, or even crops from the fields were all occasionally stolen.

Mingja of Asonanggri had 45 rupees stolen from him. He told Jengnon, his sister's husband, about it and they inquired among Mingja's neighbors. One of the neighbors had seen a boy named Rasin, who lived in Rongram, loitering around Mingja's house, though he did not actually see him take the money. Nevertheless, the *loskor* held a trial and Rasin was found guilty. He returned the 45 rupees to Mingja and also had to pay Mingja and his family a compensation of 25 rupees, some of which was turned over to the *loskor* as an informal gift in return for his help.

In this case, Mingja made most of the preliminary inquiry himself, but sometimes a *sordar* or the *loskor* makes it instead. As in the case of Rasin, a convicted thief usually has to pay a substantial compensation besides making good the value of the stolen article. The compensation varies considerably, but may equal the value of the article itself.

Damage by animals is one of the most frequent causes of disputes. During the growing season cattle are supposed to be kept tied up, and if one accidentally gets loose in the field, the owner is responsible for any damage it may do. Since it is impossible to make any accurate estimate of the damage, this can lead to acrimonious controversies, and they are likely to be especially bitter if the cattle belong to Nepalis. Occasionally a Nepali buffalo does great damage to Garo fields, and since the Nepalis are recent immigrants to the Garo hills and lack the ties of kinship and common sentiment that tie all Garos together, these quarrels may be particularly difficult to settle satisfactorily. The *loskor* may judge these cases, but they may also be taken to the district courts.

## FAMILY DISPUTES

Disputes over family rights come to formal trial more often than any others. These are more complicated than disputes arising from false accusation, violence, or theft, and they are more distinctively colored by the peculiar features of Garo social organization. Illicit intercourse and dispute over the obligation of the *a'kim* relationship (as discussed in Chapter VI) are the major causes of family litigation.

A case which rather neatly illustrates several of the Garo rules concerning both illicit intercourse and *a'kim* responsibility is that of Rimji, the daughter of Sang. Rimji was chosen as Sang's heiress, and Jingnan was brought in as her husband and as heir to her parents. Some time after they were married, he committed adultery with Salji, who was unmarried at the time and who unfortunately became pregnant, making the adultery public knowledge. In due course there was a trial, and Salji was judged to be guilty of infringing upon the rights of Rimji; so her relatives had to pay Rimji's relatives a compensation which, as reported to me, was 30 rupees. Since Salji had no husband, the boy Jingnan had not infringed upon anyone's rights and his relatives did not have to pay compensation to anyone, though both he and Salji were publicly beaten by older members of their respective lineages. This would have ended the affair if Jingnan had then settled down quietly to married life; but he did not. He abused his wife, and on a number of occasions he beat her. He did not initiate a divorce, but eventually Rimji and her family could endure no more and evicted him. Again there was a trial and this time Jingnan was judged to have been wrong to have beaten his wife, and so his relatives had to pay 30 rupees to her relatives to compensate for his abuse. In spite of the indignities suffered by Rimji, however, her family were still required to pay 60 rupees to Jingnan's family as a compensation for having initiated a divorce and for having broken the *a'kim* bond which had joined the two groups of relatives. It was no one's opinion that the beatings warranted a reduction in the compensation for divorce; the situation was rather that there were two separate and distinct compensations which were meant to settle two different grievances. Rimji's hardships did not excuse her family from the compensation, but they did soften her relatives' anger toward her. She undertook her divorce with the approval of her family, and she was not beaten at the trial as she would have been if she had been blamed for wishing it. Moreover, the boy received none of the property of their household. Rimji was later married again, this time more happily, though to a somewhat younger man, and the family was planning to adopt a younger second wife (*jikgite*) for her husband. The case of Rimji and Jingnan contains an example of divorce, or, as the Garos phrase it, of break in the *a'kim* relationship.

The permanence of the *a'kim* bond has been emphasized (Chapter VI). However, any such relationship must occasionally fail to be maintained. Garos do in fact recognize ways in which the *a'kim* bond can be broken, but a break always requires formal recognition, and generally involves a payment in compensation. The mechanism of rupture of the *a'kim* bond is illuminating for an understanding of the bond itself. The divorce which ends a marriage is also the most common way for *a'kim* to end. Most marriages, once they have been agreed to by all sides, and once the boy has settled down and agreed to stay, last until the death of one of the partners. In many elderly couples both husband and wife are each the first and only spouse of the other. Still the Garos firmly believe that it is absurd for two people to stay together if they can no longer tolerate each other's company. Marriage is meant to be permanent but the couple should also be compatible, and if they are not, then the marriage is expected to come to an end. Either partner may bring an end to a marriage at will. A man can simply walk out, and a woman can evict her husband. Eventually, however, the divorce must be formalized at a public meeting.

Divorce raises great complications because it constitutes a failure to maintain the responsibilities of *a'kim*, so whoever initiates a divorce must pay a compensation to the opposite party.

As in the case of Rimji's divorce, the amount is usually 60 rupees. The first person to break off a marriage, whether husband or wife, owes this money to the other. Like any other, this compensation is collected and distributed among the relatives of the spouses, so that the individuals' real punishment is not the financial burden of the compensation, but the disapproval and the physical beating which may also be received. As was shown in the case of Rimji, neither adultery nor beating is considered grounds for divorce, and her husband's behavior did not excuse Rimji from payment of the compensation. In fact, in Garo law grounds for divorce simply to not exist. Only if both partners and their respective families mutually agree can compensation be avoided; for if a divorce is equally desired by both sides, neither need pay. Otherwise, monetary compensation is always required, whatever the reasons. This occasionally leads to the awkward situation which the Garos describe as "mutually watching and waiting," in which each of the spouses hopes the other will precipitate a divorce, but neither wishes to do so himself.

Property division after a divorce is not well defined, but property rarely complicates settlement. Most divorces take place within a few years after marriage, before the couples have been able to amass enough property for this to be of great significance. If the husband initiates divorce by leaving his wife, she remains in undisputed possession of all the property which they formerly shared. Even if, as Rimji did, the girl initiates divorce, the man usually leaves her house. Garos suggest that if the divorce is initiated by the girl and if they have significant property, the husband may be able to claim half of it, but in practice such a division of property is most unusual. The man can return to his parents' home, and if he is young, as most divorcés are, regain much the same position he once had as a bachelor. He can expect that sooner or later he will be taken again as a husband for another girl. If the divorced girl is young, she is also likely to move back into the house of her parents, but an older woman may remain separately with her children until re-marriage. A girl who is married only briefly and who has not become pregnant may be able to marry again without her rela-tives' promising a young second wife for her new husband; but if the marriage has lasted longer, and particularly if the girl has had a child, then it is always necessary to promise a *jikgite* as a second wife in order to persuade any man other than a widower to marry her. Public payment and acceptance of the compensa-tion legalize the divorce and end the relationship of the man and woman. After this time, the partners to the marriage are free to contract new marriages, without reference to the restrictions of lineage other than the universal prohibition on marriage within the moiety.

One or both partners of thirteen broken marriages were living in Rengsanggri while I was there. Of these, seven had been marriages of non-heirs, four had been heir marriages, and two had been replacement marriages. This sample is not adequate to show whether heir or non-heir marriages are more stable; any kind of marriage may end in divorce, and the compensations paid are the same in any case. Divorce of non-heirs entails relatively few complications, since both parties are free to enter another marriage. The divorce of an heiress leaves her parents without an heir, and either another husband must be brought to her or another daughter made heiress in her place. At any rate, if the older couple are still alive when their heiress daughter is divorced, the divorce does not completely sever *a'kim*, since the lineages are still connected by the older couple. Of the same thirteen Rengsanggri marriages, eight were ended on the initia-tive of the man, and the man's family paid compensation to the woman's family. Only three were ended on the woman's initia-tive, with compensation to the man's family. Two were ended shortly after marriage by mutual agreement of the individuals and their families, and in these two cases no compensation was paid.

The compensation paid at the time of divorce is called the

*a'kim dai—dai* being the Garo word for any monetary compensation—since it is intended to serve as a recompense for breaking the *a'kim* bond. *A'kim dai* is also paid on two occasions other than divorce. These are the breaking of an engagement and the failure to provide a replacement for a dead person. During the time after a boy has run away from a girl to whom he had been taken as a prospective husband, but before he either has made it clear that he wants no part of the marriage or else has agreed to stay and be a husband to the girl, the two people are in a relation to each other which it is not inappropriate to call an engagement. It is publicly known that these two are prospective husband and wife, though it is not yet certain that they will actually be married. During this time they do not live with each other or even see much of each other. It is not possible, however, for one of the parties to break an engagement unilaterally, since the two are considered already tentatively bound by *a'kim*. If either one marries some other person, he or she is considered to have broken *a'kim*, and his or her family is responsible for paying the same compensation that is paid in the case of the divorce of fully married people.

I attended a trial resulting from one such case which occurred in Waramgri. Jangnan had been taken as a prospective husband and heir to Menjak. The ceremony of killing the chickens was performed, but Jangnan had run away. He had not, however, made clear his intention to have no more to do with the affair, and so he and Menjak were considered to be engaged. However, Jangnan began having an affair with another girl, Tijak; and when this became public knowledge, Menjak's relatives made a complaint against Tijak and the boy, and a trial was held. There was no dispute concerning the facts of the case. Everyone admitted knowing that Jangnan was engaged and therefore not eligible, but it was also clear that he had no intention of leaving Tijak and returning to Menjak. Everyone present rapidly agreed to the suggestion of the *loskor* that Menjak deserved to collect 60 rupees from Jangnan. When the money was collected, the *loskor* demanded that the money be handed personally by one girl to the other, and Tijak had to say, as she handed it over, "This is because I stole your husband." Both Jangnan and Tijak were considered to be guilty, Jangnan of breaking the *a'kim* which had tied him to Menjak, and Tijak of having committed what amounted to adultery with Menjak's potential spouse.

Such a case is much like a divorce even though the marriage had not been fully entered into, and the compensation of 60 rupees is the appropriate amount to pay for having broken *a'kim*. The situation was colored by what was considered adultery, but the compensation was larger than is usual for simple adultery, since its payment formally broke the original *a'kim* between Menjak and Jangnan and allowed his relation to Tijak to become legitimate. Whether this was regarded as a case of divorce or of adultery, the overriding consideration was that of settling the dispute. No anger was shown at the trial, except for some animosity between the two girls and the stylized fury with which Jangnan was denounced for his animal-like behavior.

A boy who honorably makes clear that he wants nothing to do with a marriage proposal would not be subject to the same legal indemnities. Jangnan's mistake was in acting surreptitiously. In a parallel fashion, a girl who is still engaged to a boy who has run away must not take a second boy, or else she will owe compensation to the first.

Death does not destroy *a'kim*; thus the family of a dead person has the obligation to provide a replacement, and the widowed person has the obligation to accept. If a widowed person unilaterally marries somebody of his own choice, then the family of the widow or widower will owe the *a'kim* compensation of 60 rupees to the family of the dead person; but if on the other hand the family of the dead person do not provide a replacement, they must compensate the family of the surviving spouse. Failure to provide a replacement is not common, and I had to search for some time before I discovered anyone who could remember an unambiguous example. Furthermore, it is possible for the families in such a situation to agree to end the *a'kim* without the payment of a compensation, but as always the agreement must be a formal one accepted by all sides. Such an agreement usually occurs only when the family of the dead person are unable to find a suitable replacement. In such a case they may, as the Garos say, "set the widow (or widower) free." This means that the surviving spouse is released by agreement from the restriction of *a'kim* and is then free to marry whomever he wishes, if he can find anybody. Kinship groups dislike setting people free, for it is an admission that the family are unable to fulfill their obligations; and widows and widowers want to be given a new spouse. "Setting free" is really a misnomer, then, since one of the most explicit reasons for maintaining the law of *a'kim* is to make sure that a person will not be left alone after the death of his spouse but will be taken care of by being given a replacement. Nevertheless, if the lineage of the dead person is genuinely unable to find a suitable person, both sides will usually agree that the *a'kim* restrictions are to be abrogated and that no compensation need be paid. Such agreements reduce the frequency with which *a'kim* compensation is paid as a result of failure to provide a replacement, and most often replacements are arranged according to the formal rules.

In each of these cases—divorce, breaking of engagements, and failure to provide replacements—compensation is paid only upon unilateral action by one of the parties. In each case the relationship can be ended by mutual agreement if all concerned are willing.

The settlement which in the case of Rimji and Jingnan, cited at the beginning of this section, required Salji to pay 30 rupees to Rimji for having committed adultery with Rimji's husband, was typical of many cases about which I heard.

When only one of the partners to adultery is married or otherwise committed, the unmarried partner must pay compensation to the spouse of the married person. No important distinction is made between the adultery of a man and of a woman. If both partners to the adultery are married, each must pay compensation to the opposite spouse. That is, a woman always pays compensation to another woman, the wife of her lover, whose rights she has infringed, while similarly a man must pay compensation to the man whose rights he has infringed. At first glance, it might seem that where both parties are married, the compensation is simply exchanged between the two households; and that that which an adulterous husband pays, his wife gains. Since compensation is always paid by and collected by the broader kinship group, however, this money does not stay within the household, but rather is distributed among the members of four different kinship groups. Publicly known and admitted adultery does not necessarily lead to divorce, and indeed it should not. I knew many men and women who had stayed married although their kinship groups had paid for their adultery. The manner in which Garos pay and receive compensation implies that the dispute is not between the spouses at all; and it would appear that an adulterous husband is somehow less to blame than his partner, since only she need pay the compensation to the wife. Of course this does not prevent a straying husband from coming under a cloud of disapproval, and he may be beaten and denounced; but unless the woman is married too, he and his kinsmen do not pay any compensation. Compensation is never paid directly from one spouse to another or between their kinship groups except in the case of divorce, for to do so would imply an inability to get along peacefully together.

The penalties for adultery apply not only to married people but to the other classes of people who are also bound by *a'kim*, those who are engaged and those who are widowed but who remain obligated to the kinship group of the deceased spouse. Tijak was considered to have infringed upon Menjak's rights by committing adultery with Menjak's prospective husband, although Menjak was not yet fully married to him. In a parallel way, if a widow or widower commits adultery, then the partner is considered to have infringed upon the rights of the deceased spouse's family just as he would have if the spouse were still living. Such cases are somewhat unusual. Widows, and especially widowers, often marry too promptly for much danger of such adultery, and if the kinship groups cannot find a replacement spouse, then the widow or widower is usually released from his or her obligation under *a'kim*. The rule, however, is clear, namely that compensation for adultery is owed by all people bound by *a'kim*, and not only married people.

Garos do not make a terminological distinction between adultery and other varieties of extra-marital intercourse, all of which are called *teleka* and all of which are considered improper. They do not react to premarital intercourse as consistently as to adultery; but even improper advance on the part of a boy to a girl is considered a punishable offense, and in theory a girl can claim a small monetary compensation from a boy who suggests sexual relations, though this compensation is rarely demanded. Even sexual relations between unmarried people rarely lead to litigation unless pregnancy results, although Garos readily cite formal rules which state that fines should be paid by the boy's family to the girl's family even if there is no pregnancy. Of course, if it is conducted with discretion, no one else need learn of an extramarital affair, though Garos are not given to consistent secrecy in these matters. If an affair lasts for any length of time a pregnancy is likely to result, but even this leads more often to a marriage than to trial and compensation. Only if the boy and girl are members of the same moiety and are therefore not appropriate marriage partners does a pregnancy have some likelihood of precipitating negotiations for the payment of compensation. Sexual relations between members of the same moiety or even sib are less strongly disapproved than is marriage, and unless the two people are closely related cousins, they cause hardly more alarm than such relations

THE SETTLEMENT OF DISPUTES

between any two unmarried people. However, they raise one
extremely unpleasant problem, since if the girl becomes pregnant the couple will be unable to marry. Sa'jak, the daughter of
Kaljing, had an illegitimate baby whose father was Tamring,
the son of Aduma of Singgat's house. Both Sa'jak and Tamring
were members of the Chambigong sib of Rengsanggri and could
not marry, or at least they were unwilling to face down their
relatives and live together. A trial was held, and both of them
were scolded and beaten and told to be good. They promised
henceforth to keep away from each other; and Tamring and his
relatives had to pay a compensation of 60 rupees to Sa'jak.

## LAND DISPUTES

No disputes arouse as much heat or go on so interminably as
those over land titles. Since the period of British rule the
government has attempted to record land titles at the district
headquarters, but the distribution of the titles is extremely
complex in practice and the records have tended to imply a
simplified system of rights. Moreover, writing them down
introduces into the system an inflexibility which is not found in
the actual feelings of Garos about their rules. For each village
or village cluster the district government recognizes a single
*nokma* who is regarded as having title to the land of those
villages. Sketch maps record the village boundaries, and the
government confirms inheritance of the title by the *nokma*'s
heir. It is also recognized that titles can be sold, though the
courts seem to have been quite consistent in demanding general
agreement among the villagers before a sale of land is recognized. That is, though he holds title, no *nokma* has been able to
sell land to another village without permission. There are
occasional legal disputes over the *nokma*ship, which are seen
primarily as disputes over title to the village land. If the choice
of the *nokma*'s heir proceeds according to the normal rule, then
there can be no question about legitimacy; but complicating

factors can arise. In one village the *nokma*'s first wife died, and he was given a replacement. Many years later the *nokma* died, and a dispute arose as to whether the replacement wife or the only daughter of the first wife should be entitled to the land. The rules for inheritance of personal property are not entirely clear in such a case, and disposition depends upon the decision of the family as to the next heiress. This particular case was decided by the district court on the reasonable basis that the land title was not entirely personal property but that the villagers had a voice in choosing the title-holder. The court concluded that the villagers preferred the replacement wife to the daughter.

In another village the *nokma* had no daughters when he died, but an adopted heiress was chosen for the widow, and Watjing was married to both women and declared to be *nokma* The daughterless widow, Khalji, lived for a while with Watjing and her adopted daughter, Sengjak; but eventually she quarreled with them, paid a divorce compensation of 60 rupees to Watjing, and went off to marry another man This marriage was fruitful, and eventually a daughter from that marriage contested the inheritance of the *nokma*ship by the adopted Sengjak and her husband The district court first decided in favor of the adopted heiress over the real daughter; but the decision was appealed to the high court of Assam, and the outcome was still in doubt when I left the district.

These rather complex disputes over inheritance are unusual. More often, the *nokma*ship passes without ambiguity to a man's heir. Similar ambiguities could arise over inheritance of personal property, but where traditional shifting agriculture is practiced this is simply not valuable enough to make a dispute worthwhile, and families are able to make amicable settlements without going to court. Only the *nokma*ship and land titles are really worth quarreling over.

One final example will demonstrate how complex and protracted disputes over land title can become. Songmagri and its daughter village of Rengsanggri have had a long dispute with some people of a village to the north—Digranggri. I pieced together the story of the dispute largely from records of the District Council court, supplemented by the memories of the villagers. In 1884, according to the Council records, a gun belonging to the *nokma* of Songmagri was burned and destroyed in a plot of land which then belonged to the *nokma* of Digranggri. The villagers know of this and still call the plot *Chandalbret*, *chandal* meaning 'a muzzle-loading gun,' and *bret* meaning 'to burst,' as the gun is reputed to have done in the fire. This much was admitted by all concerned, but there was and still is dispute as to how it happened. The Songmagri people asserted, and their relatives in Rengsanggri still maintain, that the gun was burned maliciously, while the *nokma* of Digranggri asserted at the time that the gun was deliberately concealed on the plot of land so that it would be burned and so that claims could be made against Digranggri. Songmagri claimed the plot of land as compensation, but the district court at the time decided in favor of Digranggri. This decision so infuriated the *nokma* of Songmagri that (again according to the District Council records) "after coming out of the court, he suddenly became insane or infuriated and dealt a deadly blow on a constable standing in the court compound with a *dao* [bush knife] as a result of which the constable instantly died." The *nokma* was sent to the penal colony on Andaman Island for life, and never returned. This was not, however, the end of the dispute. The next Songmagri *nokma* opened the case again in 1903, but was again unsuccessful. Some time after this, a complicating development took place. The *nokma* of Digranggri (the successor to the man who burned the gun) and the *nokma* of another village, Gongronggri, agreed to trade some land. Digranggri and Gongronggri were sister villages, just as Songmagri and Rengsanggri are, so the transaction did not involve a major change. The land traded does not seem to have included the plot now known as *Chandalbret*, but the plots were adjacent and this served to confuse everybody about the case. Then, still later, and to make matters worse, the people of Gongronggri sold out all of their land to Rengsanggri and Songmagri, and the remaining Gongronggri people moved away to a wet rice area. This sale is reputed to have been peacefully made, but it had the effect of transferring some land of the Digranggri-Gongronggri area to that of Rengsanggri-Songmagri.

Then, in 1924, the original case was reopened—on what grounds is not clear. By this time one of the most remarkable Garos of recent generations had entered the dispute. Janggin Loskor had become rich partly, at least, by recruiting men for a Garo labor battalion which was sent to France during the First World War. Some people claimed that he received a payment from the government for each man he recruited, and a bribe from each man whom he allowed to remain free, though I cannot vouch for the actual existence of this unbeatable scheme. Janggin also did road contracting, and he had the foresight to invest heavily in wet rice land. Janggin never learned to read or to write anything except his name, but he invented a private notation to keep track of his far-flung business deals, and when he died suddenly in 1956, neither his heirs nor I were able to decipher his records in order to discover who owed him what. Janggin's first wife was a Rengsanggri woman, though he lived in Rengsanggri only briefly. He somehow managed to have the district records indicate that he was the main *nokma* of the cluster of villages to which Rengsanggri belonged, though this official designation certainly did not correspond with the opinions of the Rengsanggri people, who pointed out that he was married as a non-heir and could not possibly be a *nokma*. He did, however, become *loskor* of the *eleka* to which Rengsanggri belonged. He was a very influential man, and was more consistently deferred to than any other man in the region.

Already in 1924, when the land dispute was reopened, Janggin seems to have had considerable influence at the Deputy Commissioner's office. Janggin had been granted the title of

"Member of the British Empire" in recognition of his recruiting services, and—completely unable to speak English and illiterate though he was—he was appointed as one of the early Garo representatives to the Assam Legislative Assembly. To what extent his influence was a factor in the dispute over *Chandalbret* it is impossible to say, but this time Songmagri was successful: the plot was transferred to its jurisdiction, the Digranggri *nokma* who had formerly claimed it was actually forced to leave Digranggri, and a new man assumed the *nokma*ship there. *Chandalbret* was included in the land which Rengsanggri periodically cultivated. The most recent act regarding it occurred in 1956, when the heir of the evicted Digranggri *nokma* reopened the case on the grounds that Indian independence was a new factor allowing review of the earlier decision. It did not appear that he had much chance of success, however.

This case is more complex and protracted than most disputes over land, but it illustrates how unreconcilable land quarrels can be. It is easy to imagine that heads might have been taken in the past over such a dispute; and such a recourse at least might have resolved it. Today, a dispute like this can only lead to interminable battles in courts which do not always understand the traditional land rules.

# The Market

IN CHAPTER VIII THE transactions which take place between households in the village were discussed. Though many of these might be considered "economic," none of them required the use of money, and indeed money is hardly used within the village. By contrast, most of the dealings which Garos have outside their villages, and particularly those in the market, are strictly monetary in nature. Garos sell some of their crops for cash, and purchase some essential consumer items. The people of Rengsanggri told me that even before the coming of the British, their ancestors took occasional trips to a market which was located about fifteen miles to the west, near the present market of Garobadha, where the hills end and the plains begin. They said that they went in large and well-armed parties for protection against their enemies. Market places are now more widely distributed than they used to be, and Garos have neither to go so far nor to go armed. Markets have been established wherever roads penetrate the hills, so that trucks and busses are able to deliver and pick up the dealers and their goods. Many areas in the hills still have no roads, and some villagers must walk twenty miles or more to reach a market place; but everyone is dependent upon the market, and all make the trip from time to time whatever the distance.

Each of the markets in the Garo Hills is held on a particular day in the seven-day week. They are staggered to allow the traders to make the rounds of several markets, staying just one

THE MARKET 273

day at each before moving on. The traders are plains men, mostly Bengalis. The Rengsanggri people deal primarily with two markets. The most important is the Friday market at Rongram, which is on the road about three miles from the village; but a few villagers always attend the Saturday market which is held in Tura, another nine miles along the road to the south. More rarely one or two men from Rengsanggri visit the market which is held at Garobadha, to the west of Tura. The Rongram market has been opened only since the partition of India, following which a new road was put through to Tura to avoid the threat of disrupted communications raised by the partition. Formerly most marketing was done in Tura, but the one at Rongram is more convenient and has become one of the most important markets of the Garo Hills. It draws people from all sides—particularly from the north and east, since in those directions there are no markets for many miles, while it has competition from Tura and Garobadha in the south and west. People are already streaming into the market area by Thursday afternoon, since the Friday market really begins then. Those who come from a great distance camp for the night in the market area and cook their supper at open fires from food that they bring with them. On Friday morning they are joined by many more people from the villages closer by. Garos walk in over the footpaths that crisscross the hills, and almost everybody carries a basket hung by a tump line from his forehead. Some carry goods to sell, others need the space to carry home their purchases, and everyone brings along a few personal possessions. Traders come by truck or by bus, bringing large burlap-wrapped bundles of their wares. Activity in Rongram reaches a peak early Friday morning, when as many as three thousand people may be milling around the market; by noon, people are leaving again. Many go back to their villages, but most of the traders, and a few of the Garos, move up to Tura for the market the next day.

Rengsanggri is closer than many villages to the market, and

some men make the trip almost every week, though attendance
drops during the heaviest agricultural seasons. Women also go
in large numbers, and they take an active part in some of the
trading. From a purely economic point of view the market has
an exceedingly important place in their lives, for it supplies
goods which are considered essential and which are available in
no other place. But the market is more than a place to buy and
sell, for it is probably the most important contact which people
in conservative villages like Rengsanggri have with the world
beyond their immediate neighbourhood. It provides an ideal
opportunity for gossip, for flirting, and for a welcome change
from the labors that occupy most days. People often dress in
their best clothes, and young people in particular deck themselves out in their finest turbans and jewelry. In Rengsanggri
no important ceremonial event was ever held on Friday because
it would conflict with the market.

The markets are under the general jurisdiction of the District
Council. The Council "sells" the right to collect certain taxes
and fees to an individual whom the Garos speak of as the
'owner' of the market, though he has to renew his contract with
the District Council each year. The 'owner' pays a fixed sum to
the Council, and this provides an important source of revenue,
as much as several thousand rupees from each market. The
'owner' has to ensure his profit by enforcing the collection of
fees as rigidly as possible, and an able man can make a considerable profit in a year of market operations. The District Council
fixes the legal fees. These are mostly levied on the seller of any
merchandise, and may be determined by the quantity sold.
Four annas, for instance, are charged to the seller of each
maund of cotton that changes hands. In other cases each sales-
man is taxed regardless of what he sells; for example, each cloth
merchant pays a fixed market fee of eight annas. Many Garos
believe that unscrupulous market 'owners' charge more than
the stipulated fees and thereby line their own pockets at the
expense of the farmers who do not know the rules very well. I

was told, for instance, that the proper tax on the sale of a cow is twelve annas, but that 'owners' sometimes manage to charge this fee to both the buyer and seller, thereby collecting twice the amount they are entitled to. The 'owner' has certain responsibilities in addition to paying a sum to the District Council. He must keep the sheds in repair, and must hire somebody to sweep up the debris after the people have left. The 'owner' of the Rongram market also had to hire several assistants to make the rounds and collect the taxes for him.

Most market transactions are between a Garo on the one hand and a Bengali on the other, for Garos only rarely buy and sell to one another. The Garos bring in their crops to the market, where Bengali merchants buy them and take them to the plains. From other Bengali merchants they purchase the goods they require. The Bengalis are always specialists, who buy a single crop or a few similar crops, or who sell just one sort of commodity. Except for the cotton merchants, the Bengalis are private dealers who live by buying their goods in one place and selling them somewhere else. Those who sell manufactured goods seldom have any idea of the ultimate source of their wares, which they simply buy from wholesalers in the plains. Even the dried-fish merchants could give me no clear idea of where or by whom the dried fish was produced. Conversely, the Garos have no idea where their crops go, and I was asked a number of times whether I knew where their cotton was taken. They speculated that it was probably taken somewhere and made into thread, but they were not really sure even of this.

The specialization of the Bengalis gives them a considerable advantage over the Garos. They often make the rounds of several markets in the course of a single week, and they have an intimate knowledge of the qualities of their goods and of the fluctuation of prices. On the other hand, at the Rongram market at least, the Bengalis must learn the Garo language if they are to be successful in business. Few Garos in this area speak enough Bengali to make a purchase, so all bargaining is done in Garo.

The merchant who does not learn Garo is not likely to survive the competition for very long.

The Rongram market really begins on the road several miles from the market center, for a few commodities, particularly rice beer and betel leaves, are frequently sold there; but the market place proper is located at the junction of several footpaths with the one-lane, but all-weather, gravel motor road. Several rows of sheds are provided, in which some of the merchants spread their wares, but many others have to squat on the ground with their goods heaped about them. At the height of the market on Friday morning, people swirl about in apparent confusion with their crops, their purchases, and their children. They all talk and shout, and the noise is often compounded by the presence of a small pickup truck, decorated with advertisements and equipped with a loudspeaker, which sends recorded Indian music blaring through the market place. Periodically the music stops, to be replaced for a few minutes by shouted exhortations in the Garo language to smoke a particular brand of *biri* cigarettes.

The permanent sheds have floors and roofs, but no walls. They are about ten feet wide and six feet deep, just the size which allows a single merchant to sit cross-legged at the center within reach of all his wares. Most of these sheds are occupied either by cloth dealers or by merchants who handle a range of goods such as might be found in an American variety or ten-cent store. There were even a few dealers who styled themselves *dos anna kompani*—literally "ten-anna company"—and who sold all their products for no more than that amount, but most dealers were not so inflexible. The cloth dealers seldom sell anything but cloth and often specialize on a few particular items, such as ready-made goods—shorts and shirts for men and dresses for small girls—or untailored piece goods. They adjust their stock to the taste of the customers, and some carry large amounts of the plain blue cloth Garos admire so much. Cloth merchants drape their goods about their stalls, each with perhaps a few hundred rupees' worth of stock in all, and try to lure customers from the crowds that wander by. The variety salesmen carry a much more diversified stock. A single merchant may display mirrors, spoons, scissors, bobby pins, padlocks, several kinds of hair oil and soap, razor blades, safety pins, buttons, twine, clothing snaps, pencils, pen points, ink tablets (to be dissolved in water), a couple of kinds of small notebooks, flashlight batteries, pocket knives, candles, cigarettes and *biris*, matches, and playing cards.

An important part of every market, one which is always off to one side, is occupied by the dried-fish dealers. Like most other products, dried fish is carried into the market in gunny sacks, and spread out on the ground for inspection. Still other men sell rice in bulk, to people who have enough cash to supplement the products of their own fields. Cattle are driven into the market and sold to the Garos in substantial numbers, and one part of the market is reserved for the cattle dealers, who are mostly Moslems from the plains. Other animals—pigs, chickens, or goats—are less frequently traded, since Garos raise about as many as they consume. Occasionally Garos bring them into the market, and they are traded in small quantities.

A few dealers specialize in the iron blades of tools. They spread their wares in the open, since their products do not take up enough space to justify the higher market fee that they would have to pay for a shed. They all sell the standard blades— bamboo knives, axheads, spearheads, sickles—and tripod stands for holding a pot over a fire. A few also sell iron points to be attached to a digging stick. The purchaser always hafts the blade himself.

Many kinds of food are retailed in small amounts, supplementing the Garos' own agriculture. A few dealers concentrate on exotic vegetables, such as tomatoes or potatoes, which Garos seldom grow. Others sell fried sweets, nutty delicacies, or packaged crackers, and others gaudily colored sugar candy. Dry-food merchants sell flour, pulse, sugar, and various kinds

of spices. None of these are considered staples or are purchased
often. Other dealers sell what are locally known as *biskets*.
These are slightly sweetened bread rolls, which are about as
hard as zwieback, and which it is considered elegant to dunk in
tea. Like most other commodities, these are carried to the
market in gunny sacks, and dealers sell as many as they can one
day and keep the rest to sell the next day or week. From these
or other dealers one may also buy puffed rice—in bulk or rolled
into candy balls—crudely processed brown sugar, and areca
nuts or the leaves and lime with which they are eaten. A few
dealers specialize in tobacco of various sorts, especially the kind
which is purchased in bulk and smoked in water pipes. There
may be patent-medicine salesmen with dozens of boxes and
bottles of potions, pills, elixirs, and such related products as
shampoo and mothballs. Pills may be taken from their boxes and
sold one or two at a time. Once I saw a Sikh, wearing a distin-
guished-looking white turban, who offered an assortment of
false teeth. For one rupee he would select an appropriate tooth
and with his pliers would wire it into the mouth of his customer,
all the while surrounded by an admiring crowd of shoppers.
The same man also did tattooing with a needle powered by a
flashlight battery. A few salesmen are always on hand to supply
the jewelry that Garos like to wear. Some of this is manufactured locally by Nepalis, but most is imported from the plains.

Tea stalls constitute a more permanent part of the Rongram
market. A few are operated throughout the week, mostly by
Nepalis who are the only permanent residents of the market
area. Other tea stalls are operated only on the market day, however—a few of them by Garos. They are mostly built of bamboo,
and while they may be partially walled, they are often open
toward the market. A fire at one side or in an adjoining room
keeps tea brewing continuously, and the proprietors can also
supply snacks to go with the tea. The benches and occasional
chair and table of the tea stalls provide the only convenient
place to sit down and relax near the market. All the goods des-

cribed are paid for with cash which Garos earn by selling their products.

*Cotton.* This is the most important cash crop for the people of Rengsanggri and most of the villages in its vicinity, and Rongram is now one of the principal cotton markets in the Garo Hills. Garos carry their cotton to market in immense openwork baskets, which are carried by the usual tump line. Each contains one hundred or even as much as one hundred and fifty pounds of cotton, which is all sold for cash. Many men carry their own cotton to market and sell it themselves; or cotton may be bought and sold among the villagers first, and a man with a lot of cotton which he either has grown himself or has purchased may hire others to help him carry it to market. A man who buys cotton in the village to sell in the market always assumes a risk, since the selling price in the market fluctuates and cannot be safely predicted. He may make a considerable profit, but he may sometimes also take a loss.

One day I was sitting in the house of Ringin, an old lady who lived with her adopted daughter and son-in-law, Rongsin, when another youth, Anang, came bounding in. Ringin had been ginning cotton to obtain the seeds for the next year's planting, and Anang was interested in buying the ginned cotton. He and Rongsin went to weigh it; they talked a bit, and then Anang asked how much they wanted for it. They bargained and discussed the matter at some length. Rongsin's wife, though present, took no part in the discussion, but the old lady and her son-in-law both argued with Anang, and took an equal part in deciding how much to ask. Rongsin ventured that they would like 34 rupees, but Anang made a startled noise to indicate that he found this unreasonable, and eventually he offered 26 rupees. The two men embarked on a considerable discussion of the market, the vagaries of the price, the difficulties of selling cotton, and the risks Anang would be taking. Anang was a fluent and eloquent debater, and had a ready answer for every point the others raised. He spoke more than the rather shy and quiet Rongsin or even than the latter's usually ebullient mother-in-law. Rongsin eventually suggested 30 rupees, but Anang was still firm; then Ringin came down to 28 rupees, but this only evoked more vigorous argument from Anang, and assertions that he couldn't possibly pay more than 26 rupees. Anang had with him two ten-rupee notes, which he placed beside the fireplace from time to time, flourishing them with a good deal of emphasis, but each time Ringin slowly picked them up and gave them back to him. She and her son-in-law went down to 27 rupees, pleaded for at least half a rupee more than the twenty-six that were originally offered, and after perhaps half an hour of discussion agreed on the original price offered by Anang. Anang left with Ringin the twenty rupees he had been flourishing and hurried out with the promise to bring the rest of the money and pick up the cotton the next morning.

This was typical of the cotton deals which regularly take place in the village, and which are obviously very different from the transactions discussed in Chapter VIII. However, the fact that these are monetary transactions between households is a direct reflection of the use of money in the market, since all the cotton is destined ultimately to be carried into the market and sold. As with purchases at the market, agreement is usually reached only after vigorous bargaining. Traditional labor exchange follows well-defined but entirely different principles, and it would be extremely ungracious to appear to calculate and haggle over its terms; but on the occasion of any cash transaction it is expected that both buyer and seller will push as hard as they can to get a good price.

Growers, purchasers, or porters carry the cotton into the market, and there, unlike any other crop, it is sold under close governmental supervision. The District Council sends a representative to the market to supervise the trading. The cotton purchasers are not usually private traders, but are large firms, represented by agents who reputedly come from as far away as Bombay. The firms have international connections, so the fluctuations of the international cotton market affect the Garo farmer directly—though he understands nothing of this, and must take whatever price he can get. The price is actually determined by bids of the representatives of the firms. Whoever makes the highest bid is able to take most of the cotton that day, though if the others are willing, they are permitted to buy a smaller portion at the same price. All Garos sell at the price fixed for that day in the market. They can refuse to sell if they feel the price is not high enough; but there is little to be done with unsold cotton, and it is risky to wait until the next week in the hope of a higher price. One week it did happen that no offers were made that satisfied the Garos, and the several dozen Garo men who had cotton all cooperated with each other in refusing to sell until the next day, when the buyers finally offered one rupee more per maund. When the agreement is finally made, the purchasers have the baskets of cotton loaded on to trucks, and it is shipped off to find its way to world markets.

*Other Cash Crops.* Neither ginger, nor chili peppers, nor any of the other crops which Rengsanggri people sell compares in importance to cotton in total cash value. Other villages earn more from oranges or areca nuts, but neither is important in Rengsanggri. Cash crops other than cotton are most often carried into the market by the man who has grown them. They are taken to the part of the market where the particular commodity is sold, and buyer and seller haggle over the price of each transaction individually. Prices are discussed widely enough so that each commodity tends to sell at a fairly steady price over the short run; but other than for cotton, there is no organized way by which prices are made public, and so they may vary somewhat from sale to sale. As in all the other market transactions, the buyer's knowledge of general market conditions and his skill with figures is apt to be so much greater than that of the farmer that the latter is at a distinct disadvantage.

*Rice Beer.* The women of Rengsanggri are in the fortunate position of living beside a major pathway, near convenient resting places a few miles from the market. People who come in from further away often want to rest before the final stage of the trip to market, or afterward on their way home. Every week a few Rengsanggri women prepare pots of rice beer which they carry to the roadside and sell to the travelers by the bottle or glass. Since beer varies in quality, the buyers are given the opportunity of sampling a small amount in a cup before purchasing it. It is therefore necessary to prepare a good brew, and for this purpose women who make beer for sale usually purchase high-quality rice at the market. This may cost them about 5 rupees, but if they are able to sell all of the beer made from it they may take in as much as 10 rupees, which gives them a very satisfactory profit. If the brew turns out badly, or if there is a surplus of beer at the road one week, they may not make so much, and may even take a loss, though the beer can always be finished at home.

It is illegal to sell rice beer in the market place itself, and it is the existence of this regulation—even though some beer may be sold under cover—which gives the Rengsanggri women a favorable opportunity to do business. They have two favorite spots, one immediately adjacent to the village and one about a mile closer to the market, at the junction of two paths. Women from another village sometimes sell beer at this latter place also, but the Rengsanggri women always sit together, stirring their pots of the brew, and chatting gaily with each other and with the travelers who stop to rest and sometimes to have a drink.

*Market Snacks.* Some women, though rarely those from Rengsanggri, boil vegetables—most often sweet potatoes or sweet manioc—and sell them in the market place as snacks. They are peeled and sold a piece at a time for one anna each. Other women sell prepared packets of betel mixture ready for chewing.

*Betel-leaf Dealers.* Considerable quantities of betel leaf are picked in the villages to the east of Rengsanggri, where the elevation is greater and apparently more suitable for this plant.

Men from those villages carry it in large baskets as far as a fork in the path near Rengsanggri, where men from the latter village buy the baskets from them and carry them further. Most of them take their purchases straight through the Rongram market on Friday, and on up to Tura for the one on Saturday. Here they sell it to Tura people and to shopkeepers, who resell it throughout the week. This carrying trade is almost a monopoly of Rengsanggri men, and almost every week six or eight of them are found in the Tura market, where they always sit together with the leaves spread around them. The pickers tie the leaves together in packets of twenty, and then twenty of these packets are tied into larger bundles which may sell on the Rongram path for a rupee and eight annas, and which may be worth 2/8 by the time they reach Tura. Several bundles can be carried by a single man, so they hope to make a profit of 5 or even 10 rupees on a trip; but the market fluctuates according to whether there is a surplus or a scarcity that week, so they sometimes take a loss. The leaves must be kept moist and carefully tended by the carrier, or they will wither and be impossible to sell. Since the leaves stay fresh for no more than a week, there is an ever new demand in Tura.

*Butchers.* Every week in the market two or three Garos butcher a cow and sell its meat. This is one of the few transactions entirely in the hands of the Garos, since most of the plains people consider butchering, and especially the butchering of cattle, a degrading occupation. The slaughtering is done at a rather remote corner of the market. The cow is killed and then divided into pieces of standard weight but unpredictable anatomical provenance, and these are displayed on a mat spread upon the ground. Less frequently a pig is butchered and sold in the same fashion.

*Wage Labor.* Opportunities for wage labor, though not plentiful, are available by the day for a few men. A few can work as porters for fellow villagers, or for men of neighboring villages who have a large amount of cotton to carry into market.

Occasionally the 'owner' of the market, or a Bengali merchant, hires a few Garos to build a tea stall or other kind of market shed. In 1956 a new motor road was being cut through the hills in the neighborhood of Rengsanggri. It was divided into lengths of one-eighth to one-half mile, which were assigned to contractors, each of whom had to hire laborers to do the actual digging and carrying of earth. Some of the labor was paid for by the day, while some was subcontracted in small amounts, so that a worker would be paid a fixed sum for digging or filling a stretch of road no more than fifteen feet long; and a few of these subcontractors even hired a neighbor to help them dig. Wage labor most often brought a rupee per day, but heavy labor might be paid at one rupee eight annas or even two rupees per day.

Most of the money which Garos earn in these ways is spent in petty purchases of various items which they need or want through the year. Except for a few things such as small amounts of salt or singly purchased snacks, for which there is a more or less standard price, the purchaser must expect to haggle for everything he buys. The atmosphere of the market place can be most readily conveyed by accounts of a few transactions which I overheard.

A Garo who wished to buy some dried fish of a particularly high quality surveyed the offerings of the Bengali dried-fish merchants who were lined up along the side of the road, sitting on the ground behind their merchandise. This kind of fish comes in bundles each weighing one seer (about two pounds), and consists of much larger specimens than the ordinary variety. One seller was vigorously talking about his fish, emphatically declaring that he would sell it for 2 rupees per bundle and could not come down a single *pice* (a coin worth 1/4 anna, which was obsolete at the time). Not taking his declaration on the price too seriously, the Garo youth counted out ten bundles, suggested that since he was buying a large quantity he should get a special price, and offered 15 rupees; but the seller was firm at 20 rupees. Then they quietly went into a huddle, where they spoke privately, the buyer giving the seller a chance to make an agreement that would not jeopardize his position with other buyers. The seller would come down only 8 annas, however, so the buyer moved on and counted out 10 bundles from the assortment of another dealer. This dealer gave as his price 19 rupees, and the buyer now countered with an offer of 17. The seller came down to 18; but when the buyer suggested Rs. 17/8, the seller said no. The buyer started to walk away, but called out the price of Rs. 17/8, to give the dealer one more chance. This time the latter nodded agreement, and the sale was made. The man had spent almost half an hour making this purchase.

Not all purchases take so long. A Garo went to a stall where the dealer had hung out the colored strings which Garo men tie around the knot of their long hair. The Garo counted out ten of these, asked the price, and was told one rupee and four annas (two annas each, which is more or less the standard price). The man said that he wouldn't give it, and the shopkeeper suggested Rs. 1/2. The man said with determination that he would give him only one rupee, and the shopkeeper agreed. The whole discussion took no more than thirty seconds. The shopkeeper afterward turned to me and explained that he had given a special price because the man had purchased so many of them.

The quality of most commodities varies considerably, and this, as well as size and amount, affects the price. Knowledge of such variations gives an advantage to the merchants, but Garos are happy to take advantage of any knowledge they have. Once I went with my friend Bitak to a cloth merchant to buy a length of the ordinary blue cloth which Garos tie around their heads as turbans. I asked the merchant the price and he told me twelve annas per yard. Bitak thought this reasonable, so I agreed and asked for two yards. Bitak suggested that I measure it on my arm, the length from the elbow to the tip of the middle finger being reckoned as one-half yard. I measured out four such lengths; the shopkeeper accepted my measurements and tore off the cloth, and I gave him his rupee and a half. Bitak and I walked a short distance away from the shop and then, with immense satisfaction, Bitak measured the cloth on his own arm and found that it came to four and a half lengths of his own arm. He had been aware of the extraordinary length of my arm, and was delighted to think that we had put something over on the shopkeeper.

Most purchases are made on behalf of a single household, and most are for immediate use. Dried fish may be an exception on both these scores, for it is generally purchased in large quantities once a year and then stored until needed. Two families sometimes purchase it together, and then divide it in proportion to the contribution of each when they get home. The largest purchases are made in February and March, when a household may buy as much as a maund of fish—an amount which should last for an entire year. The Garos dry it further in the warm sun and then pound it vigorously into cylinders of bamboo which are plugged with clay to keep out the air. Preserved in this manner, dried fish should still be edible after a year or more. The only other purchase at which households commonly cooperate is that of cattle, which are bought in order to be butchered and divided.

One of the few cash purchases regularly made by Rengsanggri people away from the market was that of paddy. Rengsanggri had a slight rice deficit, but the people sold enough cotton and other cash crops to be able to balance this by purchase. Paddy was occasionally purchased at the market, but more often an agreement was made with some man from a village a few miles away, where rice was more plentiful, to purchase a large quantity in a single batch. This saved money since it avoided the labor of carrying the loads into the market and out again. These purchases were often for several maunds of paddy, but it was measured by volume rather than by weight. A standard method of storing the paddy is to make a cylindrical container by bending a large, flexible mat into a circle, standing this on the floor, and tying it in place. Paddy is then simply poured into the cylinder. People without granaries sometimes even store paddy in the back of their houses in this way. The rolled mat is filled with paddy to a standard height, which each man measures separately on his own body; thus it may be the height to the bridge of one man's nose, but only to the chin of a taller man—actually about four feet seven inches. The height is standard, but the girth, which is measured by forearm lengths, varies, and the price is agreed to on the basis of the girth.

Large sales and large purchases at the market are both almost always handled by the men. Men carry most of the cotton to market, and even if his wife helps, it is the husband who makes the sale to the trader and who receives the money. It is the man who dickers for the price at which he sells his chilis and ginger; and when a large quantity of dried fish are to be purchased, it is almost always the man who bargains for the price and who actually receives the fish from the seller. But women do much of the smaller-scale marketing. The money a woman earns from her sales is considered rather specially hers, and she is likely to use it herself to buy things. While some of it may be spent on cloth or even on jewelry for herself, women also use their money for household necessities or treats, such as small quantities of especially tasty dried fish, or of salt or sugar, to be used by the whole family. Furthermore a woman can readily spend from the general family budget so long as there is general agreement between herself and her husband. Even if her husband actually spends the money, he may buy personal items for his wife and children as well as things for himself or for general family use.

Without noting sales and purchases in a detailed way for at least a year it would be difficult to get a complete picture of the monetary side of household budgets, and even then the variation in both harvests and prices in successive years would leave one without a secure average. Even modest households often have a cash income of five hundred rupees or more over the course of the year. Typically, well over half of this comes from the sale of cotton, but the cash is spent in small amounts for a multitude of miscellaneous goods. Of course, money income constitutes only a small fraction of the budget, since Garos grow most of their own food and manufacture many other essential items without the expenditure of a single rupee; but for other goods which the Garos consider equally essential, money must be used.

The market place where most money is earned and spent is a cosmopolitan center. Here the most remote villager deals with Bengalis, Nepalis, and sometimes people from other parts of India. He hears different languages spoken and sees different clothes. New manufactured goods appear which he either buys and incorporates into his life or looks at longingly, feeling that in some way he is on the outer periphery of a vast and varied world. The market is one channel by which new ideas have penetrated the district, bringing changes to the life of all Garos.

# ❧ XII ❧

## *New Ideas*

THE STUDY OF A single community at a single time leaves an unjustifiable impression of permanence. The Garos have not been isolated from the rest of the world; indeed, contact with the civilization of north India undoubtedly stretches back for many hundreds of years. There are no records in existence to substantiate this, but it is clear that innumerable cultural traits found in other parts of India have made their way into Garo culture and have now become Garo traits as well. The Garo language contains hundreds, perhaps thousands, of loan words from Bengali and other languages of north India. The phenomena covered by these terms range from such esoteric modern matters as governmental affairs, all the way through the names for many plants which have come in from the plains, down to so intimate a word as that for mother's brother (i.e., *mama*, a term occurring in many north Indian languages), and that most useful of Indian expressions, *achcha*, which has some of the same meanings as the American "O.K." Like other people of India, Garos greet each other with the question which to the uninitiated Westerner seems such an invasion of privacy: "Where are you going?" Some of their religious concepts, such as their belief in the possibility of rebirth and their uncertainty as to whether two names stand for two gods or only one, seem reminiscent of Hindu thought. From resemblances so fundamental it may be inferred that close contact with peoples in the world around them has existed for a long period, though the nature of their earlier contact is now obscure. More recently, both Western and Indian civilizations have had increasingly direct influence upon the Garos. Three major sources of change have affected them over the past few decades and continue to affect them today: the imposition of external political control, new methods of agriculture requiring permanent land tenure, and proselytizing Christianity. Each will be discussed in turn.

### IMPOSITION OF EXTERNAL POLITICAL CONTROL

It is difficult to form a clear idea of the Garo political system in pre-British times, since the earliest reports are at best fragmentary and at worst contradictory; but I will attempt to piece together as much information as possible from them. All early British observers were concerned with finding men of authority among the Garos with whom they had to deal. The men they found were variously referred to as "chief," "headman," "Booneah," "nokma," "lushkor"—probably a term applied by the British rather than one used by the Garos of the time—and "Lokma," presumably either a variant or a misunderstanding of *nokma*. The extent of the authority of these men is unfortunately not very clear. The widest estimate of their authority was given by Mills, who wrote, "In former times for three or four generations past, the chiefs of Rangtoghiri and Dolanghiri were acknowledged lords paramount in the hills, and they had considerable power in the great number of slaves they possessed and were always willing to exercise that power in aid of the Government, but the last great chief Tokul Lushkur died four or five years ago, and has been succeeded by a man deficient in ability and energy, and I believe his power has been greatly diminished by division of property, and by the escape of his slaves, at any rate we are now unable to obtain much assistance, and there seems to be no other chief who has any considerable authority and is willing to use it at our direction."[1] Mills also wrote, concerning certain chiefs who were believed to be extending their power over neighboring regions, "... We have reason to believe that some of the western Garrow chiefs have extended their authority over many of the neighboring clans of Garrows."[2] How such widespread or even "paramount" authority, if it really existed, could have been wielded is difficult to understand, considering the difficulty of moving about most parts of the hills and the ferocious independence which all observers attributed to the Garos at that time. Possibly these quotations are somewhat exaggerated in their implications, for in 1849 Reynolds reported disillusionment in trying to get compliance from the Garos without reference to the "Lokma" or "chief" of the particular village concerned.[3] He makes almost no reference to the duties or prerogatives of these "chiefs." Eliot, in a very early report, stated that the "Booneahs decide on all complaints except adultery, murder and robbery, which are tried by a general assembly of the neighboring chiefs ..."[4] It would seem that adultery, murder, and robbery might comprise a large portion of the disputes that had to be settled. Reynolds wrote of a chief called Moonkual, "The power this man possesses over the people is astonishing, and his will is law"; but this author does not state the occasions upon which Moonkual exercised power, or the sanctions which he might apply if he were defied.[5] Throughout the reports, however, runs the implication that when these important men were willing to cooperate, the British were able to accomplish their tasks of punishing the instigators of head-hunting raids, collecting tax, or obtaining labor, but that without their aid almost nothing was possible. However widespread their jurisdiction, and however they may have enforced their will, these men seem to have had some genuine power, but they can hardly have been despots, for observers sometimes remarked on the humanity of the chiefs. A chief called Oodassey was "by no means a violent or artful man. He is far from possessing a bad disposition, is a mild man, and by all accounts takes great pains to do justice, and keep up unanimity with his people."[6] The absence of strict observation of rank was also remarked upon by Eliot in connection with marriages, marriage being permissible even though "the disparity of age or rank be ever so great."[7]

The reports are more explicit as to the mode of recruitment to office. Eliot reported that in one village "... the rightful chief is Momee, a woman, and her power being, by established usage, transferable by marriage to her husband, he ought in consequence to preside."[8] Fifty years later, around 1850, some of the Garo chiefs were being officially recognized, though hardly controlled, by the British, for Mills states, "The office of Lushkar is hereditary; it descends, according to the Garrow law of descent, to the deceased's son-in-law, who on succession receives a perwannah from this office, executing at the same time an agreement, that he will abstain from war and will not himself keep, nor allow those subservient to him to keep human skulls in his or their possession; that he will report immediately all murders, or cases of homicide that occur in his jurisdiction, that he will apprehend all offenders therein; that he will not allow any parties of independent Garrows on predatory expeditions to pass through his country, and that he will watch those who do so, and report the circumstance. This agreement is a mere dead letter, not acted up to, I believe, in any one particular."[9] However poorly these men may have lived up to the expectations of the British, the method of inheritance of this office was no doubt precisely that of the inheritance to the nokmaship today.

It would seem, however, that these "chiefs" or "Lushkors" may have had rather more authority than the nokmas do today. If so, the contradictions of the office, inherited in its peculiar way, may have been more serious than they are now. Could a man who obtains office by marrying the correct daughter of the correct man be consistently assigned significant authority? In the light of this question it is interesting to note that two of the earliest men to leave first-hand reports of expeditions into the hills tell of instances in which the rule of inheritance had been defied, and a different man had assumed the office. Eliot reported that in one village "Oodassey Booneah is looked on as the headman of this pass at present, having most influence with his sect; the rightful chief is a young and silly man, the chiefship is usurped by Oodassey, and his usurpation is submitted to by the rightful chief."[10] In a similar vein Reynolds reported, "The chief of the village is Moonkual; he has, however, no real title to the distinction, but being a clever intriguing man, he had gradually usurped the authority of the old hereditary chief, who is in his dotage, and his heir and son-in-law being weak in intellect, the people have chosen for themselves a man capable of directing their counsels and managing them. They still, as a matter of form, submit any important subject for the consideration of the old chief, but I query whether his opinion is attended to when it is at variance with that of Moonkual."[11] One can hardly draw firm conclusions from so few cases, but certain basic facts do seem clear: legitimate succession was to the son-in-law, but there were ways of circumventing legitimate succession when the proper heir proved to be ineffectual.

The British first met the Garos who lived along the borders of Bengal and shortly thereafter made contact with those near the Assamese plains. These are the same areas where Garos had long had the most intimate contact with Indian plains people— a contact which seems sometimes to have been accompanied by mutual hostility, and intermittently by head-hunting on the part of the Garos. Violence, however, did not prohibit a degree of regularity in the relationship. For one thing, for as long as anything is known of them the Garos appear to have been dependent upon markets.[12] Before the British built roads into the region, markets were held only at the foot of the hills; but then as today, the Garos carried down their cotton and other crops and traded them for dried fish, salt, and other essential items, and the markets were already places where the Garos met plains people. The markets were apparently held under the auspices of important men in the plains. By the middle of the last century, and no doubt earlier, certain zemindars made claims to duties on the trade with the hills.[13] The ethnic affiliation of the zemindars is often unclear, but presumably they were not Garos; some are referred to as Bengalis, and one is described as a Mech, a term used today for one of the so-called "plains tribes" of Assam who speak, or recently spoke, a Tibeto-Burman language but who are Hindus and live in the plains.[14] This zemindar was reported to have made continual attempts, in the early part of the nineteenth century, to bring the Garos near to his domain under subjection, and to have kept his border area in a turmoil. Thus it would seem that not all violence at the time originated with the Garos. The border areas were, in fact, characterized by an endemic instability.[15] The zemindars were able to exert authority at times, but difficult topography and the relative mobility of the Garos would set limits upon how far into the hills their authority could consistently reach. At times the Garos were able to throw off the authority of the zemindars and even to raid the plains, but the relatively dense plains population and the ability of their foes to marshal their defense prevented them from ever leaving their hills very far behind. In the border areas disturbance was almost continual. It is probable that further back in the hills the Garos were vigorously taking each other's heads at every opportunity, but we know nothing of the dynamics of this fighting.

The early sources give us only a partial picture of the real sources of power, the means of settling disputes, and the organization of head-hunting. No Garo is alive today who can remember how these were accomplished. The most coherent description of head-hunting that I ever obtained was from an old man of Songmagri who said he had heard about it from his father and father-in-law, both of whom he described as 'men choppers.' This man, Raki, was certain that there had been traditional enmity between certain villages, and that, in particular, Songmagri (which at the time included the ancestors of the people who eventually went to Rengsanggri) was the enemy of Digranggri and Gongronggri to the north. If this is true, it could mean that the dispute between these villages over land some years ago had had an ancient origin, though it is not impossible that Raki was projecting a later quarrel backwards. Raki described head-hunting as being largely a matter of sneaking through the jungle and attacking people at work in their fields. He said that nobody would ever dare to attack the village itself. He was able to show me some of the small splints of bamboo which were once inserted into the ground so as to impale the barefooted attackers. Before a raid and, if successful, after their return from it, the warriors would perform a ceremony at a sacred spot in or near their own village where a number of small stones were clustered. Each village still possesses this cluster of stones, but with the passing of head-hunting they have been largely abandoned except for a small sacrifice held there once in three or four years. The object of the head-hunting was to bring back heads from a hit-and-run attack and then to celebrate the success of the raid by beating the drums and killing a cow. Raki was of the opinion that it was the *nokma*s who led the head-hunting expeditions.

There is nothing unreasonable about this description of head-hunting. The most questionable part may be that played by the *nokma*, but perhaps the *nokma*s really did have more authority then than they do now. The authority which the new office of the *loskor* has accumulated today may have been acquired at the expense of that of the *nokma*. This would seem particularly reasonable if the *nokma*ship was once somewhat more readily transferable than it is today, so that any *nokma* who was not completely competent could be replaced. This still leaves unanswered the question of how matrilocal residence, and particularly the *nokma*s' matrilocal residence, harmonized with the exercise of violence by the village men. The *nokma* of a lineage today is so clearly a man from *another* lineage who has married into it that it would be impossible to imagine that this is a recent phrasing of his position, even if it were not for the descriptions that earlier observers left of the methods of recruiting a new chief.

The fullest early description of the means of settling disputes among the Garos was given in a remarkable account by Francis Hamilton, who was sent to the borders of Assam by the East India Company between 1809 and 1814 to undertake a survey of the territories adjacent to those under its control. Hamilton was unable to visit the territory himself, but he spoke with natives of the company's territories who had visited the areas, and to others whose home was in Assam, among the latter of whom were a number of Garos. In regards their means of settling disputes he said:

"The chiefs known as *nokma*s and the head men of families assemble in a council called *jingma changga* [which in modern Garo simply means "to assemble in a crowd"] and endeavor to reconcile all those of the clan who have disputes; for it would not appear that they have a right to inflict any punishment unless a man should be detected in uttering a falsehood before them, in which case he would be put to instant death, more from popular indignation than from a regular progress of justice. Dishonesty or stealing seem rarely to be practiced, and almost the only source of dispute seems to be murder, which would appear to be an ordinary crime. But the relations of the person killed are, by custom, held bound to demand blood for blood, and ought to put to death either the murderer or one of his kindred, or at least one of his slaves. The other family then is bound to pursue a similar mode of retaliation, and the feud would thus continue endless, unless the council interfered and brought about a mutual reconciliation, which it is usually able to effectuate, by inducing the parties to accept a price for the blood that has been spilt. Although every head of a family has an equal right to sit in their assemblies, the influence of the chiefs, or of one or two wise men usually decides everything.

"When a man of one clan murders a person belonging to a

different community, the matter is arranged with more difficulty, and often produces a war, unless the chiefs mutually
endeavour to reconcile matters, in which case their influence
generally prevails; but they have no authority to declare peace
or war, nor even in the field do they pretend to command any
free man. If any man complains of an injury, such as one of his
family having been murdered by a foreigner, the whole clan is
ready to avenge his cause, or to fight until their companion is
satisfied. No compulsion can be used; but the man who refuses
to take the field would be entirely disgraced."[16]

Garos today often say that adjudication of disputes was
formerly the *nokma*'s job, but it seems reasonable to suggest that
disputes were more frequently settled by negotiation between
kinship groups, with a less significant part played by any
neutral party, and this seems to be implied by Hamilton, who
mentions "headmen of families" and "wise men" in addition
to the "chiefs" themselves. In most of the Garo area today,
only the most petty cases are decided without the presence of a
neutral representative of the government. Chondu told me of a
time when he and some of his relatives met in order to settle a
dispute which had arisen when some children had stolen a few
eggs. They met without any governmental representative, but
Chondu described the meeting in exactly the same terms used
to describe court cases, and the relatives collected money for a
compensation, just as they do in more serious matters.

There are Garos living in what is today the Mymensingh
district of East Pakistan who apparently settle disputes somewhat differently from their relatives in the Garo Hills District.
Ever since the British took over administration, Mymensingh
has been governed as part of Bengal, while the Garo Hills District itself has been part of the State of Assam; so although
Garos have been straddling an international border only since
the independence of India and Pakistan, they have been
straddling a state border for much longer. Such legal devices as
the *loskor*ships and the special provisions for dealing with cases

under Garo customary law have not been established in Bengal. I was unable to visit the Garo area of East Pakistan, but I was told that even today the Garos there often settle their own disputes without recourse to government intervention, though in the last resort they may appeal to the government, if the parties cannot otherwise become reconciled. I was told that among the Mymensingh Garos cases are argued between the two parties to the dispute and their respective kinship groups. The two principals to the dispute are said to be represented in the discussion by "speakers" who are usually, but perhaps not always, members of the matrilineal descent groups of the principals. Elders of the two sides may also speak up, raising as many points of law as they can and citing previous cases in support of their arguments. Such discussions are said usually to lead to agreement between the two sides, and to settlement by means of a monetary compensation.

The older men in the Garo Hills proper remember the time when "speakers" played a more important role in legal disputes than they do now. Speakers are said generally to have been older 'brothers' (ada) or 'uncles' (mama) of the principals. To be a "speaker" is described as a skilled job, requiring intimate knowledge of the fine points of law in addition to the ability to speak well. Most people were unable to handle it. Today, older members of the kinship groups still state their opinions at trials, but with less formality than seems to have been the case formerly. Today much of the power has shifted away from kinship groups and their speakers to the ideally neutral loskors. Of course even in Mymensingh disputes can be taken to the government courts, but recourse to the courts seems to come at a later stage in the proceedings. Before the assumption of administration by the British, the only appeal from disagreement at such a meeting was presumably violence.

As British power became more pervasive toward the middle of the last century, and as the government came into increasing contact and conflict with the Garos, it inherited the ancient violence of the frontier area. The British divided the Garos into three classes: the zemindary Garos, whose country formed part of a zemindary estate since it had been subdued by forceful action on the part of the zemindar, who exacted some degree of allegiance from them; the "Nazrana" or tributary Garos, who in theory owed tribute to the British government rather than to the zemindar; and finally the independent Garos, living further in the interior, who owed nothing, and about whom virtually nothing was known, much of the area still not having been visited by any European.[17] The boundaries between the three areas were, however, very imperfectly defined. The British were continually frustrated in their attempts to collect agreed taxes, and were intermittently disturbed by more violent action on the part of the Garos. It was a thoroughly unsatisfactory situation, from the government's point of view, and government officers made constant references to the difficulty of controlling the violence in the hills. But the British faced a serious dilemma since they felt it to be impossible to occupy the hills, the only way in which the violence could finally be controlled. Mills made this very clear: "The chief cause of the barbarous conditions of the Garrows and their violent incursions has arisen from the terrible unhealthiness of the climate of the tract they inhabit, which will not admit of officers or troops being sent into the Garrow hills except at an extreme risk of life.... Nothing but dire necessity should, in my opinion, induce us to occupy and administer this country; its climate is most deadly, and unless a European functionary can reside in the interior, and superintend the administration, which it is known he could not do, we should not attempt to extend our rule over unprofitable hills. All past experience proves that we cannot trust entirely to native agency in the management of wild tribes. There is nothing to be gained by occupying the country; the revenue that could be derived from it would not cover one sixth of the cost of maintaining the police force; the expense of Government would be considerable, and the loss of life in all probability appalling. Matters have not yet, I think, come to that pass."[18]

Within twenty years after this statement, however, matters did finally come to that pass, and the British determined to take the territory under their administration. Once they resolved to do so, the move went smoothly. Several columns of troops moved into the hills from different directions, and in 1867 an administrative center was set up at the place which came to be known as Tura. Head-hunting and feuding continued for a few years, but in 1876 the government rounded up two hundred skulls and publicly destroyed them.[19] Apparently the symbolism of this maneuver was effective, for today Garos speak of this as the end of head-hunting, and in fact since that time, peace in the Garo Hills has never been seriously threatened.

If peace was to be maintained, some method of settling disputes other than a resort to violence had to be established, and the new British administration was forced to guarantee the settlement of all legal cases, even petty ones. A dispute that could not be settled by traditional methods could not be allowed to lead to inter-village warfare. Inevitably the British government had to give some supervision to the settlement of trouble cases, and they had to provide a system of higher courts to which decisions that could not be settled at the village level could be appealed. They also, of course, had an interest in collecting taxes, and in building roads to allow for the development of the district. The solution to these needs was found in the system of *loskor*ships with their petty courts at the lowest level, and the district courts above them to which their decisions could be appealed.

There is no evidence that the British administration was anything but completely sincere in its effort to settle disputes according to traditional Garo law. The *loskor*s have always been Garos, and their job has always been explicitly defined as the administration of customary law according to traditional practice. Even in the district courts, which have generally been presided over by non-Garos, an attempt has been made to apply traditional law. Old men, who were presumed to be knowledgeable in Garo tradition, have been called in to give their opinion, and in the records of cases in the District Council, references have occasionally been made to a published ethnological article on Garo law. However sincere the attempt to follow traditional laws, the imposition of neutral judicial officers, the guarantee of settlement by the district government, and the reservation of force by the government authorities, could not help but bring changes. The office of *loskor* appears gradually to have accumulated power, probably at the expense both of the *nokma*s and of the matrilineal descent groups. This does not mean that the latter are no longer significant institutions, but only that their relative importance has probably declined somewhat as that of the *loskor* has risen. Today the *loskor*s and their courts, and the administration above them are so much a part of the Garo social organization that it is quite inaccurate to describe the Garos as forming anything but a dependent non-sovereign unit in a much larger society. Significant power over the Garos was for eighty years concentrated in London; with Indian independence, this power has been inherited by New Delhi.

Today the courts of the *loskor*s are formally established under regulations passed by the District Council and approved by the governor of Assam; however, in 1956 Indian independence and the shift in jurisdiction over the *loskor*s' courts from the Deputy Commissioner's office to the District Council were only beginning to have any effect on the villages in the district. Disputes were still settled in the same manner as during the period of British rule.

## NEW AGRICULTURAL METHODS

Much of the discussion of the legal changes which have come about with the British occupation is necessarily inferential, on the one hand since no territory has escaped its effect, and on the other no one remembers how disputes were settled before the British came, or how head-hunting expeditions were organized. The other important ways in which the world has impinged upon the Garos have been less pervasive, and by comparing areas more and less Christianized and more and less dependent upon wet rice, one may obtain a reasonably comprehensive picture of the resulting changes. The agriculture and religion of Rengsanggri are reasonably typical of the more conservative Garos, though there are numerous variations in detail even where neither wet rice nor Christianity has had appreciable influence. Where these have had influence, the variation is much greater.

The Garo Hills are not excessively rugged, and even in the center of the district, a few flat river valleys can be profitably converted into paddy land; but it seems that before the British established peace, the Garos never practiced wet rice agriculture, or that if they did, they ceased being Garos and merged into the plains population.[20]

Ever since the British took over, however, some Garos in most parts of the hills have been gradually converting land to wet cultivation. The system of wet rice agriculture now used by these Garos closely follows that practiced by the plains people around them. Wet rice requires techniques and work habits so different from those required by dry rice that the problems of shifting to its cultivation are considerable. The preliminary task of preparing the ground is a barrier to all but the exceptionally enterprising man, for the jungle has to be cleared far more thoroughly than is ever necessary for hill rice. The ground must be leveled; and in order to assure a water supply there must be a proper choice of fields, and both irrigation ditches and dikes around the fields must be built. This large initial investment in labor may eventually be handsomely repaid, but for the first few years the crops may not even be as great as those possible from the same amount of labor on hill plots. What is needed, therefore, is a degree of foresight and planning, a willingness to work hard now for a rather distant goal, which is not necessary to the traditional types of agriculture. Even after the fields are constructed, all is not assured; for example, one man cited the danger of destruction of the fields by marauding elephants as inhibiting his desire to undertake the necessary labor. Beyond the initial labor, moreover, new techniques must be mastered. Preparation of wet fields for planting requires plowing, and this in turn necessitates the use of draft animals. A Garo who wishes to open wet land must maintain a team of oxen, and both the expense and the labor involved go beyond those required for dry agriculturalists. Skill in guiding animals before the plow must be acquired, and adjustment made to the patterns of work which this demands. The preparation of the ground for wet rice has a tedious monotony by comparison with the clearing of hill fields. Even the times of planting and harvesting are different. Seed must be sown in a seed bed in April or May, and then transplanted between June and August—an entirely new agricultural task. As with preparing the fields, transplanting requires intensive labor—though, since the paddy fields are not weeded after planting, once the transplanting is finished there is little work except for maintaining the dikes and regulating the irrigation. The fields are kept continually under water until about November, at which time they are drained. In the following month the rice ripens and is harvested—at least two months later than the harvest of hill rice. Even the methods of harvesting and threshing must be different, since the variety of rice used in wet cultivation is tougher and the grains cannot be milked off the stalks like those of hill rice. Instead, it must be cut with a sickle and carried to a special threshing floor in the village. Here the rice is spread so that cattle may be driven around and around over it, gradually beating the grain off the stalk—another new technical operation which hill rice growers can omit completely. Not only is the wet-rice kernel more firmly attached to the stalk, but also the husks are tougher, so that wet rice growers often build efficient, but rather complex foot-operated rice pounders to replace the simpler mortar and pestle used by the hill rice growers.

It is true that most Garos who take up wet rice agriculture still farm some hill land to supplement the other, since it cannot produce the variety of crops that Garos are accustomed to. While this practice softens the abruptness of the change, the technical factors involved are all obstacles to the shift to wet rice agriculture, and it is easy to understand why the Garos have sometimes been slow to adopt the newer and in the long run more productive methods.

But while some Garos do make such changes, difficult though they are, the technical innovations are only the first stage of the transition; for with it comes a series of changes in the rights of individuals to land and in the social relationships of men to each other. The transition has been so difficult that new wet fields have often been cleared by people accustomed to these techniques who have moved in from other areas rather than by local hill rice farmers. The complications of changing residence appear to be less formidable than those of changing techniques. As a result, there has been considerable population movement connected with wet rice growing. Garos from areas of established wet rice cultivation, as well as members of neighboring ethnic groups, have both frequently moved many miles in search of suitable land. As a result the wet rice areas are generally a good deal more cosmopolitan than those where dry rice alone is grown. A single village in a wet rice area often includes men from several parts of the hills, and the ties of friendship and kinship which such people retain with the places of their origin help to give such villages a broader perspective upon the world.

Hill farmers seem to have had little opposition to the clearing of some land for wet rice, even though this has meant that it could no longer be used for dry cultivation. In most villages the areas in which wet cultivation is possible are more or less limited, it never yet having occurred to a Garo that hillsides might be terraced; and the threat of alienation of the land has not yet seemed particularly serious. Strangers, and sometimes even non-Garos, have been allowed to settle and clear new land. At the present time the laws passed by the Garo Hills District Council in an effort to encourage wet rice cultivation provide that if local villagers do not take advantage of suitable land, others will have the right to convert it to paddy fields. In some cases new settlers have probably paid the *nokma* or even the *a'king* owners (title-holders) a fee to permit its use and alienation. Some might interpret this as *a'wil*, the fee that is traditionally paid to the *a'king* owner by non-villagers who wish to use dry fields, though ordinarily *a'wil* confers only a temporary right. Others might interpret it as purchase price for the land; or, finally, it might be considered a bribe, since no such purchase is recognized as legal by the government. However regarded, such a fee might help to smooth over any antagonism toward the new arrival, though in practice it appears that the villagers have often failed to appreciate the value of potential paddy land and have let it go with little or no opposition.

Once land has been prepared for wet cultivation it can, of course, be cultivated year after year and need no longer be retired periodically like dry fields. The district government has recognized the right of the man who clears land to use it continuously, but has demanded the payment of an annual land tax. Within a few years after preparation, the clearer can expect his lands to be surveyed by the district government, and thereafter to be taxed. This arrangement is not entirely unwelcome, since his name is recorded at the same time and he is thus officially recognized as having the right to cultivate the land. However, the clearer does not immediately have full ownership. Rather, his rights first amount only to what is locally known as "temporary patta," which is a grant of rights of usufruct. Normally such land can be inherited in the usual fashion but cannot be sold, and if timber should be standing on the land, the government reserves the right to prevent its being cut.

Moreover, if the government should require the use of the land for such purposes as road-building, the cultivator must surrender his plot without compensation. After a good many years the land may be converted to "permanent patta." The cultivator then has full ownership rights, including the right of sale and the right to compensation if the land is needed for government purposes. He continues to pay a tax to the district government in proportion to the amount of land registered in his name. Tax on wet rice land is collected by a number of special tax officials called *mausidars*, each of whom has jurisdiction over a certain area. Under the *mausidars* are lesser officials in charge of the land records of the smaller "circles." Villagers in plains areas may pay a land tax but no house tax. House tax alone is collected in villages with no wet rice, but some villages have to pay both. House tax, unlike land tax, however, is channeled through the *loskor*. Land held under "permanent patta" is bought and sold from time to time. The price paid for the land is agreed to by buyer and seller. Such prices have not been exorbitant in terms of the value of the crop which it can produce; they rarely amount to more than three times the value of the annual crop, and are sometimes even less. New land potentially usable for wet cultivation has been available readily enough to prevent serious bidding up of the land values, and Garos have not been cultivating in this manner long enough to have come to place great faith in land as an investment. Even so, this type of private land ownership has helped to alter the distribution of wealth quite sharply in villages where it has become important. Inevitably some people show more foresight than others in opening wet plots, and in many areas of long-established wet rice cultivation a few large proprietors own more land than they are able to cultivate by their own labor. They therefore either hire labor or, more often, let their land out on shares to others who have failed to acquire wet fields. When land is thus worked on shares, the owner generally provides the seed, but the harvest is split equally between the

owner and the cultivator. The owner may also advance rice for
the cultivator and his family to eat, without changing any
interest; but the rice must be paid back at the time of the harvest. Such a loan is looked upon as a distinct advantage for the
cultivator, since only in this way can he avoid heavy interest on
a rice loan. Working on shares has not yet led to a serious problem of absentee land ownership, for even the largest proprietor
usually lets out only part of his land, and retains enough for his
family to work themselves. He and his tenant continue to do the
same kind of labor, to live in the same village, and to treat each
other as social equals, the contractual relationship not giving
rise to any marked status differences. Nevertheless, such an
agreement gives a pronounced economic advantage to the owner,
for he gets half his tenant's harvest in return for very little work
or responsibility. Since many villages with large areas of wet
rice land include a number of families who own no wet fields at
all, while there are other families who control three or four
times as much land as they require for their own use, these
villages are often  marked by a greater disparity in income than
are those which depend entirely upon traditional methods of
cultivation. In wet rice areas this variation in wealth is often
immediately apparent to the most casual visitor. Such a village
may have two or three large plank houses with corrugated iron
roofs—structures more solid, permanent, and elegant than the
traditional bamboo houses, if not much more comfortable. At
the same time, other villagers are likely to live in small bamboo
shacks which the people of Rengsanggri would hardly consider
decent.

The inheritance pattern does nothing to break up sizable land
holdings. Traditional Garos had heirlooms and expendable
household possessions to inherit, but these did not give a reliable permanent income. The pattern of inheritance to a single
daughter and her family did not, therefore, drastically bias the
distribution of wealth in favor of a few families. Owners of
wet rice land generally retain the custom of inheritance by a

single daughter, so that large holdings tend to stay intact. This is not a strict rule. Holdings of wet rice land are so recent an innovation that the rules of inheritance of the land seem thus far to remain somewhat uncodified. A man with extensive holdings is likely to give token amounts to all his daughters, and may even manage to let his sons take a little, though the relatives of his daughters are likely to object if this practice goes very far. The bulk of the land usually goes to the heiress and her husband, and if the land holding is modest, they usually receive all of it. Garos from wet rice areas expressed to me the sentiment that it was much better to keep the land together, because if it were split up, everyone would become poor. Of course, if it is kept together the other children may become even poorer; but they are advised to go to a different place and open some new land for themselves, or else to work hard and purchase land.

A few Garos have managed to accumulate extensive tracts of land and have become quite wealthy. They have been able to build large houses and to have certain luxuries well beyond the means of most people. But to a Garo, beyond a certain limit there is little use for money. No one thinks of investing it in capital goods which might increase productivity, and in the end the only thing to do with wealth is to buy more land, thereby further concentrating it into a few hands.

Permanent land ownership has a slight bearing upon kinship relations, though the effects have not been radical; and, by and large, even in areas where wet rice land has been used for two or three generations, the kinship patterns remain similar to those in an area such as Rengsanggri. Children in wet rice areas may be a bit more dependent upon their parents economically than those in purely dry rice areas. Even in wet rice areas sons and daughters sometimes sell a few crops and use the money for their personal needs, and, of course, in most villages they are able to open some dry land in addition to that under wet cultivation; but where a large part of the income comes from wet land, it is no longer possible for a son to operate his own plot in virtual independence of his family, as is commonly done by the older bachelors in Rengsanggri. As children become more dependent upon their parents they approach, even if only slightly, the kinship patterns of the plains people around them. Possibly more important is the effect of all this upon the attitude toward the rights of the kinship groups to property. Husband and wife, of course, cultivate their property together. This gives the kinship groups both of the husband and of the wife an interest in the property, which amounts to a strong additional incentive for providing replacements if one of the spouses should die. Even in traditional Garo areas the family of a dead man ought to provide a replacement to marry his widow; but where the dead man had been working a considerable area of wet rice land, his family will be especially eager and happy to provide a replacement so that they may continue to have some use of and control over it. It is clearly recognized that both families have a stake in the property, and the rules of inheritance and replacement can be nicely adapted to ensure that the rights are preserved. It can even happen that the rights of the husband and his family are so well recognized that in the case of a divorce some of the land will go to the husband, though more of it is likely to stay with the wife. The husbands have considerable control over the property which is formally handed down in the families of their wives. I was told of one instance where a son was given temporary use of a plot of land. It was agreed that he and his wife were to use the land for as long as they needed it, but that it was eventually to revert to the son's matrilineal kinship group and was under no circumstances to be inherited by his children. In this case, the son let the land fall into disuse when he moved to another area, and—what was still worse—actually tried to sell the plot. At this point one of the husbands of a woman of his matrilineal descent group stepped in and forced him to return the money, and the land was reclaimed for use by the women of the descent group and their husbands. The dispute caused considerable hard feeling, but it showed clearly that the husbands of a lineage are sometimes able to enforce their claims to land at the expense of the brothers and sons.

Whether it is the brothers or the husbands of a matrilineage who control the property, the principle of matrilineal inheritance is of course maintained. Sons are occasionally given small patches of land and even allowed to receive full ownership of them if the holdings of the parents are unusually large, but inheritance by the son of a large proportion of the estate is virtually unknown. I heard of two cases in which a son brought his wife to live in the home of his parents. This was an almost intolerably awkward arrangement, and caused conflict and quarreling in both cases. In one case the son and his wife were eventually allowed to keep and use the parental land, though not without opposition on the part of the girl's relatives, who did not want the land alienated. This could never have happened if the son had had sisters; and even so, it was most exceptional. All Garos are quite aware that the plains people around them are patrilineal and patrilocal, but even those Garos who have taken over the plains methods of agriculture most completely have no tendency to copy them.

There would appear to be somewhat less mutuality in labor exchange in areas of intensive wet rice agriculture. Not only can land be loaned to others on a sharecropping basis, but agricultural labor can sometimes be hired, especially at transplanting and harvest, when the demands of labor are particularly heavy. Labor is also sometimes hired for house-building, a practice unknown in Rengsanggri. Even when labor is given without payment, it is more often calculated and paid back in closely equivalent amounts, and less often given freely, than in the more traditional areas. In some plains areas, unlike Rengsanggri, money is also loaned at interest. Perhaps the relatively diverse origins of the people of wet rice areas makes traditional free labor exchange more difficult. One cannot so easily rely on the ancient bonds of kinship to supply the help that may be needed.

Though paddy agriculture is certainly the most important new technique to affect the Garos, there are a number of other new crops which, though less widespread, have had parallel results, since all of them allow permanent use of the same plot of land. Extensive areca-palm and orange groves have been planted in some areas. Traditionally, the man who plants a tree has first rights to its fruit, and this principle is adhered to in commercial orchards. Some men with foresight and ambition have planted large orchards, and have in practice become the owners of the land as well as of the trees, since the land cannot be used for other crops. Orchards require considerable foresight, since several years must pass before they start producing and they need a degree of continuous care. Brush must occasionally be cleared from between the trees, and gathering the fruit may be a large task. Labor may be hired for these jobs, or the crop may be sold on the tree to traders, who then organize the picking and take the fruit. Orchards vary in size from a few trees, hardly more than enough to supply the household, to several hundred. Land usable for orchards is not as limited as paddy land, though oranges require considerable altitude and cannot be grown successfully in all villages. However, anyone willing to do the work is free to plant trees; and in the long run, if ownership rules remain as they are, the orchards may add considerable imbalance to the distribution of income. In a few areas pineapple gardens have also been successfully established, with similar potential results.

In the long run, the development of these specialized cash crops is probably of economic advantage to the Garos. It can bring cash income well beyond the potentialities of slash-and-burn agriculture. It has proved profitable for traders to air-freight Garo oranges out of Assam to Calcutta. Surely rice can be more profitably grown in the flat lands of the plains, and so long as the means of transportation continue to expand, it may gradually prove profitable for the Garos to concentrate on specialized crops such as are grown more easily in the hills than in the lowlands which cover so much of north India. Such a concentration will, of course, tie them more and more intimately with the economy of India, and make them increasingly sensitive to fluctuations in that economy. It may also contribute to an imbalance in the internal distribution of wealth among the Garos. In 1956, the government was establishing community development projects and rural development blocks in parts of the district. These so far had had only limited effects, but as agricultural guidance become more intensive, it seems likely that the pace of agricultural development will quicken.

## CHRISTIANITY

The third major influence on the Garos, and in some ways the most important, has been that of Christianity. American Baptist missionaries began to have a few peripheral contacts with the Garos even before their hills were occupied by the British. Missionaries were stationed in Goalpara, a town on the Brahmaputra just north of the Garo Hills, and some of their work was with Garos. However, intensive Christianization began only after the occupation of the hills. American missionaries followed the government officers into the hills and like them set up their headquarters in the town of Tura, which remains the center of Garo Christian activities today. The missionaries not only evangelized, but from the beginning carried out extensive medical and educational work. They established a hospital in Tura, and set up dispensaries at various other points in the district. At first almost all of the education in the district was in the hands of the missionaries. They first used the Bengali alphabet for writing the language, on the principle that this was the alphabet used by the people surrounding the Garos; but they later switched to the Roman alphabet, and today the latter is used exclusively.[21] Today, although the largest part of Garo education is actually administered and paid for by the district or state governments, the legacy of missionary work continues to permeate the educational system. It apparently became established very early that an essential ingredient of all education was the teaching of Christianity. Mission teachers have been expected to teach Christianity as well as reading and arithmetic, and today Garos accept without question that becoming educated is an adequate reason for becoming a Christian. Non-Christian Garos, or *Songsareks*, as the adherents of the older religion are called, have little opposition to Christianity. Parents of children who have become Christian never express sorrow over the fact but simply point out that after all the child went to school, and so naturally he became a Christian. So completely has this attitude been accepted that the change to government-supported schools has made little difference. Village teachers, whether paid by a missionary society or by the government, are certain to be Christians, since they themselves have had some education, and they almost always see it as part of their job to teach Christianity, even though the government may not require them to do so.

The cultural changes that come with a switch to Christianity do not all seem to be very intimately associated with the new religion, but any aspects of the culture that either the early missionaries or the Garos themselves considered to be somehow connected with the traditional religion have been replaced. These include almost all of the traditional arts of the Garos— their music, their dancing, and their wood-carving where that was important. Christians do not build bachelors' houses and they are not supposed to drink rice beer. The traditional village festivals always have a ceremonial aspect. The climax is usually a sacrifice, and a supplication of the spirits or gods. Christianity can hardly coexist with sacrifices to the spirits, and as a result the whole festival—music, dancing, feasting, and merrymaking —is abandoned. Of course, Christians substitute new activities for those that are lost. They have church services on Sundays, and sometimes prayer meetings on other days. They observe

Sunday as a day of rest, just as non-Christians sometimes take days of rest in connection with their village festivals. Christians have their own feast days, and on Christmas especially all Christians of a village usually participate in a communal feast to which they all contribute. The delight taken in such feasts is no different from that of *Songsarek* festivals, except that no rice beer stimulates the Christian's gaiety. The variety of Protestantism which has influenced the Garos has been rigid in its disapproval of alcohol, and perhaps the Garos have exaggerated the ideas of their teachers more dogmatically than was intended. Today, Christians and *Songsareks* alike often cite the shunning of rice beer as the primary sign of Christianity, and in answer to the question "Is he a Christian?" the answer is often "No, he is a rice-beer drinker." If a Christian drinks today, and some of them do, he does it surreptitiously. Christians substitute tea, very milky and sugary, for rice beer, and the two drinks are clearly equivalent. Tea has become a hospitality symbol among the Christians. If one visits six Christian houses in the course of an afternoon, he will almost surely drink six cups of tea; and in some areas at least, tea is served to large parties of visitors at the Christian holidays, just as visitors during *Songsarek* festivals are served rice beer.

Christian hymns form an obvious substitute for the traditional music. Both are connected with their respective religions, and both are vigorously enjoyed. Bachelors' houses are deemed to be closely associated with the traditional religion since ceremonies were conducted in them and rice beer was drunk there. The need for a place for the boys to sleep remains, since even Christians may find it awkward for a boy to have to sleep in his parents' house. Frequently the school teacher's house in a Christian village becomes an informal substitute for the bachelors' house, and the school boys who are considered on their way to becoming Christians bring their blankets and sleep on a porch or in a spare room of the teacher's house. His house, like the bachelors' house, becomes a center for the activities of youths, and plays a parallel educational role in the village life. In older Christian areas some people manage to overcome the dislike of having the boys sleep in the parents' home, but this is not easy if the parents remain *Songsareks*.

Even the houses of Christians are generally constructed differently from those of *Songsareks*. Garos usually say that this is because the entertainment patterns are different, and that it is no longer necessary to entertain large drinking parties; but the contrast seems primarily to be a symbolic matter. By building a house in a different style one announces to the world that this is a Christian home, where one need not expect to be served rice beer. Christian houses are usually less long and narrow, and often have roofed porches of one sort or another; but since they are much more varied than the traditional ones, it is difficult to make generalizations about them other than that they are nearly always different from the houses of the *Songsareks*. Christian men always cut their hair in the short, modern style, while most *Songsareks* still tie theirs in a knot at the back of the head. Christians never wear the traditional earrings, since these are specifically destined to be thrown to an ogre who demands them of the dead man as he works his way to the after-world, while Christians presumably have no need of them. Otherwise, the clothing of Christians does not change much, and this is one part of the world where Christianity has not required women always to cover their breasts. As a man moves closer to Christianity, he generally sells any of the traditional heirlooms which his family possesses, since these too have some connotation of the older religious system. There is no real Christian substitute for these heirlooms, though one man suggested to me that converts invest in wet rice land instead.

Christians of course no longer sacrifice, and since most sacrifices are directed toward the curing of disease, Christians must turn to other methods. All Garos make some use of jungle medicines, but Christians probably use them more consistently. I suspect that these have about the same curative value as the sacrifices which they replace, but Christians are probably also more receptive to modern drugs than the *Songsareks*. Penicillin and quinine are as popular with some Garos as they are anywhere in the world. An anthropologist cannot help being saddened at the loss of traditional dancing and music, especially when it is replaced by rather hackneyed American Protestant hymns; but it is unrealistic to expect people who can recognize the value of modern drugs to retain unaltered their faith in sacrifices or in the spirits toward whom the sacrifices are directed.

Some Christian Garos hold their Christian values very deeply, while some, of course, have drifted into Christianity with little genuine thought. But for everyone Christianity is a symbol of participation in a much larger world than the old one of their relatively isolated villages. Christians travel to other parts of the hills and occasionally beyond to attend religious meetings, and they become acquainted with people from the whole district. They are better educated and know much more about the world. People with ambitions, people who hope for innovations to bring improvements into their lives, turn naturally to Christianity. Often the same people who become wet rice farmers also become Christians, since both innovations require something of the same willingness to experiment with new techniques. Christianity and wet rice agriculture do not always go together, for many Christians have only hill farms and a few non-Christians have paddy land; but more often than not, the same ambitions people take to both. Even in non-Christian villages it is often possible to judge which people are moving in the direction of Christianity. Even before they are baptized they are likely to cut their hair and to abandon their earrings. They may continue to drink rice beer for a while, but gradually give it up and to some extent cut themselves off from the social affairs of the other villagers. In some areas Christians and *Songsareks* tend to segregate themselves in separate sections of the village, or in separate villages. It is said that Christians do not like the noise of the *Songsareks'* drinking parties, and that the *Songsareks* may be annoyed by the nonparticipation of the Christians. The village of Asonanggri in the Rengsanggri area may have been an incipient Christian village; and in other regions Christian villages are firmly established. The split into separate villages does not imply enmity or discord. Both groups continue to assist each other where assistance is necessary. At funerals, for instance, both groups help each other as freely as co-religionists. The *Songsareks* tolerantly accept the Christian inability to serve rice beer, and the Christians politely decline to join in the drinking when they visit the *Songsareks*.

One implication of Christianity, namely its effect on the *nokma*ship, extends beyond the purely religious sphere. The *nokma* is largely a ritual leader, so if the *nokma* becomes a Christian, someone else must take over his ceremonial duties for the sake of the remaining *Songsareks*. This is one modern reason for the transfer of effective *nokma*ship, even if the title itself is not shifted. The government usually continues to recognize the old *nokma* as the official head of the village, since in the government's eyes his religion is irrelevant to his office. The villagers also speak of it in this way, but without ritual duties the *nokma*ship is a rather empty title, and Garos point out that the pastor and school teacher in Christian villages do some tasks similar to those of a *nokma*. A Christian *nokma* no longer entertains lavishly, and in fact Christianity tends to de-emphasize the importance of entertainment as a means to prestige. When Christians hold feasts, they are usually supported by subscription and not by mutual or competitive hospitality. Thus Christianity may tend to diminish the redistribution of wealth and, like the ownership of wet rice land, to accentuate economic inequality.

Though many Christians also are wet rice cultivators, Christianity itself has little bearing on the methods of subsistence. Neither new agricultural techniques nor Christianity has any great impact upon kinship relations, and thus kinship remains one of the most durable aspects of Garo culture. Christianity impinges directly upon the family organization only in its rules regarding marriage and divorce, but even here the effect is less than overwhelming. Christians are not allowed to have two wives, of course. Rarely, a man appears to have retired one wife when he became a Christian, but few Garos have more than one wife anyway. A good many non-Christian Garos do have aged widowed mothers-in-law whom they *call* wife, and the main change effected by a Christian is to cease calling this woman by the same term as is used for a wife. He continues to allow his wife's mother to live with them, and to take care of her economic needs just as faithfully as do non-Christians, but he no longer maintains the fiction that she is a wife. The essentials of the system of heirship, the care of people in their old age, are maintained.

Negotiations for a marriage must be different among Christians than among *Songsareks*. Christians no longer feel that it is appropriate to send out the bachelors to bring in a son-in-law. Rather, a marriage should be peacefully arranged between the couple or their respective families. By and large, there is probably some shift in the direction of greater initiative on the part of the potential spouses themselves and away from the influence of the parents, even though Christian parents continue to choose an heiress, whose husband becomes the heir to the family. Whatever influence the parents have continues to be most strongly exerted over the heiress daughter, and she is still expected to marry a classificatory cousin from the proper lineage. Among Christians as among *Songsareks*, the initiative in arranging marriages comes from the girl's side, but now that the young men of the village no longer go to bring in the bridegroom, the girl may have to take direct action herself. A Christian girl's most frequent maneuver is to write a letter to the boy of her fancy. The latter may be more or less directly a proposal of marriage, but any letter from a girl to an unmarried boy is interpreted as a proposal. If the boy is completely uninterested he is best advised to ignore it entirely, since any answer at all may be taken as interest or even acceptance. Even the most highly educated Garo boys say that they could not possibly write the first letter in such an exchange, but must wait for the girl to take the first move. A number of educated and sophisticated Garo women have married members of other Assamese hill tribes—Lusheis, Mikirs, and Khasis. Few Garo men have married non-Garos, however, and it would seem that with both Garo women and the men from the other tribes able to take initiative (in none of these other tribes do women habitually make the first move), a romance can start easily, but a Garo man has no way to approach a girl who is not used to taking the initiative. Well established Christians solemnize their marriage at a ceremony involving a pastor, rings, and traditional Christian vows, but not uncommonly the solemnization follows rather than precedes consummation. The girl may present herself at the sleeping place of the man, and a few nights together are taken as intention to marry. The Christian attitude toward premarital sexual relations seems to be not too different from that of the *Songsareks*, though perhaps Christians follow with a marriage ceremony a bit more regularly.

Among people who are moving toward Christianity but who have either not yet been baptized or have not long been members of the Christian community, special problems arise. They no longer feel that it is appropriate to go through the traditional *Songsarek* marriage ceremony, but they may be unable or unwilling to undergo a formal Christian marriage, which has such stringent legal provisions that divorce is almost impossible. These people often start to live together in a type of marriage to which Rengsanggri people sometimes refer a bit contemptuously as a "sneaked" marriage. The marriage may be formalized with a feast, even if neither a Christian or *Songsarek* ceremony is held. Such couples are recognized as legitimately married, and relationships of inheritance, replacement, and divorce are conducted according to traditional Garo practices.

Christian divorce is encumbered with more serious problems than the relatively simple divorce of non-Christians. Christian marriages are governed by the Indian Christian Marriage Act, under which obtaining a divorce requires court proceedings beyond the competence of any court within the district. In effect, this makes legal divorce impossible for any but the most wealthy Garos, however legitimate the grievance may be. The old Garo attitude that it is better for a man and woman to separate than to continue living unhappily together hardly disappears with Christianity, and the result is that separation, if not legal divorce, is not uncommon among Christians, and is not looked upon with great disapproval. Serious difficulties arise only when one of the separated individuals starts living with someone else, a procedure that is by no means unknown. In the eyes of the law this is, of course, adultery, and it may lead to expulsion from the church. To many Garos, however, it is somewhat less sinful than is implied by the rules of the church or the laws of the country. Garos speak of these people as husband and wife, and generally accept them as such. There is some sentiment among Christian Garos for the easing of the divorce laws, so that divorces could be handled within the district, and the impossible position of separated spouses be mitigated.

The earliest Christian denomination to reach the Garos was that of the American Baptists, and consequently their influence has penetrated furthest. My comments have applied most specifically to that denomination. Roman Catholics have also carried on missionary work, and many Garos have now become Catholics. There are also a few villages of Hindu Garos. These Hindus are a numerically insignificant group and have no tendency to expand at the present time, but they are interesting in the light they throw on the process of religious change. Both Catholics and Hindus have lost virtually the same set of cultural traits as the Baptists, no doubt because the same things were everywhere considered to be too intimately associated with the

earlier religion to be continued by converts. Catholics and
Hindus replace them with other practices; but while Catholic
hymns are different, they have superseded the old music just as
effectively. Like Baptists, Catholic Garos cut their hair short
and stop wearing earrings, but they have been less adamant
about rice beer than the Baptists. Hindus substitute Bengali
religious songs for the older Garo music, and frequently wear
Bengali clothes—dhotis and saris.

Today, every educated Garo is a Christian; both Garos and
non-Garos often view Christianity as the distinguishing sign
by which the Garos are set apart from the other people of the
country. Garos express their concern at being encircled and
ruled by a non-Christian population, and non-Garos speak with
distaste of the proselytization that has resulted in the alien
religion in their midst. But the differences that separate the
Garos and other hill people from the plains people of Assam are
much older than the religious differences. Christianity is as
much a result of the differences as it is their cause, and Christianity may have succeeded partly because Garos have sometimes
looked upon it as a means of defense against the threat of being
overwhelmed by the plains population surrounding them.
Today, considerable mistrust continues to divide the plains
people from the Garos. Garos tend to view the plains people as
arrogant, and in return are looked upon as backward and igno-
rant. Similar feelings of mistrust resulted in years of bloody
insurrection in the Naga Hills. The Garos have happily avoided
bloodshed, but many have hoped for the establishment of a
separate state which would comprise the hill districts of Assam
but be separate from the plains areas. Though the plan has not
been accepted, agitation in its favor became a major political
effort on the part of a number of Garo leaders, and the new District Council rapidly became a new focus for Garo initiative
and Garo nationalism. In the fall of 1956, the country was preparing for its second general election. The continuing distrust
of the plains people was evident in the utter defeat of the

Congress Party in the Garo Hills District elections the next year. A local party, the Garo National Council, won most of the seats in the District Council, as well as all four of the Garo constituencies in the Legislative Assembly of the State of Assam.

The last hundred years have seen the incorporation of the Garos into a larger political and economic unit than they had belonged to before. In the process many Garos have had their range of vision widened from the village to the entire Garo district, but few Garos today have yet acquired any deep realization that for better or worse, the Garo Hills District has become and will remain politically and economically a part of India. There is simply no other place for it to go. More and more Garos are becoming educated. A number have received the B.A. degree and more are attending Gauhati and Calcutta Universities; but almost all Garos think of themselves as Garos only and not at all as Indians. Rural development is being pushed by the government. This will hasten changes in Garo agriculture and perhaps in other aspects of their culture. Economic and political developments will inevitably bring Garos into an ever closer relationship with the rest of the country, but adjustments will be necessary on both sides before the Garos can achieve a secure place within the nation. It is not yet clear how many of the essentials of their culture can be retained in the face of ever-increasing contact with the rest of India.

# APPENDICES

# Appendices

Certain data, not amenable to incorporation within the text but bearing upon its conclusions, are assembled in these appendices. The first two consist of tables of statistics on various aspects of kinship, marriage, and household composition for the single village of Rengsanggri. The data in these tables can be compared by means of the first column of numbers on the lists, which in all cases refer to the serial number of the household. These numbers have been assigned according to genealogical relationship rather than by geographical proximity, as will be evident by comparing the segmentation diagram (page 180) where the numbers run consecutively, and the village map (page 26), on which the numbers are jumbled.

## Appendix A.   Household Composition

Table 1 lists the households of the village of Rengsanggri and gives certain information about their composition under the following headings:

(1) Household number.
(2) Name of the head of the household (eldest married man, if present; otherwise, widow).
(3) Number of people living in the household.
(4) Number of adults (those approximately past puberty).
(5) Number of married couples.
(6) Number, if any, of *jikgite*s (young second wives—see Chapter VI) in the household.
(7) Number, if any, of widowed mothers-in-law living in the household.
(8) Comments on special peculiarities of the household.

Summaries of the data follow the table.

## TABLE 1

| (1) Household Serial No. | (2) Head of Household | (3) Number in Household | (4) Number of Adults | (5) Number of Married Couples | (6) *Jikgites* | (7) Widowed Mothers-in-law | (8) Special Comments |
|---|---|---|---|---|---|---|---|
| 1. | Gajang | 6 | 4 | 1 | – | 1 | |
| 2. | Mineng | 3 | 2 | 1 | – | – | |
| 3. | Toja | 6 | 4 | 2 | – | – | Household includes Toja's married but non-heiress daughter and her husband who will soon move out. |
| 4. | Dingman | 3 | 3 | 1 | – | 1 | |
| 5. | Tanggeng | 4 | 4 | 1 | – | 1 | |
| 6. | Anat | 4 | 2 | 1 | – | – | |
| 7. | Kakan | 4 | 4 | 2 | – | – | |
| 8. | Rangjan | 4 | 2 | 1 | – | – | |
| 9. | Wajang | 11 | 5 | 2 | – | 1 | |
| 10. | Kingjeng | 5 | 3 | 1 | – | – | |
| 11. | Jingnang | 8 | 5 | 1 | 1 | – | |
| 12. | Galma | 2 | 2 | 1 | – | – | |
| 13. | Bano | 7 | 3 | 1 | 1 | – | |
| 14. | Jusang | 3 | 3 | 1 | – | – | Household includes Naban, the widowed father of Jusang's wife. |
| 15. | Gojing | 4 | 2 | 1 | – | – | |
| 16. | Nemnem | 2 | 2 | – | – | – | Widow without husband. |
| 17. | Singat | 7 | 6 | 1 | 1 | 2 | Household includes both a widowed mother and a widowed grandmother. |
| 18. | Tanggan | 7 | 4 | 2 | – | – | |

TABLE I (*continued*)

| (1) Household Serial No. | (2) Head of Household | (3) Number in Household | (4) Number of Adults | (5) Number of Married Couples | (6) *Jikgies* | (7) Widowed Mothers-in-law | (8) Special Comments |
|---|---|---|---|---|---|---|---|
| 19. | Chondu | 6 | 4 | 1 | – | 1 | |
| 20. | Dingkam | 4 | 2 | 1 | – | – | |
| 21. | Saljing | 8 | 5 | 2 | – | – | The two couples occupy separate though adjacent houses. |
| 22. | Kam | 6 | 3 | 1 | 1 | – | |
| 23. | Rangjeng | 5 | 2 | 1 | – | – | |
| 24. | Jusin | 2 | 2 | 1 | – | – | |
| 25. | Kaljing | 5 | 3 | 1 | – | – | Household includes Kaljing's divorced daughter and her illegitimate child. |
| 26. | Ansing | 2 | 2 | 1 | – | – | |
| 27. | Nangban | 5 | 2 | 1 | – | – | |
| 28. | Rangman | 3 | 2 | 1 | – | – | |
| 29. | Gurang | 5 | 2 | 1 | – | – | |
| 30. | Singron | 8 | 6 | 2 | 1 | 1 | Household includes Singron's wife's divorced sister and her daughter, and another married sister and her husband, who will soon move out. |
| 31. | Ranjeng | 4 | 2 | 1 | – | – | |
| 32. | Jangon | 7 | 4 | 2 | – | – | Household includes Jangon's wife's mother's sister and her husband, who reside here temporarily. |

TABLE I (*continued*)

| (1) Household Serial No. | (2) Head of Household | (3) Number in Household | (4) Number of Adults | (5) Number of Married Couples | (6) *fikgites* | (7) Widowed Mothers-in-law | (8) Special Comments |
|---|---|---|---|---|---|---|---|
| 33. | Jengnon | 8 | 5 | 1 | – | 1 | Household includes Jan'mi, Jengnon's wife's mother's sister, who is divorced and not remarried, and Jengnon's wife's brother, Gonan, who has been divorced. |
| 34. | Polen | 6 | 2 | 1 | 1 | – | |
| 35. | Nanggan | 6 | 4 | 2 | – | – | |
| 36. | Jigat | 6 | 4 | 1 | – | – | |
| 37. | Rongsin | 4 | 3 | 1 | – | 1 | |
| 38. | Aling | 10 | 5 | 2 | – | – | The two couples occupy separate but adjacent houses. |
| 39. | Miman | 8 | 5 | 2 | – | – | |
| 40. | Malsing | 2 | 2 | 1 | – | – | |
| 41. | Chenggan | 4 | 2 | 1 | – | – | |
| 42. | Manchok | 4 | 2 | 1 | – | – | |
| 43. | Kandok | 6 | 4 | 1 | – | – | One resident son, Kaljam has been divorced. |
| 44. | Maljing | 2 | 2 | 1 | – | – | |
| 45. | Binan | 5 | 4 | 1 | – | 1 | Household includes Mingcheng, the son of Giting (44), who is too poor to feed him. |
| 46. | Snang | 4 | 3 | 1 | – | – | |

TABLE I (*continued*)

| (1) Household Serial No. | (2) Head of Household | (3) Number in Household | (4) Number of Adults | (5) Number of Married Couples | (6) *Jikgites* | (7) Widowed Mothers-in-law | (8) Special Comments |
|---|---|---|---|---|---|---|---|
| 47. | Gatman | 5 | 3 | 1 | – | – | Household includes Chiman, the son of Maljing (44), whose father's house is too poor to feed him. |
| 48. | Mingsan | 2 | 2 | 1 | – | – | |
| 49. | Manjing | 4 | 4 | 2 | – | – | |
| 50. | Tang'jing | 7 | 6 | 2 | – | – | |
| 51. | Guan | 3 | 3 | 1 | – | – | |
| 52. | Seng'jan | 4 | 4 | 1 | 1 | – | |
| 53. | Ti'man | 4 | 3 | 1 | – | – | |
| 54. | Sang | 6 | 6 | 2 | – | – | |
| 55. | Chengram | 5 | 2 | 1 | – | – | |
| 56. | Nata | 2 | 1 | – | – | – | Widow without husband. |
| 57. | Jongram | 6 | 3 | 1 | 1 | – | |
| 58. | Jengdon | 3 | 2 | 1 | – | – | |
| 59. | Morison | 2 | 2 | 1 | – | – | |
| 60. | Sujon | 5 | 3 | – | 1 | – | Widow without husband, but with *jikgite* already chosen. |

TOTALS

| | |
|---|---|
| Number of households .. .. .. .. .. .. | 60 |
| Village population .. .. .. .. .. .. .. | 293 |
| Adults (past puberty) .. .. .. .. .. .. | 192 |

Households consisting of a single nuclear family—total    ..    27

    Nuclear families which are remnants of formerly larger households    ..    ..    ..    ..    ..    ..    8

      (Of these, #6, 23, 43, 44, and 48 have had the older couple die, while the older couple of #29 and 58 moved away, and the widowed mother of the wife of #46 also moved away.)

    Nuclear families resulting from the marriages of a non-heiress daughter    ..    ..    ..    ..    ..    ..    19

      (#2, 8, 10, 12, 15, 20, 24, 26, 27, 28, 31, 36, 40, 41, 42, 51, 53, 55, 59.)

Households including a widowed mother of the wife ..    ..    10

    (#1, 4, 5, 9, 17, 19, 30, 33, 37, 45. #9, 17, 33, and 45 are also included in categories below.)

Household including a widowed father of the wife    ..    ..    1

    (#14).

Households including a man with two wives, one of them a *jikgite*    ..    ..    ..    ..    ..    ..    ..    8

    (#11, 13, 17, 22, 30, 34, 52, 57. #17 and 30 are also included in other categories below.)

Households of widows without a married man    ..    ..    3

    (#16, 56, 60.)

Households with an extra couple in temporary residence    ..    3

    (#3, 30, 32.)

Households with single individuals not usually included in a household    ..    ..    ..    ..    ..    ..    5

    (#25, 30, 33, 45, 47.)

Households with remnants of three generations of married people    ..    ..    ..    ..    ..    ..    ..    2

    (#9, 17.)

Stem Families: Households with two complete married couples, man, wife, heiress and heir    ..    ..    ..    ..    9

    (#7, 18, 21, 35, 38, 39, 49, 50, 54.)

## Appendix B. Marriage and Residence

Table 2 gives data for the marriages which existed in the village of Rengsanggri in May 1956, including the genealogical relationship of the spouses to one another and the type of residence pattern they follow. The data are presented in columns as follows:

1) Serial number of the household.

2) Name of the husband. Since in a number of cases a man has two wives, some men are listed twice, each time with a different woman. Italicized names indicate couples in which the *man* is a member of the main village lineage (i.e., a Chambigong of Reng-sanggri) rather than the woman, as in the most usual situation. In a number of cases these individuals had contracted earlier marriages which had been terminated by the time to which these tables refer. In such cases the letters below the name give basic data about these *earlier* marriages as follows: d, marriage ended in divorce; w, marriage terminated by the death of the other partner leaving this person widowed; H, heir; n-h, non-heir.

3) Name of the wife. Symbols are the same as under 2).

4) Type of marriage. H, heir; n-h, non-heir; J, *Jikgite* (marriage of a man to a younger second wife); R-M, Replacement-male (i.e., the woman was married earlier to another man and subsequently either widowed or divorced); R-F, Replacement-female. Joining indicates that both husband and wife were widowed and their house-holds joined by the present marriage. Full explanations of these marriage types will be found in Chapters III and VI.

5)-10) These columns are designed to give an indication of the relationship of the husband to his wife's father, and hence of the closeness of the spouses as *matrilateral* cross-cousins. To specify this relationship the village and sib of the wife's father must be known, and this information is given in columns 5) and 6). In these columns the symbol (\*) indicates that the girl's adopted father rather than biological father is considered, and the symbol (+) that the girl's mother's husband rather than her biological father is considered. Similarly the village and sib of the husband are given in 7) and 9). A key to the abbreviations in these columns is given below. In some cases the man was raised in a village other than that of his own line-age. The village where he actually lived as a child is given in 8). Column 10) gives index numbers summarizing the closeness of the relationship of the husband to his father-in-law. Of these, 1 indi-cates that the father-in-law is the real mother's brother of his son-in-law, which means, of course, that the spouses are first matrilateral cross-cousins; 2, that the father-in-law and son-in-law are close relatives, members of the same minimal lineage as closely as can be determined, but not real mother's brother and sister's son; 3, that the two men come from the same village but are apparently not related closely enough to be considered as belonging to the same minimal lineage; 4, that the two men come from the same village cluster but not the same village (see below for villages regarded as belonging to the same village cluster); 5, that the men are of different village clusters but at least of the same sib; and finally, 6 indicates that the two men are of entirely different sibs, though since these tables include no case of moiety endogamy, the men are always of the same moiety.

11)-16) These columns give data similar to that in columns 5)-10), but indicate the degree of relationship of the husband and wife to one another when they are considered as *patrilateral* cross-cousins. Columns 11) and 12) give the village and sib of the husband's father, while 13) and 15) give the village and sib of the wife; 14) indicates the village where the wife spent her childhood; 16) gives an index of the relationship of the wife to her husband's father, with the numbers indicating the same degrees of relationship for these two relatives as the numbers of 10) indicated for husband and wife's father.

17)-28) These columns indicate other relationships which are significant in understanding the choice of spouses in certain types of marriages. If a woman dies and is replaced by another woman, the relationship of the two women to one another is the most important one for understanding the new marriage. Columns 17) and 18) give data for the previous wife where that is pertinent, and 19) gives an index of the nearness of relationship of the former and present wife. If, on the other hand, a widow is married to a man who replaces her former husband, the relationship of the first and present husband is the important one, and columns 20), 21), and 22) give data for this type of marriage. In the Garo view of marriage, the important relationship is between an individual and the person he or she replaces. Women must have either a daughter or adopted daughter as heiress. Columns 23), 24), and 25) give data for the relationship of a woman to the woman from whom she inherits, whether as an ordinary heiress or as a *jikgite*. In most cases these

women are mother and daughter, and this is indicated simply as
such with the index number 1. In a few cases, however, when the
older woman had no daughter, it was necessary for her to adopt
another girl; in such cases the relationship of the two women is indicated in these three columns. If a widower is given a second wife as
replacement for a deceased earlier wife, his relationship to the
second wife's father is less significant for his own original marriage
than his relationship to the father of the original wife, for whom the
second wife is only a replacement anyway. The relationship of the
husband to the father of his first wife is given in 26), 27), and 28)
where this is appropriate.

29) In this final column is given the residence of the couple after
marriage, with respect to their individual residences before marriage.
Data concerning the latter appear in columns 7), 8), 13) and 14).
"Normal" residence implies that the man moved into Rengsanggri
from another village at the time of his marriage and married a girl
from the village lineage of Rengsanggri. This happened in over half
of the cases. The residence of other couples is described individually.

Residence with respect to the household is implied in column 4)
by the type of marriage. Heirs always move in to join the economy of
their wife's household, while non-heirs never permanently do so. A
replacement spouse joins the residence of the widow or widower.

*Explanation of symbols.* Villages are indicated in Table 2 by
abbreviations consisting of a capital letter followed by one lower-
case letter. Villages which have particular importance to Rengsanggri people or which are nearby are shown on the map on
page 26.

Re  Rengsanggri  —⎫
So  Songmagri    —⎪
Mi  Misimagri    —⎬  Regarded as belonging to the
No  Nokwatgri    —⎪  same village cluster
As  Asonanggri   —⎭

Far  Indicates that the village in question is a long way from Reng-
     sanggri, and beyond the usual radius of marriage ties—generally
     a distance of more than twenty miles.

Ag  Aguragri                    Cd  Chidekgri
Ap  Ampanggri                   Ck  Chokagri
Bb  Bibragri                    Cn  Chandigri

| Bd | Bodrenggri | Co | Chibonggri |
|---|---|---|---|
| Bn | Bandigri | Dg | Digranggri |
| Cb | Chibragri | | |

Dk Dirakantragri —⎫
Dr Diragri          —⎬ Belong to same village cluster

| Gg | Gongginagri | Rk | Rongkonggri |
|---|---|---|---|
| Gl | Galwanggri | Rm | Rombagri |
| Gn | Ganolgri | Rr | Rongramgri |
| Gr | Gongronggri | Sm | Samingri |
| Jd | Jendragri | Sr | Soragri |
| Mc | Machugri | Sw | Sawilgri |
| Md | Mandalgri | Tb | Timbugri |
| Mg | Megapgri | Tu | Tura |
| Mp | Marakhapara | Wa | Waramgri |
| Mr | Marakgri | Wb | Waribokgri |
| Rg | Renggigri | | |

Sib Names: Columns 6), 9), 12), 15), 18), 21), 24), and 27) of Table 2 indicate sib membership according to the following abbreviations (Sangma and Marak are the names of the two local moieties, to one or the other of which each sib belongs): C, Chambigong Marak. B, Bolwari Marak. R, Rangsa Marak. O, Mrong Marak. A, Agitdok Sangma. T, Tigite Sangma. M, Manda Sangma. G, Gabil. This last, Gabil, is considered, in those parts of the hills where it is most often found, to be a member of a third exogomous group, the Momin. The few Gabils found in the area of Rengsanggri have apparently come in recently from these areas. Since the local people are not accustomed to deal with more than two exogamous groups, they tend to classify Gabil as Marak.
Totals:

| | | |
|---|---|---|
| Number of Married Women in Rengsanggri.. | .. | 78 |
| Number of Married Men in Rengsanggri | .. | 70 |
| Heir Marriages | .. | 28 |
| Non-heir Marriages .. | .. | 24 |
| Total "New" Marriages | .. | 52 |
| Number of Secondary (*jikgite*) Marriages | .. | 9 |
| Number of Male-Replacement Marriages | .. | 9 |
| Number of Female-Replacement Marriages .. | .. | 7 |
| Number of Joining Marriages .. | .. | 1 |

TABLE 2

| (1) Serial Number of Household | (2) Husband's Name | (3) Wife's Name | (4) Type of Marriage | (5) Wife's Father's Village | (6) Wife's Father's Sib | (7) Village of Husband's Lineage | (8) Village of Husband's Childhood | (9) Husband's Sib | (10) Index of Mother's Brother's Daughter's marriage | (11) Husband's Father's Village | (12) Husband's Father's Sib | (13) Village of Wife's Lineage | (14) Village of Wife's Childhood |
|---|---|---|---|---|---|---|---|---|---|---|---|---|---|
| 1. Gajang | | – Singwil | H | So | M | So | So | M | 2 | So | C | Re | Re |
| 2. Mineng | | – Samri | n–h | So | M | Wa | Re | A | 6 | Re | C | Re | Re |
| 3. Toja (w/n–h) | | – Salji | R–F | Jd | A | So | So | M | 6 | So | C | Re | Re |
| 3. Chimin | | – Miri | n–h | So | M | Mr | Tu | T | 6 | Far | ? | Re | Re |
| 4. Dingman | | – Songdi | H | So | M | So | So | M | 2 | Re | C | Re | Re |
| 5. Tanggeng (d/H) | | – Panjak | H | Mi | C | Re | Re | C | 4 | So | M | Dk | Dk |
| 6. Anat (w/H) | | – Sanjak | R–F | ? | B | Re | Re | C | 6 | Dg | T | Wa | Wa |
| 7. Kakan | | – Rongji | H | Gl | A | Ap | Ap | A | 1 | ? | O | Re | Re |
| 7. Donjeng | | – Kimri | H | Ap | A | Ap | Ap | A | 2 | ? | B | Re | Re |
| 8. Rangjan | | – Ginmi | n–h | Re | C | Re | Re | C | 3 | Ap | A | Wa | Re |
| 9. Wajang (w/n–h) | | – Watji | R–F | ? | ? | Mi | Mi | M | ? | Mi | C | So | So |
| 9. Wilson | | – Nengji | H | Mi | M | Mi | Mi | M | 2 | Mi | C | Re | Re |
| 10. Kinjeng | | – Snajing | n–h | Mi | M | Rg | Rg | T | 6 | Sm | C | Re | Re |

| (18) Former Wife's Sib | (19) Relation of Former to Present Wife | (20) Former Husband's Village | (21) Former Husband's Sib | (22) Relation of Former to Present Husband | (23) & (24) Village and Sib of the Woman from whom Wife inherits unless real mother, in which case so indicated | (25) Relation of Wife to Woman from whom she inherits | (26) Village of Former Wife's Father | (27) Sib of Former Wife's Father | (28) Relation of Husband to Former Wife's Father | (29) Residence |
|---|---|---|---|---|---|---|---|---|---|---|
|  |  |  |  |  | Daughter 1 |  |  |  |  | Normal |
|  |  |  |  |  |  |  |  |  |  | Both raised in Rengsanggri, he of foreign lineage |
| C | 3 |  |  |  |  |  | So | M | 3 | Normal |
|  |  |  |  |  |  |  |  |  |  | Normal |
|  |  |  |  |  | Daughter 1 |  |  |  |  | Normal |
|  |  |  |  |  | Daughter 1 |  |  |  |  | Wife brought to husband's village sometime *after* marriage |
| A | 2 |  |  |  |  |  | Re | C | 3 | Wife moved to husband's village at marriage |
|  |  |  |  |  | Daughter 1 |  |  |  |  | Normal |
|  |  |  |  |  | Daughter 1 |  |  |  |  | Normal |
| C | 4 |  |  |  |  |  | Gl | A | 6 | Both raised in Rengsanggri, she of foreign lineage. Both belong to non-Rengsanggri lineages |
|  |  |  |  |  | Daughter 1 |  |  |  |  | Normal |
|  |  |  |  |  |  |  |  |  |  | Normal |

TABLE 2 (*continued*)

| (1) Serial Number of Household | (2) Husband's Name | (3) Wife's Name | (4) Type of Marriage | (5) Wife's Father's Village | (6) Wife's Father's Sib | (7) Village of Husband's Lineage | (8) Village of Husband's Childhood | (9) Husband's Sib | (10) Index of Mother's Brother's Daughter's marriage | (11) Husband's Father's Village | (12) Husband's Father's Sib | (13) Village of Wife's Lineage | (14) Village of Wife's Childhood |
|---|---|---|---|---|---|---|---|---|---|---|---|---|---|
| 11. | Jingnang | – Smijing (w/n–h) | R–M | Mi | M | So | So | M | 4 | So | C | Re | Re |
| 11. | Jingnang | – Ponpon | J | So | M | So | So | M | 2 | So | C | Re | Re ( |
| 12. | *Galma* | – *Palmi* | n–h | Re | C | Re | Re | C | 3 | Mi | M | Wa | Re |
| 13. | Bano | – Mala (w/H) | R–M | Dr | A | Wa | Wa | A | 5 | Re | C | Re | Re |
| 13. | Bano | – Ranchok | J | ? | ? | Wa | Wa | A | ? | Re | C | Re | Re |
| 14. | Jusang | – Jing'si | H | Wa | A | Cd | Cd | A | 5 | ? | B | Re | Re |
| 15. | Gojing (d/n–h) | – Tangri | n–h | Wa | A | Jd | Jd | A | 5 | Mg | B | Re | Re |
| 17. | Singgat | – Wilwil (d/H) | R–M | Dg | T | Cn | Cn | T | 5 | ? | G | Re | Re |
| 17. | Singgat | – Rangsi | J | Mi | M | Cn | Cn | T | 6 | ? | G | Re | Re |
| 18. | Tanggan | – Silji | n–h | Cd | A | Gn | Gn | T | 6 | Cn | B | Re | Re |
| 18. | Chengbon | – Namnam | H | Cn | T | Cn | Cn | T | 3 | Bn | C | Re | Re |
| 19. | Chondu | – Kiljak | H | Wa | A | Wa | Wa | A | 2 | ? | R | Re | Re |
| 20. | Dingkam | – Kinkin | n–h | Wa | A | Bb | So | T | 6 | So | C | Re | Re |
| 21. | Saljing | – Wila | n–h | Wa | A | Mi | Mi | M | 6 | Mi | C | Re | Re |

| (19) Relation of Former to Present Wife | (20) Former Husband's Village | (21) Former Husband's Sib | (22) Relation of Former to Present Husband | (23) Village and Sib of the Woman from whom Wife inherits unless real mother, in which case so indicated & (24) | (25) Relation of Wife to Woman from whom she inherits | (26) Village of Former Wife's Father | (27) Sib of Former Wife's Father | (28) Relation of Husband to Former Wife's Father | (29) Residence |
|---|---|---|---|---|---|---|---|---|---|
| | So | M | 2 | | | | | | Normal |
| | | | | Daughter 1 | | | | | Normal |
| | | | | | | | | | Both raised in Rengsanggri, she of foreign lineage |
| | Dr | A | 5 | Daughter 1 | | | | | Normal |
| | | | | Re C 2 | | | | | Normal |
| | | | | Daughter 1 | | | | | Normal |
| | | | | | | | | | Normal |
| | Dg | T | 5 | Daughter 1 | | | | | Normal |
| | | | | Re C 3 | | | | | Normal |
| | | | | | | | | | Normal |
| | | | | Daughter 1 | | | | | Normal |
| | | | | Daughter 1 | | | | | Normal |
| | | | | | | | | | Normal |
| | | | | | | | | | Normal |

**TABLE 2** (*continued*)

| (1) Serial Number of Household | (2) Husband's Name | (3) Wife's Name | (4) Type of Marriage | (5) Wife's Father's Village | (6) Wife's Father's Sib | (7) Village of Husband's Lineage | (8) Village of Husband's Childhood | (9) Husband's Sib | (10) Index of Mother's Brother's Daughter's marriage | (11) Husband's Father's Village | (12) Husband's Father's Sib | (13) Village of Wife's Lineage | (14) Village of Wife's Childhood |
|---|---|---|---|---|---|---|---|---|---|---|---|---|---|
| 21. | San | – Nokan | H | Mi | M | Mi | Mi | M | 2 | Mi | C | Re | Re |
| 22. | Kam | – Changmi (d/n–h) | R–M | Mi | M | Rm | Rm | M | 5 | Rm | C | Re | Re |
| 22. | Kam | – Dijak | J | Dg | T | Rm | Rm | M | 6 | Rm | C | Re | Re |
| 23. | Rangjeng | – Gatmi | J | Wa | A | Gl | Re | A | 5 | Re | C | Re | Re |
| 24. | *Jusin* | – *Nonmi* | n–h | Re | C | Re | Re | C | 3 | Gl | A | Wa | Re |
| 25. | Kaljing (w/n–h) | Jiring – (w/n–h) | joining | ? | ? | Mi | Mi | M | ? | Mi | C | Mi | Mi |
| 26. | Ansing | – Satri | n–h | Mi | M | So | So | M | 4 | So | C | Re | Re |
| 27. | Nangban | – Kokem | n–h | Mi | M | Md | Md | M | 5 | Wr | C | Re | Re |
| 28. | Rangman | – Chekmi | n–h | Md | M | So | So | M | 5 | ? | G | Re | Re |
| 29. | *Gurang* | – *Sinring* | H | Re | C | Re | Re | C | 3 | Wa | A | Cd | Re |
| 30. | Singron | – Bitji (w/H) | R–M | Far | A | Gn | Gn | A | 5 | Gn | C | Re | Re |
| 30. | Singron | – Natmi | J | Dr | A | Gn | Gn | A | 5 | Gn | C | Re | Re |
| 30. | Siman | – Sinjak | n–h | Far | A | Dr | Dr | A | 5 | So | C | Re | Re |
| 31. | *Ranjeng* | – *Gaji* | n–h | Ck | C | Re | Re | C | 5 | Far | A | Md | Re |
| 32. | *Jangon* | – *Watji* | H | Re | C | Re | Re | C | 2 | Gr | T | Wa | Re |

| (19) Relation of Former to Present Wife | (20) Former Husband's Village | (21) Former Husband's Sib | (22) Relation of Former to Present Husband | (23) Village and Sib of the Woman & from whom Wife inherits unless real mother, in which case so indicated | (24) | (25) Relation of Wife to Woman from whom she inherits | (26) Village of Former Wife's Father | (27) Sib of Former Wife's Father | (28) Relation of Husband to Former Wife's Father | (29) Residence |
|---|---|---|---|---|---|---|---|---|---|---|
| | | | Daughter 1 | | | | | | | Normal |
| | Dg | T 6 | | | | | | | | Normal |
| | | | Daughter 1 | | | | | | | Normal |
| | | | Daughter 1 | | | | | | | Both raised in Rengsanggri, he of foreign lineage. |
| | | | | | | | | | | Both raised in Rengsanggri, she of foreign lineage |
| 4 | Mi | M 3 | | | | | Wa | A 6 | | Both belong to non-Rengsanggri lineages |
| | | | | | | | | | | Normal |
| | | | | | | | | | | Normal |
| | | | | | | | | | | Normal |
| | | | Daughter 1 | | | | | | | Both raised in Rengsanggri, she of foreign lineage |
| | Dr | A 5 | Daughter 1 | | | | | | | Normal |
| | | | Daughter 1 | | | | | | | Normal |
| | | | | | | | | | | Normal |
| | | | | | | | | | | Wife moved to Rengsanggri as child |
| | | | Daughter 1 | | | | | | | Both raised in Rengsanggri, she of foreign lineage |

TABLE 2 *(continued)*

| (1) Serial Number of Household | (2) Husband's Name | (3) Wife's Name | (4) Type of Marriage | (5) Wife's Father's Village | (6) Wife's Father's Sib | (7) Village of Husband's Lineage | (8) Village of Husband's Childhood | (9) Husband's Sib | (10) Index of Mother's Brother's Daughter's marriage | (11) Husband's Father's Village | (12) Husband's Father's Sib | (13) Village of Wife's Lineage | (14) Village of Wife's Childhood |
|---|---|---|---|---|---|---|---|---|---|---|---|---|---|
| 32. | Tapa | – Senjak | n–h | Re | C | Far | Far | – | 6 | Far | – | Wa | Re |
| 33. | Jengnon | – Gan'mi | H | Cd | A | Cd | Cd | A | 3 | Sr | B | Re | Re |
| 34. | Polen | – Mejing (d/n–h) | R–M | Cd | A | Wa | Wa | A | 5 | Re | C | Re | Re |
| 34. | Polen | – Mami | J | ? | ? | Wa | Wa | A | ? | Re | C | Re | Re |
| 35. | Nanggan | – Nuri | H | Wa | A | Wa | Wa | A | 2 | ? | R | Re | Re |
| 35. | Ajeng | – Rami | H | Wa* | A* | Wa | Wa | A | 2 | Wa | R | Re | Re |
| 36. | Jigat | – Pangri | n–h | Wa | A | Wa | Re | A | 3 | Re | C | Re | Re |
| 37. | Rongsin | – Ginri | H | So | M | So | So | M | 2 | Re | C | Re | Re |
| 38. | *Aling* | – *Bangji* | H | Re | C | Re | Re | C | 2 | Wa | A | Wa | Wa |
| 38. | *Jurang* | – *Chaji* | H | Re | C | Re | Re | C | 1 | Wa | A | Wa | Re |
| 39. | Miman (w/n–h) | – Changrit | R–F | Cb | A | Dg | Dg | T | 6 | Rk | C | Re | Re |
| 39. | Bitak | – Numin | H | Dg | T | Dg | Dg | T | 3 | Co | B | Re | Re |
| 40. | Malsing | – Ringmi | n–h | Dg | T | Cn | Cn | T | 5 | Bb | C | Re | Re |
| 41. | Chenggan | – Mingti | n–h | Dg | T | So | So | M | 6 | Re | C | Re | Re |
| 42. | Manchok | – Singrit | n–h | Dg | T | Wa | Re | A | 6 | Re | C | Re | Re |

| (19) Relation of Former to Present Wife | (20) Former Husband's Village | (21) Former Husband's Sib | (22) Relation of Former to Present Husband | (23)(24) Village and Sib of the Woman from whom Wife inherits unless real mother, in which case so indicated | | (25) Relation of Wife to Woman from whom she inherits | (26) Village of Former Wife's Father | (27) Sib of Former Wife's Father | (28) Relation of Husband to Former Wife's Father | (29) Residence |
|---|---|---|---|---|---|---|---|---|---|---|
|  |  |  |  | Daughter |  | 1 |  |  |  | Both of foreign lineages, she raised locally / Normal |
|  | Cd | A | 5 |  |  |  |  |  |  | Normal |
|  |  |  |  | Re | C | 2 |  |  |  | Normal |
|  |  |  |  | Daughter |  | 1 |  |  |  | Normal |
|  |  |  |  | Re | C | 2 |  |  |  | Normal |
|  |  |  |  | Daughter |  | 1 |  |  |  | Both raised in Rengsanggri, he of foreign lineage / Normal |
|  |  |  |  | Daughter |  | 1 |  |  |  | Wife moved to Rengsanggri shortly before marriage |
| 2 |  |  |  | Daughter |  | 1 | Cd | A | 6 | Both raised in Rengsanggri, she of foreign lineage / Normal |
|  |  |  |  | Daughter |  | 1 |  |  |  | Normal |
|  |  |  |  |  |  |  |  |  |  | Normal |
|  |  |  |  |  |  |  |  |  |  | Normal |
|  |  |  |  |  |  |  |  |  |  | Both raised in Rengsanggri, he of foreign lineage |

TABLE 2 (*continued*)

| (1) Serial Number of Household | (2) Husband's Name | (3) Wife's Name | (4) Type of Marriage | (5) Wife's Father's Village | (6) Wife's Father's Sib | (7) Village of Husband's Lineage | (8) Village of Husband's Childhood | (9) Husband's Sib | (10) Index of Mother's Brother's Daughter's marriage | (11) Husband's Father's Village | (12) Husband's Father's Sib | (13) Village of Wife's Lineage | (14) Village of Wife's Childhood |
|---|---|---|---|---|---|---|---|---|---|---|---|---|---|
| 43. | *Kandok* | – *Nengmi* | H | Re | C | Re | Re | C | 3 | Dg | T | Wa | Re |
| 44. | Maljing (w/H) | – Giting | R–F | Dg | T | Cb | Cb | A | 6 | Wb | C | Re | Re |
| 45. | Binan | – Dimdik | H | Dg | T | Cn | Cn | T | 5 | ? | B | Re | Re |
| 46. | *Snang* | – *Galmi* | H | Re | C | Re | Re | C | 2 | Dg | T | Bd | Bd |
| 47. | Gatman | – Chanmi | H | Gg | M | Gg | Gg | M | 2 | Mc | C | Re | Re |
| 48. | Mingsan (w/H) | – Miktot | R–F | Wa | A | Wa | Wa | A | 2 | ? | R | Re | Re |
| 49. | *Manjing* | – *Radik* | H | Re | C | Re | Re | C | 1 | Wa | A | Ag | Ag |
| 49. | *Chongrin* | – *Manmi* | H | Re★ | C★ | Re | Re | C | 3 | Wa | A | Ag | Ag |
| 50. | Tang'jing | – Nojak | H | Dr | A | Dr | Dr | A | 2 | So | C | Re | Re |
| 50. | Anang | – Jingdi | H | Dr | A | Dr | Dr | A | 2 | Tb | C | Re | Re |
| 51. | Guan | – Rujoni | n–h | Dr | A | Dk | Dk | A | 4 | Mi | C | Re | Re |
| 52. | Seng'jan | – Dabang (w/n–h) | R–M | Dr | A | Mi | Mi | M | 6 | ? | G | Re | Re |
| 52. | Seng'jan | – Bengbot | J | Mi | M | Mi | Mi | M | 1 | ? | G | Re | Re |
| 53. | *Ti'man* | – *Gatgat* | n–h | ? | B | Re | Re | C | 6 | Mi | M | Wa | W |

| (19) Relation of Former to Present Wife | (20) Former Husband's Village | (21) Former Husband's Sib | (22) Relation of Former to Present Husband | (23) Village and Sib of the Woman & (24) from whom Wife inherits unless real mother, in which case so indicated | (25) Relation of Wife to Woman from whom she inherits | (26) Village of Former Wife's Father | (27) Sib of Former Wife's Father | (28) Relation of Husband to Former Wife's Father | (29) Residence |
|---|---|---|---|---|---|---|---|---|---|
|  |  |  |  | Daughter | 1 |  |  |  | Both raised in Rengsanggri, she of foreign lineage |
| 3 |  |  |  |  |  | Cb | A | 1 | Normal |
|  |  |  |  | Daughter | 1 |  |  |  | Normal |
|  |  |  |  | Daughter | 1 |  |  |  | Wife brought to husband's village after marriage |
|  |  |  |  | Daughter | 1 |  |  |  | Normal |
| 2 |  |  |  |  |  | Wa | A | 2 | Normal |
|  |  |  |  | Daughter | 1 |  |  |  | Wife brought by parents to Rengsanggri during childhood |
|  |  |  |  | Ag | T | 2 |  |  | Wife brought to Rengsanggri at Marriage |
|  |  |  |  | Daughter | 1 |  |  |  | Normal |
|  |  |  |  | Daughter | 1 |  |  |  | Normal |
|  |  |  |  |  |  |  |  |  | Normal |
|  | Mi | M | 1 |  |  |  |  |  | Normal |
|  |  |  |  |  |  |  |  |  | Normal |
|  |  |  |  | Daughter | 1 |  |  |  | Wife brought to Rengsanggri a year after marriage |

TABLE 2 (*continued*) 3

| (1) Serial Number of Household | (2) Husband's Name | (3) Wife's Name | (4) Type of Marriage | (5) Wife's Father's Village | (6) Wife's Father's Sib | (7) Village of Husband's Lineage | (8) Village of Husband's Childhood | (9) Husband's Sib | (10) Index of Mother's Brother's Daughter's marriage | (11) Husband's Father's Village | (12) Husband's Father's Sib | (13) Village of Wife's Lineage | (14) Village of Wife's Childhood |
|---|---|---|---|---|---|---|---|---|---|---|---|---|---|
| 54. | Sang | – Tari – Rimji | n–h | Mr | T | Mi | Mi | M | 6 | Mi | C | Re | Re |
| 54. | Donjang | (d/H) | R–M | Mi | M | So | So | M | 4 | So | C | Re | Re |
| 55. | *Chengram* (w/n–h) | – *Nangji* | R–F | Re | C | Re | Re | C | 3 | Mr | T | Ag | Ag |
| 57. | Jongram | – Kimring (w/n–h) | R–M | Jd | A | Wa | Wa | A | 5 | Bn | R | Re | Re |
| 57. | Jongram | – Salchi | J | ? | T+ | Wa | Wa | A | 6 | Bn | R | Re | Re |
| 58. | Jengdon | – Pari | H | Sw | M | Rr | Rr | M | 5 | Rm | C | Re | Re |
| 59. | Morison | – Nakji | n–h | Mp | A | Far | Far | A | 5 | ? | Ar-Re eng | | Far |

| (19) Relation of Former to Present Wife | (20) Former Husband's Village | (21) Former Husband's Sib | (22) Relation of Former to Present Husband | (23) & (24) Village and Sib of the Woman from whom Wife inherits unless real mother, in which case so indicated | (25) Relation of Wife to Woman from whom she inherits | (26) Village of Former Wife's Father | (27) Sib of Former Wife's Father | (28) Relation of Husband to Former Wife's Father | (29) Residence |
|---|---|---|---|---|---|---|---|---|---|
| | | | | | | | | | Normal |
| | Mi | M | 4 | Daughter | 1 | | | | Normal |
| 2 | | | | | | Re | C | 3 | Wife brought to Rengsanggri at marriage |
| | ? | T | 6 | | | | | | Normal |
| | | | | Daughter | 1 | | | | Normal |
| | | | | Daughter | 1 | | | | Normal |
| | | | | | | | | | Both raised elsewhere but came to wife's village after marriage |

CROSS-COUSIN MARRIAGE AND REPLACEMENT. The data of Table 2 can serve to indicate the degree of relationship of married people to each other when they are considered as either matrilateral or patrilateral cross-cousins. Tables 3 and 4 summarize the degree of relationship of the spouses according to the type of marriage which joins them. Table 3 shows the degree of relationship between the wife and the father of her husband. The indices of relationship are the same as those used in Columns 10), 16), 19), 22), 25), and 28) of Table 2.

### TABLE 3
#### Spouses Considered as MATRILATERAL Cross-Cousins

|  | 1 | 2 | 3 | 4 | 5 | 6 | ? | Totals |
|---|---|---|---|---|---|---|---|---|
| Heir Marriages | 3 | 15 | 6 | 1 | 3 | – |  | 28 |
| Non-heir Marriages | – | – | 4 | 2 | 7 | 11 |  | 24 |
| Replacement-male Marriages | – | – | – | 2 | 6 | 1 |  | 9 |
| Replacement-female Marriages | – | 1 | 1 | – | – | 4 | 1 | 7 |
| *Jikgite* Marriages | 1 | 1 | – | – | 2 | 3 | 2 | 9 |
| Joining Marriages | – | – | – | – | – | – | 1 | 1 |
| Totals | 4 | 17 | 11 | 5 | 18 | 19 | 4 | 78 |

### TABLE 4
#### Spouses Considered as PATRILATERAL Cross-Cousins

|  | 1 | 2 | 3 | 4 | 5 | 6 | Totals |
|---|---|---|---|---|---|---|---|
| Heir Marriages | – | 1 | 3 | 4 | 5 | 15 | 28 |
| Non-heir Marriages | – | – | 4 | 6 | 5 | 9 | 24 |
| Replacement-male Marriages | – | 1 | 1 | 2 | 2 | 3 | 9 |
| Replacement-female Marriages | – | – | – | 2 | 3 | 2 | 7 |
| *Jikgite* Marriages | – | 1 | 2 | 1 | 2 | 3 | 9 |
| Joining Marriages | – | – | 1 | – | – | – | 1 |
| Totals | – | 3 | 11 | 15 | 17 | 32 | 78 |

From the Garo point of view, the cross-cousin relationship is less important than the relationship between a man or woman and the person from whom he or she inherits. A man may inherit from or succeed to the position of his wife's former husband if he is brought in as a replacement for a man who has died. If, on the other hand, a man is married to a second woman after his first wife dies, his own marriage is more properly understood from the point of view of the *first* wife's, rather than the second wife's, father, except that men who are originally married as non-heirs do not replace anybody or succeed to anyone's position. Table 5 summarizes all types of male replacement. Only those men who were originally married as heirs or replacements are shown. Men who marry a divorced woman are not included since they are not considered proper replacements; but men who marry widows are shown. Men married at present to replacement wives are counted only if their *first* marriage was an heir marriage.

TABLE 5

Total Male Replacement

Summary of the Relationship of Men to their Heirs or Successors

|  | 1 | 2 | 3 | 4 | 5 | 6 | Totals |
|---|---|---|---|---|---|---|---|
| Ordinary Heirs | 3 | 15 | 6 | 1 | 3 | – | 28 |
| Relation of a man to his wife's former husband in R–M and joining marriages *other* than those following a divorce. | 1 | 1 | 1 | – | 2 | 1 | 6 |
| Relation of men formerly married as heirs, to former wife's father. | 1 | 1 | 1 | – | – | – | 3 |
| Totals | 5 | 17 | 8 | 1 | 5 | 1 | 37 |

A woman inherits from an older woman, most often from her mother, but occasionally from someone else. An adopted heiress inherits from her adopted mother. A *jikgite* inherits from the older wife, and a replacement wife succeeds to the position of her husband's former wife after he is widowed. The marriages of these women are summarized in Table 6.

TABLE 6

Total Female Replacement

Summary of the Relationship of Women to their Heiresses and Successors

|  | 1 | 2 | 3 | 4 | 5 | 6 | Totals |
|---|---|---|---|---|---|---|---|
| Ordinary heiresses in present marriage | 26 | 2 | – | – | – | – | 28 |
| Relationship of woman to husband's deceased former wife | – | 4 | 2 | 2 | – | – | 8 |
| Relationship of heiresses now in R–M marriages to the woman from whom she inherits | 4 | – | – | – | – | – | 4 |
| Relationship of *jikgite* to older wife | 6 | 2 | 1 | – | – | – | 9 |
| Totals | 36 | 8 | 3 | 2 | – | – | 49 |

Appendix C.   Kinship Terminology

GROUP 1.   Certain kinship terms used by the Garos form a set which is broad enough so that any Garo can readily be assigned a term. These terms can be considered to form a system which classifies kinsmen according to the following nine principles.

1) *Sex*. Most Garo kinship terms are used for relatives of only one sex. The only exceptions are the terms for 'grandchild,' and 'child.'

2) *Generation*. Most terms are unambiguous about the generation of the kinsman relative to that of ego. The most interesting exception to this rule is that when the man or woman from whom a person inherits (here called "testator") dies, the 'heir' assumes a few of the terms that were formerly appropriate to the testator, and the heir inherits, as it were, a new kinship status (see under group III below). Otherwise, only three terms (*mosa, chra,* and *namchik*) can be used without modification for kinsmen of more than a single generation, though *mama* and *gri* are used in compound terms, for kinsmen of a different generation than those denoted by the simple term. However, Garos are not very precise in their reckoning of generation, and one may not even know the exact generation of a remote kinsman in comparison with one's own. Moreover, because of multiple inter-marriages among the kin groups, it is possible to be related to a person in two or more different ways. It is quite possible, for instance, for a man to be a classificatory 'brother' if counted in one way, but a classificatory 'nephew' if counted in another. In these cases of uncertain or ambiguous generational membership, relative age is likely to be the deciding factor. If a man is the right age to be considered a nephew, the term *gri* will normally be used, though a complex genealogical discussion might persuade the speaker that *jong* or *angsu* would be more correct.

3) *Relative age*. Siblings, and parent's siblings of the same sex are distinguished according to their relative age—relative age with respect to ego in the case of siblings, and with respect to the parent in the case of aunts and uncles. A man's brothers-in-law may also be differentiated according to the relative age of the brother and sister, ElSiHu being differentiated from YoSiHu (regardless of the relative age of the brother-in-law himself to ego) and WiElBr being differentiated from WiYoBr. The principle that secondary and more distant relatives are distinguished according to the relative age of an intermediate sibling pair is followed in the case of parallel cousins: e.g., FaElBrSo is equivalent to ElBr, regardless of the relative age of the cousins themselves. However, remote relatives may not be able to trace their exact genealogical connection, or even if able, may not

bother to do so, and in such a case, the relative age of the individuals themselves will tend to be decisive.

4) *Moiety membership*. Rengsanggri people regularly cite the moiety membership of a relative in justification for the use of a particular kinship term. Thus a man may explain that an older man is his *mama* because both men are in the same moiety, even if their exact relationship is not known. If moiety exogamy is consistently maintained, every term for relatives in ego's own generation and in the first ascending and descending generations shows moiety membership unambiguously. Only the terms for grandparents and grandchildren are in any way ambiguous, and even here the ambiguity can be easily resolved by adding a qualifying term—*jakasi* or *chongka*.

5) *Collaterality*. In the first ascending generation, a distinction is made between lineal relatives (parents) and non-lineal relatives (classificatory brothers of the father and classificatory sisters of the mother). No corresponding distinction is made in other generations.

6) *Heirship*. Sons-in-law are distinguished according to whether they are or are not one's heir. There is also a special term for heiress, but the heiress may alternatively be called by the usual term for any daughter.

7) *Type of wife*. Most wives are termed *jik*, a term used only by men but generally extendable to all women of the opposite moiety from ego's but of ego's own generation. A special term exists for younger secondary wives, however. The distinction is explained fully in Chapter VI.

8) *Intimacy of relationship*. Many terms can be used both for very close and very remote relatives. For instance, *jong* can mean one's own younger brother, or younger parallel cousin, and also any younger man of one's own generation and one's own moiety, whether or not the kinship connection is traceable. Of course, Garos make a behavioral distinction in their relations with these various kinsmen, and when necessary they can make a verbal distinction as well. The modifier *nanga* means 'distant' literally 'by force' or 'with some effort' (perhaps 'effort of the imagination'), so that *jong nanga* would be a distant *jong*. *Chongmot* 'proper', 'real,' indicates a close relative but not necessarily only the closest one possible. Thus *jong chongmot* would be a close lineage 'brother' but need not necessarily be a child of the same mother. To specify that two 'brothers' had the same

mother, Garos use some such expression as "they drank from the same breast" or "they came down the same road."

In all these cases the term by itself can denote either near or distant relatives and *nanga* or *chongmot* (or some other comparable term) is only added in case closer specification is necessary. Some terms, however, can denote only a close relative or only a distant relative. An example is *mamaachu* which is used for men of one's grandparents' generation who are in one's own lineage (i.e., MoMoBr and similar close relatives). It cannot be extended to all men of that generation and moiety. Since the boundaries of kinship groups such as a lineage are not precise, the limits to which these terms can be applied are not precise either, but it can at least be said that they are not extended infinitely as some other terms are.

9) *Speakers sex.* A few terms are limited in their use to speakers of only one sex, some being used only by men, and others only by women: *sari, boning, mosa, jik, se.*

| Term | Definition and Examples |
|------|------------------------|
| ambi | All relatives called either *ambichongka* or *ambijakasi*. Great-grandmother, remote female ancestor, old woman. |
| ambichongka | MoMo, MoMoSi, FaFaSi, FaMoBrWi, MoFaBrWi. Any woman of MoMo's generation and moiety. |
| ambijakasi | FaMo, FaMoSi, MoFaSi, MoMoBrWi, FaFaBrWi. Any woman of FaMo's generation and moiety. |
| achu | All relatives called either *achuchongka* or *achujakasi*. Remote male ancestor, old man. |
| achuchongka | MoFa, MoFaBr, MoMoSiHu, FaMoBr, FaFaSiHu. Any man of MoFa generation and moiety. |
| achujakasi | FaFa, FaFaBr, FaMoSiHu, MoMoBr, MoFaSiHu. Any man of FaFa generation and moiety. |
| mamaachu | MoMoBr, MoMoMoSiSo, MoMoMoBr. Man of ego's lineage two or more generations older. |
| ama | All relatives called either *ma', majong,* or *made*. |
| ma' | Mother. |

| Term | Definition and Examples |
|------|------------------------|
| majong | MoElSi, FaElBrWi, MoMoElSiDa, FaFaElSiDa, WiFaElSi, HuFaElSi. Daughter of *ambichongka* or *achuchongka* who is older than ego's mother. |
| made | MoYoSi. As for *majong* except younger relatives instead of older. |
| ✓ mani | FaSi, MoBrWi, MoMoBrDa, MoFaSiDa, WiMo, HuMo. Daughter of *ambijakasi* or *achujakasi*. Woman of opposite moiety to ego who is in parent's generation. |
| apa | All relatives called either *pa*, *pajong*, or *wang*. |
| pa | Father. |
| pajong | FaElBr, MoElSiHu. Husband of any *majong*, son of *ambijakasi* or *achujakasi* who is older than father. |
| wang | FaYoBr, MoYoSiHu. Husband of any *made*. |
| mama | MoBr, FaSiHu, WiFa, HuFa, MoMoSiSo, MoMoMoSiDaSo. Husband of any *mani*. Son of any *ambichongka* or *achuchongka*. Older man of ego's lineage or moiety. |
| abi | ElSi, MoElSiDa, FaElBrDa, MoMoElSiDaDa. Daughter of any *majong*, or *pajong*. Any slightly elder woman of ego's moiety. |
| no | YoSi. As for *abi*, except younger relatives instead of elder. |
| ✓ jik | Wife, MoBrDa (m.s.), FaSiDa (m.s.), WiSi, BrWi (m.s.), Daughter of *mama* or *mani* (m.s.). Marriageable girl. |
| jikgite | Second and younger wife given to a man who marries a widow or divorcee as his first wife. |
| ✓ sari | HuSi, BrWi (w.s.), female cross-cousin (w.s.). Daughter of *mama* or *mani* (w.s.). |
| ada | ElBr, MoElSiSo, FaElBrSo, MoMoElSiDaSo, Son of any *majong*, or *pajong*. Any slightly elder man of ego's moiety. |
| jong | YoBr. As for *ada*, except younger relatives instead of elder. |

| Term | Definition and Examples |
|------|-------------------------|
| se | Husband, HuBr, SiHu (w.s.), FaSiSo (w.s.), MoBrSo (w.s.), Son of *mama* or *mani* (w.s.). Marriageable man. |
| boning | FaSiSo (m.s.), MoBrSo (m.s.), son of a closely related *mama* or *mani* (m.s.). |
| mosa | Man of the moiety opposite to ego's who is not closely related (m.s.). |
| bisa | So, Da, BrSo (m.s.), BrDa (m.s.), SiSo (w.s.), BrSo (w.s.). Used both as a kinship term and as a general word meaning child. |
| de | Synonymous with *bisa*, except that it is used only as a kinship term. |
| demechik | Da, BrDa (m.s.), SiDa (w.s.), SiSoWi (m.s.), BrSoWi (w.s.), MoBrDaDa (m.s.), FaSiDaDa (m.s.), MoBrSoDa (w.s.), FaSiSoDa (w.s.). |
| nokna | Heiress. That particular *demechik* chosen to be heiress. |
| depante | So, BrSo (m.s.), SiSo (w.s.), Brother of any *demechik*. |
| gri | SiSo (m.s.), BrSo (w.s.), HuSiSo (w.s.), Son of any *abi* or *no* (m.s.), son of any *ada* or *jong* (w.s.), DaHu is a *gri* but more specific terms exist for him. |
| namchik | Daughter of any *abi* or *no* (m.s.), Daughter of any *ada* or *jong* (w.s.), Sister of *gri*. SoWi. |
| angsu | Grandchild. Any child of the same age or generation as ego's grandchildren. |
| angsuchongka | DaChild, BrDaChild (m.s.), SiSoChild (m.s.), SiDaChild (w.s.), BrSoChild (w.s.). Any child who calls ego *achuchongka* or *ambichongka*. |
| angsujakasi | SoChild, BrSoChild (m.s.), SiDaChild (m.s.), SiSoChild (w.s.), BrDaChild (w.s.). Any child who calls ego *achujakasi*, or *ambijakasi*. |
| namchikangsu | SiDaDa (m.s.). Girl who calls ego *mamaachu*. |
| griangsu | SiDaSo (m.s.). Boy who calls ego *mamaachu*. |

These terms can be displayed on a chart as shown. They are not, however, the only terms which the Garos use for their kinsmen.

R—M

| Generation | (a) Own moiety in own and ascending generations. Children's moiety in descending. | | | (b) Opposite moiety in own and ascending generations. Moiety opposite to children's moiety in descending generations. | | |
|---|---|---|---|---|---|---|
| | *Male* | *Female* Non-lineal | *Female* Lineal | *Male* Lineal | *Male* Non-lineal | *Female* |
| 2nd Ascending Generation | achu achujakasi mamaachu | ambi ambichongka | | achu achuchongka | | ambi ambijakasi |
| 1st Ascending Generation — Elder | mama | majong | ama ma' | pa apa | pajong | mani |
| 1st Ascending Generation — Younger | ada | made | ama | | wang | |
| Own Generation — Elder | | abi | | se (w.s.) boning (m.s.) mosa (m.s.) | apa | jik (m.s.) jikgite (m.s.) sari (w.s.) |
| Own Generation — Younger | jong | no | | | | |
| 1st Descending Generation | depante | demechik nokna | | gri | | namchik |
| 2nd Descending Generation | angsuchongka | | | griangsu | | angsujakasi namchikangsu |

de bisa · angsuchongka · angsu

GROUP II. *Affinal terms.* A few of the terms already listed together with a number of others have meanings which denote affinal relatives which have not yet been indicated. These are relatives of one's spouse, spouses of one's relatives, or even spouses of the relatives of one's spouse. It is convenient to define these terms by building upon the definitions already given for the terms of Group I. Thus the simplest way to define *sadu*, for instance, is "wife's classificatory sister's husband," (*se* of *no* or *abi* of one's *jik*).

These terms differ from those given earlier in not being extended to such a wide range of kinsmen. This is because those previously given are sufficient to cover all kinsmen, since if one knows a person's sex, age, generation, and moiety, these are enough to place him, and give him a kin term. By contrast, the following terms are used only for fairly close relatives.

| *Term* | *Definition and Examples* |
|---|---|
| namchik | Real *jik*'s close *ada* or *jong*'s real *jik*. WiBrWi, used in this sense only by men. |
| namchikangsu | Real *se*'s *namchikangsu*. HuSiDaDa, any *namchikangsu* of one's husband. |
| griangsu | Real *se*'s *griangsu*. HuSiDaSo, any *griangsu* of one's husband. |
| boning | Real *jik*'s close *ada*, or close *no*'s real *se*. WiElBr, YoSiHu (m.s.). |
| gume | Close *abi*'s real *se*. ElSiHu. The husband of an elder lineage sister. |
| jongsari | Real *jik*'s close *jong*. WiYoBr (m.s.). Younger man of wife's lineage. |
| nosari | Real *jik*'s close *no*. WiYoSi. Younger woman of wife's lineage. |
| sadu | Real *jik*'s close *no* or *abi*'s real *se*. WiSiHu. Man who is married into the same lineage as ego. Used reciprocally. |
| chra | Real *jik*'s close male relative. WiBr, WiMoBr, WiMoMoSiSo, WiMoMoBr, So. Wife's close male relative. |

| Term | Definition and Examples |
|------|------------------------|
| chawari | Close *demechik*'s real *se*, except not the *nokna*'s *se*. Also *chawari*'s *chawari*. DaHu, DaDaHu. Son-in-law who is not an heir. |
| nokrom | *Nokna*'s real *se*. Heir. |
| obide | Real *jik* or *se*'s close *apa*. Also *obite*'s *obite*. WiFa, HuFa, WiMoFa. |
| nio | Real *jik* or *se*'s close *ama*. Also *obite*'s *nio*. WiMo, HuMo, WiMoMo. |

GROUP III. *Inheritable terms.* A few of the terms already given are used in a broader sense than has been indicated so far. This is due to the assumption of kinship terms by the heir and heiress when the man or woman from whom he or she inherits (testator) dies. Thus, a man may be called by kinship terms which others formerly used for his testator, and conversely he uses a few kinship terms for others which his testator formerly used. However, a man does not use *all* the terms which were formerly used by his testator but only certain ones. These are as follows.

| | |
|---|---|
| jik | Deceased testator's wife (*jik*) |
| se | Deceased husband's (*se*) heir |
| wang | Deceased father's (*pa*) heir |
| obite | Deceased father-in-law's (*obite*) heir |
| nio | Deceased mother-in-law's (*nio*) heiress |
| chawari | Deceased testator's son-in-law (*chawari*) |
| gume | Deceased older sister's husband's (*gume*) heir |

*Conclusions.* A few points, implicit in these lists, deserve clarification. The term *obite*, has been defined among other things as 'wife's father' and also as the man who inherits from wife's father (assuming, of course, that ego is not the heir himself). It has also been noted that the *obite* of one's *obite* (wife's father's wife's father) is also called *obite*. As this should imply, this is a recursive formula, so that the *obite* of the *obite* of one's *obite* is also *obite*, etc. If it were not for the inheritance of kin terms, most of these rather remote *obites* would be much older than ego, and would long since have been dead. However, the term *obite* can be inherited and even inherited repeatedly, and the result is that one may actually refer to several men as *obite*.

In more concrete terms, this can be understood as related to the pattern by which households emerge from one another. Thus a man speaks of the incumbent husband in the house from which his own house emerged as *obite*. This may be his wife's own father, or his wife's father's heir. He also speaks of the men of more ancient houses from which the house emerged that his own house emerged from as *obite*. For this reason, men who have married into Rengsanggri, and married a woman of the Rengsanggri lineage sometimes say that the *nokma* is the *obite* of the whole village, because all of the houses in the village ultimately came out of his house at one or more steps, or at least this is true of all of the houses in which the women belong to the Rengsanggri lineage. Conversely, all the inmarried men of Rengsanggri can be said to be the *chawaris* (sister's son, etc.) of the *nokma*. This is one way in which the hierarchy of households and the pattern of segmentation that was referred to in Chapter VII is discussed and kept sorted out by the Garos.

It may be noticed that there is no special term for co-wife. In the most common case, in which mother and daughter are co-wives, they naturally continue to refer to each other by the usual terms for mother and daughter. In the somewhat unusual case in which the co-wives are less than a generation apart in age, they may refer to each other as 'sisters' (*abi* and *no*) but the terminology is not well standardized.

One of the characteristics of this system is that there is often more than a single term which can stand for the same individual. This is implied in many instances in the lists given, but it may be well to cite a few cases. Wife's mother is most specifically *nio* but according to her generation, moiety and sex, she is also *mani*, and this term can indeed be used for her also, though it is less precise. The same is true of *mama* and *obite*, which can both be used for the father-in-law. *Sadu* meaning WiSiHu, refers to a man of ego's own moiety, and so the terms for 'brother' can also be applied to him. There is considerable overlapping in the terms *chra*, *mosa*, and *boning*, all of which apply to men of the opposite moiety to that of ego. SiDaDa is specifically *namchikangsu*, but she may also be referred to simply as *angsu* 'grandchild.' In most cases, these terms differ in their degree of specificity. The choice of which one to use is dependent upon how specific one needs to be for the particular purpose at hand.

## Appendix D.   Regional Variation

A study based largely upon a single village or region within an extensive society runs the risk of leaving the impression that what holds for this village must necessarily hold for other areas as well. The impression is not always justified, and so I feel that it is important to suggest, however briefly, a few of the variable features of Garo culture. The Garos divide themselves into a number of geographical subgroups. Dialectal differences are important in defining these, but there are other distinguishing cultural features as well. The western third of the hill region is occupied by people known as Abengs or Am'bengs. Those in the central and east-central hill regions are known respectively as Matchi and Dual. To the north of the Matchi and Dual are the Chisak, and still further to the north, where the hills flatten into plains, are the Akawe, the literal meaning of the word being "plains." In the southeastern part of the hills, south of the Machi and Dual but east of the Abeng, are a number of rather more divergent groups. The Ruga, a small group in the central south, and the Atong, a larger group along the Simsang River in the southeasternmost corner of the district, actually speak languages quite unintelligible to other Garos, but they nevertheless consider themselves to be Garos and share most other cultural traits with them. Most of the intervening region between the Ruga and Atong is occupied by people who refer to themselves as Gara or Ganching, or even as Gara-Ganching. On the periphery of the hills are a number of other groups, generally known as plains tribes. These latter do not consider themselves to be Garos, and they speak languages quite different from Garo, though one set of these plains tribes, the Koch (sometimes known as Pani-Koch), speak languages similar to Atong and Ruga. To the north are the Rabha and Kachari, to the west Koch and Hajong, and to the west and south a few people who call themselves Dalu. These various plains tribes are not found in well-defined territories; rather, their villages are often scrambled with one another, and with Garos, Bengalis, and Assamese as well. They all show varying degrees of Hinduization, practice wet rice agriculture, and tend to be somewhat less mongoloid in feature than the Garos. To the east of the Garo Hills District lies that of the Khasis. The bordering regions of the Khasi Hills are occupied by a group known to the Garos as Megam and to the Khasis as Lyng-ngam. These people speak a dialect of Khasi, and reasonably enough are generally considered to be Khasis; but they do share a number of cultural characteristics with the Garos. All Garos except the Atong and Ruga speak mutually intelligible dialects.

*Subsistence.* The most important subsistence variations are those resulting from the introduction of wet rice and some new fruits, as described in Chapter XII. In certain parts of the district, including some of the Gara-Ganching area and the central portion of the hills, cotton is not grown. Some of these areas depend instead upon betel leaf or chili peppers as a cash crop. Where cotton is not grown it is usually the practice to use the fields for only a single year before abandoning them to the jungle, but I was told that the land is left fallow for a shorter time than in cotton areas—only about five years. There seems to be no climatic reason why cotton could not be grown in these regions; but they are somewhat remote, often lying as much as two days' walk from a market or motorable road, and perhaps the difficulty of transporting the cotton discourages its cultivation.

The largest river penetrating the district, and the only one large enough to make boats practicable, is the Simsang (or Someswari), which emerges from the southeast corner of the hills. Most of the Atong villages are strung along the lower part of this river, and their inhabitants and other Garos who live near by have a riverine aspect to their culture quite different from that in any other area. Canoe-building is a thriving industry along the river. Logs are floated from many miles upstream, and then skillfully hollowed out to make heavy but seaworthy dugouts, which are used for both transportation and fishing. Fishing is a much more important activity here than anywhere else in the district, and the people of the river villages prepare particularly savory types of dried fish which they sell to other Garos.

*Technology.* Numerous technological details vary from one section of the hills to another. One of the most evident of these is in architecture. The same basic houseplan is followed by most non-Christians, and Eliot, as early as 1792, gave a description of Garo houses which could serve as a description of most Garo houses today.[1] However, the proportions of the house and the internal arrangements are somewhat variable. Some of the Atong build particularly large houses, and in the Gara-Ganching area the eaves at the front end are extended to form a larger roofed-in area than in other regions. In the northernmost part of the hills even non-Christians may build their houses on a plan similar to those of the plains Assamese, which are rather more square than the houses of most Garos; and outbuildings are likely to be grouped together in a family compound which is set off from its neighbors by a light fence.

In a few areas women continue to wear the short Garo skirt, but elsewhere this has been almost completely displaced by a longer skirt which reaches below the knees, and some modern women even wear a modified version of the Assamese chadar—a light cloth draped around the upper part of the body giving somewhat the same effect as a sari, though unlike a sari it is worn with a separate skirt cloth. Hand loom weaving has been re-introduced from the plains, and a few Garo women now produce dark-colored cotton skirts with distinctive woven patterns which are becoming popular among women able to afford them. In some areas short pants have almost replaced the man's traditional loin cloth, and a few men occasionally even sport long trousers. Smaller manufactured articles are remarkably uniform throughout the district. The same kinds of objects are purchased from the market and the same kinds manufactured. Once, on the Gauhati-Shillong highway, many miles east of the Garo Hills, but near what proved to be an isolated Garo village, I easily recognized a woman to be a Garo from the kind of basket she was carrying.

*Ceremonies.* Although the cosmological beliefs of the non-Christian Garos seem reasonably uniform, the ceremonies which are performed are remarkably varied. All non-Christians sacrifice for the cure of disease, though not all do so with as much fervor as the Rengsanggri people, and some put greater faith in jungle medicines. The cycle of annual ceremonies practiced in some of the eastern and central parts of the hills differs markedly from the routine in Rengsanggri, which is probably typical of the western or Abeng area. Even *Wangala* is omitted in a few places. In some of the eastern areas the post-funeral rite (*delangsoa*) is elaborated into one of the most important ceremonies, if not the most important one, and is made the occasion for much dancing and drinking. In Rengsanggri the *delangsoa* is only a minor part of one or another of the annual ceremonies. Burial customs are much the same among all Garos except where influenced by Christianity, but the Megam in the Khasi Hills to the east expose the bodies of their dead on high platforms rather than burn them. In some eastern parts of the district people are said occasionally to put on a ceremony and feast known as *jaksil gana* ('donning of the metal bracelets'), which is more deliberately designed to confer status on the feast-giver than any feast in Rengsanggri.

*Kinship.* This seems to be one of the most stable aspects of Garo culture. Wherever they live, Garos choose heirs and organize their families in much the same manner as in Rengsanggri. The few variations in kinship terminology mostly concern ego's own generation, particularly terms for various kinds of brothers-in-law and sisters-in-law of the opposite sex. Some areas have a special term—*chame*—for cross-cousin of the opposite sex, which the Rengsanggri people lack completely. In some parts of the district, particularly in the east, three major exogamous groups are found, one more than in Rengsanggri. Momin is added to Marak and Sangma, making it impossible to speak of moieties. Nevertheless, this difference entails hardly any differences in terminology, though people from these regions cannot justify the use of a certain term by the fact of membership in one of the groups, in the way the people of Rengsanggri frequently do. Where three exogamous groups practice more or less random marriage the symmetrical balance of the system is rapidly destroyed, and one's father's brother's wife, for instance, need not be in one's own exogamous group, as she would have to be in Rengsanggri. Even the neighboring Megams divide themselves into three exogomous groups, and like the Garos they refer to these as Sangma, Marak, and Momin. The Megams also have smaller groups corresponding to the Garo sibs, though the names do not correspond, and they also take an heir in a way that they consider similar to the Garo method. However, they seem always to choose the youngest daughter as heiress, a custom corresponding to the Khasi rather than the Garo practice.

In regions other than the Abeng area, a single village often includes members of more sibs than is typical among the Abengs, and on the other hand a single sib name seems to be used over a less extensive area. In the northeastern part of the hills a man and his younger

brother's wife or his wife's older sister call each other by the reciprocal term *cheksari*, which is lacking in Rengsanggri. These two are
teased about any contract they may have, while such a thing would
be ignored in Rengsanggri. On the other hand, in the northeast a
man and his wife's brother's wife are left quite alone, while the people
in Rengsanggri can laugh uproariously over this relationship. People
from the northeast, perhaps those in closest contact with the plains,
rarely use personal names except for people younger than themselves. Even husbands and wives regularly call each other "mother of
so-and-so" or "father of so-and-so," inserting the name of their
eldest living child. These people even dislike mentioning their own
names, and it is politer to ask someone else for a person's name than
to ask directly. They consider those in areas such as Rengsanggri to
be rather rustic and uncultured in their free use of personal names,
since in Rengsanggri even husband and wife call each other by name
and the technonymous terms are less often used.

Other features of Garo culture, their legal system, courtship practices (except where Christian influences have been strong), methods
of child care, agricultural techniques, food, and even such elusive
characteristics as their value system, seem remarkably uniform. The
neighboring tribes differ far more from the Garos than the various
kinds of Garos differ from each other. It is for this reason that the
term Garo can be said to represent a genuine ethnic reality. It des-
cribes a well-defined group set off clearly from its neighbors. Only
the position of the Atong and Megam is in any way ambiguous.
Neither speak the Garo language, and both have a few other divergent customs. The Atong, unlike the Megam, however, do consider
themselves to be a variety of Garo, and in most respects share traits
with other Garos more intimately than is true of the Megams.

# Notes

*Chapter I*
[1] Rai K. L. Barua Bahadur, *Early History of Kamarumpa* (Shillong, 1933).
[2] Banikanta Kakati, *Assamese, Its Formation and Development* (Gauhati, Assam, 1941), pp. 47-51.
[3] S. K. Bhuyan (ed.), *An Account of Assam*, first compiled in 1807-1814 by Francis Hamilton (Gauhati, Assam, 1941). John Eliot, "Observations on the inhabitants of the Garrow Hills," *Asiatic Researches*, III (1792), 17-37.
[4] A. J. Moffat Mills, *Report on the Province of Assam* (Calcutta, 1854), p. 46.
[5] 1951 Census of India, Vol. XII: *Assam, Manipur and Tripura* (Shillong, 1954). 1951 Census, Paper No. 1, *Languages* (1954).
[6] The 1951 Census of Pakistan lists 45,319 persons speaking "Other Assam-Burma Tongues" in the Mymensingh district. Most of these were probably Garos. Vol. 3: *East Bengal, Reports and Tables* (Karachi), Table 7-4.

*Chapter VI*
[1] Major A. Playfair, *The Garos* (London, 1909), p. 68.
[2] I stress the existence of brother exchange partly because its existence among the Garos has been denied. Miss Nakane ("Cross-Cousin Marriage among the Garo of Assam," *Man*, 1958:2) asserted its absence, and even considered this an important clue for the understanding of Garo social organization.
[3] E. R. Leach, "The Structural Implications of Matrilateral Cross-Cousin Marriage," *Journal of the Royal Anthropological Institute*, LXXXI (1952).
[4] Although the title of Leach's paper gives the superficial impression that he considers it to be cross-cousin marriage that encourages the development of ranked lineages, he eventually makes it clear that he does not consider either trait to be preliminary to the other,

but that he is simply pointing out the functional interrelations of the two traits.

⁵ Fred Eggan, *Social Organization of the Western Pueblo* (Chicago, 1950), p. 113.

## Chapter VII

¹ George Homans and David M. Schneider, *Marriage, Authority and Final Causes* (Glencoe, Ill., 1955). In an earlier article ("Garo Avuncular Authority and Matrilateral Cross-Cousin Marriage," *American Anthropologist*, LX (1958), pp. 743-749) I have pointed out somewhat more directly the implication of the Garo data for the Homans-Schneider theory. The significant point is not only that the Garos form an exception to the generalization that matrilateral cross-cousin marriage is unlikely to be found in a society with avuncular authority, but that it is precisely the authority that encourages this type of marriage. The constellation of relationships among the Garos is not unlike that expected by the theory, but a kinship system may look different from different positions in it, and the advantages and disadvantages of heirship surely look different when regarded from the position of mother's brother as contrasted with that of sister's son. The mother's brother makes the choice among the Garo, and to him matrilateral cross-cousin marriage looks very attractive indeed.

² This, of course, is the distinction which Murdock makes between unilineal descent groups and "compromise kin groups" (G. P. Murdock, *Social Structure* (New York, 1948), p. 66.) However, Garo "compromise kin groups" differ from those discussed by Murdock in that they include some of the men as well as most of the women of the unilineal descent group as their core. They cannot be said to be localized exclusively around either the men or the women of the matrilineage, but must include at least some of both sexes.

## Chapter XII

¹ A. J. Moffatt Mills, *Report on the Province of Assam* (Calcutta, 1854), p. cxix.

² *Ibid.*, p. cxix.

³ Captain C. S. Reynolds, "A Narrative of our connections with the Dusanee and Cheanee Garrows, with a short account of their country," *Journal of the Asiatic Society of Bengal*, XVIII (1849), p. 57.

[4] John Eliot, "Observations on the inhabitants of the Garrow Hills, made during a publick deputation in the years 1788 and 1789," *Asiatic Researches*, III (1792), p. 31.

[5] Reynolds, *op. cit.*, p. 52.　　[6] Eliot, *op. cit.*, p. 18.

[7] *Ibid.*, p. 25　　　　　　　　[8] *Ibid.*, p. 18.

[9] Mills, *op. cit.*, p. cxi.　　[10] Eliot, *op. cit.*, p. 18.

[11] Reyholds, *op. cit.*, p. 53.

[12] S. K. Bhuyan (ed.), *An Account of Assam*, first compiled in 1807-1814 by Francis Hamilton (Gauhati, Assam, 1941), p. 86.

[13] Mills, *op. cit.*, p. cxviii.　　[14] Bhuyan, *op. cit.*, p. 86.

[15] *Ibid.*, p. 87.　　　　　　　　[16] *Ibid.*, p. 91.

[17] Mills, *op. cit.*, p. cx.　　[18] *Ibid.*, pp. cxvii, 46.

[19] Playfair, *op. cit.*, p. 78.

[20] "Many Garrows ... are lost amongst the half tribes below the hills and this is the case with some large communities in the south of Habbraghaut settled on the edge of the plains. They have become industrious ryots, but are no longer Garrows, and cease to have influence on their countrymen in the hills." Mills, *op. cit.*, p. cxix.

[21] William Carey, *A Garo Jungle book;* or *The mission to the Garos of Assam* (Philadelphia and Boston, 1919).

*Appendix D*

[1] Eliot, *op. cit.*, p. 23.

# Bibliography of Garo Ethnography

ALLEN, B. C. *The Khasi and Jaintia Hills, the Garo Hills and the Lushai Hills.* Allahabad: Pioneer Press, 1906 (Assam District Gazetteers, X).

AVERY, JOHN. "The Hill Tribes of India: Tribes of the Northeast Border," *The American Antiquarian*, VI (1884), 307-316. (Garo: 308-311).

AYERST, W. "The Garos," *Indian Antiquary*, IX (1880), 103-106.

BERTRAND, GABRIELLE. *Terres Secrètes où règnent les femmes.* Paris: Amiot-Dumont, 1956. 233 pp. (English edition: *Secret Lands where Women Reign.* London, Robert Hale, 1958. 224 pp.)

BONNERJEA, BIREN. "Materials for the study of Garo ethnology," *Indian Antiquary*, LVIII (1929), 121-127.

———. *L'ethnologie du Bengale.* Paris: 1927. 169 pp. (Garo: 41-43).

BOSE, J. K. *Culture Change Among the Garo of Assam.* Unpublished Ph.D. Dissertation, University of London, 1947.

———. "Dual organisation in Assam," *Journal of the Department of Letters, Calcutta University*, XXV (1934), Article 8, 1-29.

———. "The Gana Nokma ceremony of the Garos of Assam," *Man in India*, XV (1935), 260-262.

———. "The Garo Law of Inheritance," *Anthropological Papers*, Calcutta University, New Series VI (1941), 81-150.

———. "Ordeals among the Garos," *Man in India*, XVIII (1938) 174-176.

———. "The Nokrom System of the Garos of Assam," *Man*, XXXVI (1936), No. 54, 44-46.

———. "Woangala festival of the Garos," *Man in India*, XVIII (1938), 168-173.

BOSE, J. K., and J. K. GAN. "Nouveaux Exemplaires indiens de cithare en radeau," *L'anthropologie*, XLVIII (1938), 539-541.

BURLING, ROBBINS. "An Incipient Caste Organization in the Garo Hills," *Man in India*, XL (1960), 283-299.

———. "Garo Avuncular Authority and Matrilateral Cross-Cousin Marriage," *American Anthropologist*, LX (1958), 743-749.

———. "Garo Cross-Cousin Marriage," *Man*, LVIII (1958), No. 159, 115-116.

———. "Garo Kinship Terminology," *Man in India*, XXXVI (1956), 203-218.

CAREY, WILLIAM, *A Garo Jungle Book; or, The Mission to the Garos of Assam*. Philadelphia, Boston: The Judson Press, 1919. 283 pp.

CHATTOPADHYAY, K. P. "The Tribal Problem and its Solution," *Eastern Anthropologist*, III (1949), 15-21 (Garos: 18-19).

CHOUDHURY, BHUPENDRANATH. *Some Cultural and Linguistic Aspects of the Garos*. Gauhati, Assam: Lawyer's Book Stall, 1958. 84 pp.

COSTA, GIULIO. "The Garo Code of Law," *Anthropos*, IL (1954), 1041-1066.

DALTON, EDWARD T. *Descriptive ethnology of Bengal*. Calcutta: Supt. of Government Printing, 1872. 327 pp. (Garo: 58-68).

DEY, SHUMBHOO CHUNDER. "An Account of the Garos," *Calcutta Review*, (1909), 153-166.

EHRENFELS, U. R. *Mother-right in India* (Osmania University Series.) Hyderabad, Deccan: Oxford University Press, 1941 (Garo: 39-43).

———. "Three Matrilineal Groups in Assam: A Study in Similarities and Differences," *American Anthropologist*, LVII (1955) 306-321.

ELIOT, JOHN. "Observations on the inhabitants of the Garrow Hills, made during a publick deputation in the years 1788 and 1789," *Asiatic Researches*, III (1792), 17-37.

ESME. "A Garo's revenge," *Calcutta Review*, LXXXIV (1887), 11-15.

———. "The Garos, their customs, and mythology," *Calcutta Review*, LXXX (1885), 47-71.

———. "Three scenes from the life of a Garo," *Calcutta Review*. LXXXV (1887), 44-88.

———. "Which was it, Dawhapa or Witch," *Calcutta Review*. LXXXV (1887), 150-154.

FRAZER, J. G. *Folk Lore in the Old Testament*. 3 vols. London: Macmillan, 1918 (Garo: Vol. 1, 462-465).

———. "Garo Marriages," *Folk Lore*, XXXII (1921), 202-209.

GOODWIN-AUSTEN, H. H. "On the Garo Hills," *Journal of the Royal Geographic Society*, XLIII (1873), 1-46.

——. "On the Garo Hills," *Proceedings of the Royal Geographic Society*, XVII (1873), 36-42.

——. "On the Garo Hill Tribes," *Journal of the Royal Anthropological Institute*, II (1873) 391-396.

GURDON, P. R. T. "Garo Wedding Chant," *Journal of the Asian Society of Bengal*, LXII (1903), p. 93.

HAMILTON, FRANCIS (formerly known as Francis Buchanan). "An Account of Assam with some notices concerning the Neighboring Territories," *Annals of Oriental Literature*, (June 1820), 193-278. Most of this was reproduced in a slightly different arrangement in: Montgomery Martin, *The History, Antiquities, Topography and Statistics of Eastern India*, vol. III (1838). More recently Hamilton's *Account* has been edited by S. K. Bhuyan and published by the Department of Historical and Antiquarian Studies, Government of Assam, Gauhati (1940).

HODSON, T. C. "The Garo and Khasi marriage systems contrasted," *Man in India*, I (1921), 106-127.

——. "Garo Marriages," *Folk Lore*, XXXII (1921), 133-135.

HUNTER, SIR WILLIAM WILSON. *A Statistical Account of Assam*. 2 vols. London: Trubner, 1879. (Garo: vol. 2, pt. 1, p.133-170).

MACKENSIE, SIR ALEXANDER. *History of the Relations of the Government with the Hill Tribes of the North-East of Bengal*. 1884. (Garo: 245-268.)

MAJUMDAR, DHIRENDRA NARAYAN. *The Garos (An Account of the Garos of the Present Day)*. Gauhati, Assam: The Lawyer's Book Stall, 1956. 27 pp.

MILLS, A. J. MOFFAT. *Report on the Province of Assam*. Calcutta: Thos. Jones, Calcutta Gazette Office, 1854.

MOOKERJI, RAJ RAJ. "The Nokrom System of the Garos of Assam," *Man*, XXXIX (1939), 167.

MUKHERJEE, BHABANDA. "Garo Family," *Eastern Anthropologist*, XI (1957) 25-30.

——. "Garo Marriage and Kinship Organization," *Anthropologist* (Delhi University), III (1956), 48-55.

——. "Machong among the Garos of Assam," *Eastern Anthropologist*, IX (1956), 112-116.

———. "Mother-in-law Marriage Among the Garo," *Man in India*, XXXV (1955), 299-302.

NAKANE, CHIE. "Changes of Matrilineal Families in Assam," *Transactions of the third World Congress of Sociology*, Vol. 4, 1956.

———. "Cross-Cousin Marriage among the Garo of Assam," *Man*, LVIII (1958), No. 2, pp. 7-12.

———. "On the Frontiers of Tibet," *Japan Quarterly*, VI (1959), 297-307. (Garo: 297-304.)

PIANAZZI, FR. A. *In Garo Land*. Calcutta: Orphan Press (no date *c*. 1934). 46 pp.

PLAYFAIR, A. *The Garos*. London: Nutt, 1909. 172 pp.

REYNOLDS, C. S. "A narrative of our connections with the Dusanee and Cheannee Garrows, with a short account of their country," *Journal of the Asiatic Society of Bengal*, XVIII (1849), 45-60.

ROBINSON, WILLIAM. *Descriptive Account of Assam*. Calcutta, 1841.

ROSE, H. A. "Garo Marriages," *Folk Lore*, XXXVI (1925), 388-391.

SCHERMAN, L. "Wohnhaustypen in Birma und Assam," *Archiv für Anthropologie*, XLII (1915), 203-234. (Garo: 231.)

SCHLAGINTWEIT, EMIL. "Die Garo-, Khassia-, und Naga-Voelker an der indischbirmanischen Grenze," *Globus* 34 (1878), 262-265, 279-282, 295-297.

STODDARD, REV. I. J. "The Garos," *Indian Antiquary*, II (1873), 336-337.

STONER, C. R. "The Use of a Model Bellows and Model Tiger to Cure Throat Sickness Among the Garos of Assam," *Man in India*, XXVII (1948), 179-80.

VAGHAIWALLA, R. B. (ed.). *Garo Hills District Census Handbook*, 1951 Census. Shillong: Assam Government Press, 1952. 122 pp.

WADDELL, M. B. "The Tribes of the Brahmaputra Valley," *Journal of the Asiatic Society of Bengal*, LXIX part III (Anthropology etc.) (1900), 1-127. (Garo: 54-57.)

WALKER, G. D. "The Garo Manufacture of Bark Cloth," *Man*, XXVII (1927), No. 5.

———. "Notes on the Garos," *Census of India, Assam*, (1931), vol. 3, pt. 1, Appendix B, pp. xv-xviii.

# Index